# HUGH MORRISON

HUGH MORRISON has been a member of the faculty of Dartmouth College since 1932. He graduated from Dartmouth, did graduate work at Princeton University, and became an instructor at the University of Chicago in 1929, where he first heard of Louis Sullivan and saw his buildings in Chicago's Loop. After several years of research, he wrote *Louis Sullivan: Prophet of Modern Architecture.* This was the first definitive biography of the now-famous architect. He has taught summer sessions at Harvard University and lectured on American architecture at MIT, and has also published a study of Planning Education in the United States. He received a Guggenheim Fellowship in 1948-49 which led to his writing *Early American Architecture,* published in 1952.

# LOUIS SULLIVAN

## PROPHET OF MODERN ARCHITECTURE

### BY HUGH MORRISON

The Norton Library

W·W·NORTON & COMPANY, INC.

PUBLISHERS·NEW YORK

Books That Live

The Norton imprint on a book means that in the publisher's
estimation it is a book not for a single season but for the years.
W. W. Norton & Company, Inc.

*Printed in the United States of America*

*To George Grant Elmslie*

# CONTENTS

# FOREWORD

AT an architects' dinner in the early 1890's, an acute critic remarked: "American architecture is the art of covering one thing with another thing to imitate a third thing, which, if genuine, would not be desirable." He might have gone much further; he was talking about contemporary architecture, but he might have included most of the architecture of the nineteenth century; he confined his indictment to America when he might as justly have included Europe; and if he had been a prophet, he could have applied it to the greater part of the architecture of the first generation of the twentieth century.

The besetting architectural sin of the nineteenth century was the imitation of historic styles. Today we are again beginning to regard *style* as something always changing and always modern. When Louis IX instructed his architect to design the Sainte Chapelle he doubtless said nothing about the "Gothic" style—since the term had not been invented—nor indeed about any "style." He probably said: "Build me a good modern chapel." All architecture during Greek and medieval times was *modern* architecture. Certainly it did not imitate the Egyptian style, and least of all did it build one building in Egyptian, one in Assyrian, one in Minoan, and one in Neolithic, as we do today. Eclecticism is a distinctly modern phenomenon, and when viewed in the whole panorama of the history of architecture it appears but a momentary aberration, caused, most probably, by the failure to realize sound values based on a discerning study of the experience of the past. The trouble, paradoxically, was not too much history, but not enough.

This confusion of values began more than a century ago. It may be placed at about the time when the last great architectural style died its destined death, and when at almost the same moment the dominant forces of democracy and industrialism, as signalized in the French Revolution and the Industrial Revolution, began to control the character of modern life. At that time we might have expected the birth of a modern architecture. And indeed, technically, the nativity occurred. An iron frame for the support of seven floors in a cotton factory in Manchester, England, was built in 1801. And before many years factories and warehouses and lofts began to assume an appearance which has hardly changed until today.

But the impact of the new forces was too sudden to be absorbed, and nineteenth-century culture entered into a strange dualism. Science and technique controlled the intellectual and material phases of life; romanticism and religion controlled the imaginative and spiritual phases; and the gulf between the two ever widened. Architecture was split into two uncongenial halves, utility and beauty, and we have the strange combination of a railroad station decorated by Gothic pinnacles, or an iron shop-front adorned by Greek columns.

Architects concerned themselves more and more only with beauty, and since there was no genuine new beauty, this could only resolve itself into an imitation of past standards of beauty. Thus eclecticism. Meanwhile, there were those who advocated a frankly utilitarian and mechanistic architecture, such as Viollet-le-Duc. But no union could be effected. The two attitudes were diametrically opposed. How combine the sense of practical truth of science with the sense of emotional truth of romanticism? How reintegrate engineering and architecture? The conflict had confounded the century; it had made impossible any genuine cultural expression of modern life as a whole.

In the field of architecture, I believe, it remained for Louis Sullivan to integrate romanticism and realism, to achieve a synthesis both in theory and in practice completely expressive of modern life, and to make possible the renewal of architecture as a creative art based on those fundamentals that have always existed in the great architecture of the past. In this sense he was the first modern architect. Lewis Mumford has said of him: "Sullivan's was perhaps the first mind in American architecture that had come to know itself with any fullness in relation to its soil, its period, its civilization, and had been able to absorb fully all the many lessons of the century." [1] Sullivan was in actual practice a very great architect, but his greatest achievement was in his emancipation of architectural thinking from the dead forms of the past and his demonstration of the possibility of the development of new forms directly out of the nature of the problems at hand.

Sullivan died in 1924. During his own lifetime his importance was never widely recognized. To be sure, some of his work was enthusiastically hailed during the nineties—many articles praised his buildings and his thinking as heralding a new movement in architecture—but it would be too much to expect that any complete estimate of his achievement could be made at such an early date. The opinions were, for the most part, expressions of hope for the future. Two decades later the tone of criticism had changed. Architecture had in the meantime made immense strides—or so it was believed—in a direction quite different from that pointed out by Sullivan: the Woolworth Building had raised its terra cotta pinnacles and gargoyles to the sky for many years; a revived medieval-

[1] Lewis Mumford: *The Brown Decades*, p. 143.

ism far more accurate than the quaint misunderstandings of nineteenth-century Gothic had been crowned in such masterpieces as
the Harkness Quadrangles at Yale and St. Thomas' Church on
Fifth Avenue; the glory that was Greece had achieved its final aura
of perfection in 'the most beautiful classic building of modern
times,' the Lincoln Memorial; and architecture in all its branches
had shown such immense progress that architects, critics, and public celebrated it in mutual felicitations.

It was easily seen now that Sullivan had been a failure—a very
interesting failure, to be sure; undoubtedly an eccentric and a
genius, a kind of romantic Don Quixote who had tilted against the
windmills of imaginary evils in a most admirable way; but after
all, a man who had little or no sense of practical realities. He was
viewed with charity, in the patronizing and complacent way with
which mediocrity regards genius which has been proven to be
wrong. Other views were more magnanimous: Sullivan was all
right in his day and his way—indeed, perhaps a great architect—
but that day was past; we had progressed to a new and better architecture, and instead of being the forerunner of a new century, Sullivan was the last great leader of the old; within his lifetime he was
shelved as an Old Master.

As late as 1927 a popular history of American architecture appeared with a chapter entitled "Louis Sullivan and the Lost Cause."
The author, Mr. Thomas Tallmadge, has lived to say that if he
were writing the book today, the chapter would be called "Louis
Sullivan and the Cause Triumphant." Within the last five years
critical opinion of Sullivan has changed amazingly. The development of the modern style of architecture has been so striking that
we may fairly say that the general public has become aware of it
as an accomplished fact. Book after book has appeared on the
"new architecture," and "functionalism" has become a by-word in

architectural parlance. Beginning with Lewis Mumford, and continuing in the writings of Henry-Russell Hitchcock, Sheldon Cheney, Bruno Taut and others, Sullivan has been viewed more and more as the great forerunner of modern architecture. But although recognized as a unique personal force, and often as the prophet of the modern style, no single book on him was written. Such magazine articles as were published often suffered from errors in fact about his buildings or incomplete interpretation of his thinking, and there were large lacunae on certain phases of his work because of lack of information.

I became interested in Sullivan five years ago while teaching at the University of Chicago. In attempting to discover more about him I found that most of the office records had been destroyed by fire many years ago; there were very few available photographs; there was no list of buildings which he had designed; and he had left no family to preserve personal effects which might have aided in piecing out the story. For these reasons the task of reconstructing the story of his life and work was difficult, and the account is not yet complete.

Sullivan's youth and training is, fortunately, well known through his *Autobiography of an Idea*. This account of his life, however, says very little about his buildings done in partnership with Adler, and virtually nothing of his work after 1893. My chief source of information on this and other phases of Sullivan's life has been Mr. George Grant Elmslie, who worked with Sullivan for the twenty years between 1889 and 1909, and who has carefully preserved not only all available records but an invaluable store of memories. It is not too much to say that without Mr. Elmslie's reverent preservation of material records and his sympathetic understanding and admiration no adequate account of Louis Sullivan could have been written.

My debt to published articles is sufficiently indicated in the footnotes and bibliography. A great part of my information, however, came from letters and personal interviews; these were so numerous that it would be impossible to recognize all my obligations here. I wish to express my appreciation, however, for the uniform courtesy with which my requests for information, both verbal and written, were met. In the early stages of the investigation I had much valued assistance from preliminary studies on Sullivan by Miss Lucile Smith and by H. Stewart Leonard. Their scholarly work afforded a nucleus of material which has proven of immense aid, and Mr. Leonard was kind enough to read several chapters of the manuscript. Mrs. Julius Weil, daughter of Dankmar Adler, was most helpful in the rediscovery of many of the early buildings of Adler & Sullivan about which few or no records existed, and particularly in contributing information on the life of her father. Adler's great importance in the work of the firm has never been adequately recognized, and although I have attempted to suggest this in the text, I deeply regret that exigencies of publication preclude a more complete account of his life and personality.

As to photographs, the largest extant collection of negatives of Sullivan's buildings is in the possession of Henry Fuermann & Sons, Chicago. Mr. Fuermann was a personal friend of Sullivan and I am obligated to him for the work which he did and his personal interest in aiding the project. There remained, however, some seventy or eighty buildings of which no photographs existed. Getting a record of these, incidentally, involved several thousand miles of travel throughout Illinois, Wisconsin, Minnesota, Iowa, Indiana, and Ohio, not to mention innumerable expeditions in and about Chicago. I was fortunate in having as companion on these architectural pilgrimages Mr. Joseph Barron, whose excellent photography, no less than his knowledge of the history of American architecture, was invaluable. The Barron collection of negatives includes several score on Sullivan's buildings.

Sullivan manuscripts in the Burnham Library of the Art Institute of Chicago were placed at my disposal by Miss Etheldred Abbot, whose interest and help were unfailing. For personal interviews I am most indebted to the late Paul Mueller, engineer in the office of Adler & Sullivan for many years, Mr. Arthur Woltersdorf, Mr. Richard E. Schmidt, and Mr. Irving K. Pond. Professor Henry-Russell Hitchcock was kind enough to go over the entire manuscript with me and I owe many helpful suggestions to him.

Finally I should like to express my very warm gratitude to the Museum of Modern Art, which through financial aid made the large number of illustrations possible, and to Mr. W. W. Norton, whose sympathetic coöperation in the preparation of the book has been most sincerely appreciated.

HUGH MORRISON

Dartmouth College, August, 1935

# I. YOUTH AND TRAINING

PATRICK SULLIVAN, need it be said, was Irish. Born on Christmas Day of the year 1818, he made his own way in life from the age of twelve. His mother had died when he was an infant; his father, a landscape painter of mediocre achievements, disappeared completely from his life when the two lost each other in the hurly-burly of a county fair. At first an itinerant fiddler, Patrick later became interested in dancing, found his way to London where he took lessons, and eventually established a dancing academy of his own. On July 22, 1847, he took steerage passage on the ship *Unicorn* from London to Boston. At the age of thirty he set up a dancing academy in Boston. His son Louis describes him quite candidly: "His medium size, his too-sloping shoulders, his excessive Irish face, his small repulsive eyes—the eyes of a pig—of nondescript color and no flash, sunk into his head under rough brows, all seemed unpromising enough in themselves until it is remembered that behind that same mask resided the grim will, the instinctive ambition that had brought him, alone and unaided, out of a childhood of poverty . . . he was of highly virile and sensitive powers, he wrote and spoke English in a polite way, and had acquired an excruciating French. . . . He was moderate of habit; drank a little wine, smoked an occasional cigar, and was an enthusiast regarding hygiene." [1] Three years after his arrival he met in Boston the girl whom he was to marry.

Andrienne Françoise List was born in Geneva in 1835. Her

23

father, Henri List, was German; her mother, Anna Mattheus List, was Swiss-French. The Lists were well-to-do, but they lost money in speculation, and came to America in 1850 in search of better fortune. Andrienne was a skilled piano player—"her sense of rhythm, of sweep, of accent, of the dance-cadence with its reinforcements and languishments, the *tempo rubato*—was genius itself." Patrick Sullivan met Andrienne List in Boston, was attracted by her grace of manner and her musical sense, they became engaged, and were married on August 14, 1852.

The Sullivans lived at first at 22 South Bennett Street, Boston. The older son, Albert Walter Sullivan, was born September 17, 1854; the younger son, Louis Henry Sullivan, was born September 3, 1856. There were no other children. Louis was never formally christened, and although he later called himself "Louis Henry," his mother and his grandmother preferred to call him "Louis Henri," out of respect to his grandfather, and he himself always gallicized the "Louis" in pronunciation.

When Louis was four years old he was sent to the district grammar school. Of this he had only dreary recollections. He learned his letters, he followed the routine, but the school seemed to dull his faculties, slacken his eagerness, and completely ignore his lively imagination and his abundant sympathies. In the early summer of 1862, when he was five, he went to visit his grandparents at a twenty-four-acre farm about a mile from the village of South Reading. From then until he was fourteen he spent all his summers on the farm, an experience which aided greatly in developing his independence and self-reliance, and doubtless bred into him during the formative years of his youth the almost ecstatic love of nature and the strong individualism which characterized his later years.

The Civil War did not affect him greatly, but he was sufficiently interested in it to make a "Monitor" out of a piece of lath and the bung of a flour-barrel, and to set it against a "Merrimac" in a wash-tub of water. At this time he was "abundantly freckled, and in a measure toothless; hatless, barefooted, and unkempt with activity, he was a stout, stocky, miniature ruffian, let loose upon a helpless world." But he had many moments of poignant delight in the beauties of nature, moments which left him in a quiet, self-contained mood, little able to share his experiences with the older people about him. His grandfather was disturbed by these dreamy interludes, fearing an undue precocity, but was reassured by the fact that the boy, between spells, was "ridiculously practical." Much of his time he spent alone in his "domain," a marshy tract surrounded by rolling meadows and clumps of trees, where he built dams in the brook, waded, and otherwise amused himself. Sometimes he sought out other boys to play with; more often he went on long trips of exploration by himself. Or he would visit the stove-foundry man, in town, or the cobbler, who would delight him by "extinguishing the life of a fly on the opposite wall with an unerring squirt of tobacco juice." Evenings, he would get Julia, the robust hired girl, to tell him Irish fairy tales, which he found enchanting and entirely credible.

In the summer of 1863 Patrick Sullivan took Louis away from his grandparents for a time to Newburyport, where he had established a summer school of dancing. He set about to counteract the tendency of Louis' fond grandparents to spoil him by endeavoring to instill a stronger sense of obedience, discipline and respect. Being an enthusiast regarding health, he put Louis through a regular course of physical training—rise at five, a cold wash at the town pump opposite the hotel, a run "to establish circulation," swimming, vaulting, throwing stones, through the day. Under this régime he built up a strong and supple physique, which in later years always stood him in good stead. Shortly after returning to Boston that September the family went to Halifax for six months, where Patrick opened a dancing academy. Louis recalled little but the severe cold of the Nova Scotia winter. In the spring his mother had an attack of diphtheria which compelled the family to return to Boston. Louis, to his great joy, was sent out to South Reading to live with his grandparents until the ensuing fall.

By this time he was becoming quite a youth, proud, ambitious, and with a growing sense of power. His grandfather did not worry greatly about his education, realizing that Louis was acquiring his own kind of education very rapidly. His grandmother, thinking that he needed more polish, started to teach him French, but Louis, as always, rebelled at formal education. "He became oppressed by the inanities of the grammar-book, and the imbecilities of a sort of first reader in which a wax-work father takes his wax children on daily promenades, explaining to them as they go, in terms of unctuous morality, the works of the Creator, and drawing therefrom, as from a spool, an endless thread of pious banalities." So the study was discontinued. Although his grandmother loved him, she could little realize that he was a vigorous young animal with thoughts and an impetuous will of his own.

In September, 1864, he had to go back to his parents in Boston, and was sent to school. The effect of the big city on him was, to say the least, shatteringly discouraging. Acutely sensitive to his surroundings, the crooked streets, the crowded houses, the throngs of wagons and people hurrying here and there with apparent aimlessness, confused and overwhelmed him. He was bewildered and grieved, and withdrew into himself. He was sent to the Brimmer School, on Common Street, and found it a gloomy prison. His father took up his rigorous training of cold baths, outdoor exercise —long walks to Roxbury, to Dorchester, even to Brookline—but it was a long, discouraging winter. The spring in the city had nothing of the joy which he had experienced on the farm. When the vacation came he again went eagerly to his grandparents at South Reading, and regained his former joy in life during the summer.

But again in September he had to go back to Boston. This time —he was now nine years old—he entered the Rice School, on Washington Street, where he was to spend the next three years of his primary education. His lessons seemed to him as dull and mechanical as ever, but he was much excited about Beadle's Dime Novels, which he obtained at a nearby bookstore. In school he picked up, "in addition to a bit of Geography and Arithmetic, every form of profanity, every bit of slang, and every particle of verbal garbage that he could assimilate." In 1868 the Rice School acquired a new building, on made land in the Back Bay district. When Louis was transferred there, in September, the lightness and brightness and cleanliness put him suddenly into a better humor for his lessons. For the first time he became interested in books—he discovered books; he became an earnest student, almost a recluse. He was fascinated by grammar, "took it at one dose." Once an idea had broken upon him, he foresaw consequences with extreme rapidity, and his imagination far outsped any possibility of reasonable accomplishment.

During the latter years of his primary education, his activities spread over an ever-widening field. Always inquisitive and curious, he investigated every street, alley, and wharf from end to end of Boston. Wandering about by himself, he became interested in looking at buildings—he especially admired the Masonic Temple at the corner of Tremont and Boylston Streets. One day when he was about twelve he was wandering along Commonwealth Avenue, and, according to his own account, "saw a large man of dignified bearing, with beard, top hat, and frock coat, come out of a nearby building, enter his carriage and signal the coachman to drive on. The dignity was unmistakable, all men of station in Boston were dignified; sometimes insistently so, but Louis wished to know who and what was behind the dignity." So he asked one of the workmen, who explained that the dignified man was an architect, a man who designed buildings. Having always taken buildings for granted, Louis was much impressed by the revelation that a man could make up a building out of his head. Then and there he made up his mind to become an architect. He confided his new desire to his father, who was greatly pleased that his son's ambition was centering on something definite. He suggested as a counter-proposal that Louis should study at an agricultural college and become a scientific farmer. Louis, although greatly tempted by his love of the outdoors, reflected at length and then said, "No, I have made up my mind." So it was agreed that he should become an architect, and that after he had finished his general education he should go to a technical school, and after that, perhaps, abroad.

That winter Louis' mother suffered another attack of diphtheria, and barely survived it. Since the Boston climate seemed so bad for her Patrick Sullivan decided to move inland, and in the summer of 1869 moved to Chicago, leaving Louis behind to live with his grandparents and to continue his education. During the ensuing year, his last in the grammar school, he lived at South Reading, coming into Boston daily for school. In June, 1870, he graduated with honors, and "there he received in pride, as a scholar, his first and last diploma"—an interesting fact for a man who went on to study in high school, the Massachusetts Institute of Technology, and finally the Ecole des Beaux Arts.

In September, 1870, at fourteen years of age, Louis passed the entrance examinations and was admitted to the English High

School. The English and the Latin High were then housed in a single building, rather old and dingy, merely a partition wall separating them. Louis chanced to be one of forty-odd pupils assigned to a room presided over by one Moses Woolson. It was thus in his first year in high school that he came under the influence of a personality which was to serve as an inspiration for the rest of his life. Moses Woolson was a schoolmaster. He greeted his new pupils with remarks in substance as follows: "You are here as wards in my charge; I accept that charge as sacred; I accept the responsibility involved as a high exacting duty I owe to myself and equally to you. I will give to you all that I have, you shall give to me all that you have." He insisted throughout his training on silence, strict attention, alertness, accurate listening, observation, reflection, discrimination. Louis rose to the challenge. Under Woolson's influence he became interested in things intellectual for their own sake. He disciplined himself as he had never done before. He rapidly acquired a good grounding and an interest in Algebra, Geometry, Botany, Mineralogy, English Literature, and French. Geometry particularly delighted him because of its nicety and exactitude. Sullivan's tribute to Woolson is worth quoting from the *Autobiography:*

"Impartial in judgment, fertile in illustration and expedient, clear in statement, he opened to view a new world. . . . By the end of the school year he had brought order out of disorder, definition out of what was vague, superb alertness out of mere boyish ardor; had nurtured and concentrated all that was best in the boy; had made him consciously courageous and independent; had focussed his powers of thought, feeling and action; had confirmed Louis' love of the great out of doors, as a source of inspiration; and had climaxed all by parting a great veil which opened to the view of this same boy the wonderland of Poetry. . . . There may have been teachers and teachers, but for Louis Sullivan there was and could be only one. And now, in all too feeble utterance he pleads this token, remembrance, to the memory of one long since passed on."

Toward the end of his first year in high school, Louis was left alone at South Reading. In April, 1871, his grandmother died and his grandfather and his uncle Jules broke up their home on the farm and went to live in Philadelphia. For the next two years Louis made his home with a next-door-neighbor at South Reading, John A. Thompson. He continued to go into Boston daily for his classes under Moses Woolson, and, during his second year, under a schoolmaster named Hale, whom he describes as "a scholar and a gentleman, a shining light of conscientious, conventional, virtuous routine." He seems to have acquired rather more in the way of education in his adopted home. John A. Thompson was a cultivated gentleman, whose dinner-table conversations were a liberal education in themselves. Louis felt that he had now definitely entered the cultural world. In particular, it was during this time that his taste for music developed and became a source of enjoyment for all his later years. "Thus he learned concerning chords, that the one in particular that had overwhelmed him with a sort of gorgeous sorrow was called the dominant seventh, and another that seemed eerie and that gave him a peculiar nervous thrill and chill was named the augmented fifth." He became exceedingly curious about modulations, modes, diatonic and chromatic scales, and other technicalities and names. He heard symphony concerts, soloists, and light concert music of all kinds in Boston. Especially he learned much about oratorios. He became a skilled pianist. Many years later, a catalogue of his library listed fourteen volumes of oratorios, as well as several books on musical analysis, harmony, etc.

George Thompson, the son, was slightly older than Louis, and was studying railroad engineering at the Massachusetts Institute of Technology. Through him Louis became interested in going to "Tech" for his architectural education. At George Thompson's instance he essayed the entrance examinations at the end of his second year in the English High School, passed them with ease, and accordingly entered M.I.T. in September, 1872, at the age of sixteen, to take the course in architecture.

The school was in Rogers Hall, near the corner of Boylston and Berkeley Streets, with pleasant study-rooms, a long drafting-room, library, and lecture-room. It was the first architectural school to be established in this country, and was comparatively new at the time, having been opened in 1865. It was directed by Professor William Ware, of the firm of Ware & Van Brunt. Professor Ware, in Louis' description, was "a gentleman of the old school; a bachelor, of good height, slender, bearded in the English fashion, and turning gray. He had his small affectations, harmless enough. His voice was somewhat husky, his polite bearing impeccable and kind. He had a precious sense of quiet humor, and common sense seemed to have a strong hold on him. Withal he was worthy of personal respect and affection. His attainments were moderate in scope and soundly cultural as of the day; his judgments were clear and just. The words amiability and quiet common sense sum up his personality; he was not imaginative enough to be ardent. . . . The misfortune was that in his lectures on the history of architecture he never looked his pupils in the eye, but by preference addressed an audience in his beard, in a low and confidential tone, ignoring a game of spitball under way. Yet a word or a phrase reached the open now and then concerning styles, construction, and so forth, and at times he went to the blackboard and drew this and that very neatly."

His assistant was Eugène Letang, a recent graduate of the *atelier Vaudremer* of the Ecole des Beaux Arts in Paris, and winner of the *Grand Prix de Rome*. He was about thirty, sallow and earnest, with a long and lean face and no professional air, but patient, and a student among the students. Of the latter, there were about thirty, all told—some already university graduates, almost all older and more worldly wise than Louis. He found among them agreeable companions, however, and thoroughly enjoyed the space and the freedom of the drafting-room intercourse. Under their influence he "began to put on a bit of swagger, to wear smart clothes, to shave away the down and to agitate a propaganda for inch-long side whiskers. A photograph of that date (Fig. 1) shows him as a clean-cut young man, with a rather intelligent expression, a heavy mop of black hair neatly parted for the occasion, a pearl stud set in immaculate white, and a suit up to the minute in material and cut."

Early in his career at "Tech" Louis saw from its very beginnings the famous Boston fire of November, 1872. His description of it bears repetition. It began with a small flame "curling from the wooden cornice of a building on the north side of Summer Street. There were perhaps a half a dozen persons present at the time. The street was night-still. It was early. No fire engine came. . . . All was quiet as the small flame grew into a whorl and sparks shot upward from a glow behind; the windows became lighted from within. A few more people gathered, but no engine came. Then began a gentle purring roar. The few became a crowd, but no engine came. Glass crackled and crashed, flames burst forth madly from all windows, and the lambent dark flames behind them soared high, casting multitudes of sparks and embers abroad, as they cracked and wheezed. The roof fell, the floors collapsed. A hand-drawn engine came, but too late. The front wall tottered, swayed and crumbled to the pavement, exposing to view a roaring furnace. It was too late. The city seemed doomed. Louis followed its ravages all night long. It was a magnificent but terrible pageant of wrathful fire before whose onslaught row after row of regimented buildings melted away. . . ." For two nights after the fire Louis served as a guard in the M.I.T. volunteer battalion. He was thus not unacquainted with the disorder and desolation caused by a great conflagration when he went to Chicago the next year.

The architectural training given at "Tech" was quite according to rule. Louis learned how to draw expertly—for him, we can imagine, an easy task. He learned the classic orders as the fundamentals of architectural design. He learned the historic styles. Architecture, he could see, was neatly pigeonholed in the files of the past. The classic style was something that had columns and pediments; the Gothic style had pinnacles and crockets; all of the styles were considered as vocabularies of detail rather than as modes of building. All of the styles, too, he found, were sacrosanct; it was only through them that architectural beauty could be achieved in the present. "Louis learned about diameters, modules, minutes, entablatures, columns, pediments, and so forth and so forth, with the associated minute measurements and copious vocabulary, all of which items he supposed at the time were intended to be received in unquestioning faith, as eternal verities. . . . Thus passed the days, the weeks, the months, in a sort of mischmasch of architectural theology, and Louis came to see that it was not upon the spirit but upon the word that stress was laid. . . . But the sanctity of the orders Louis considered quaint; the orders were really fairy tales of long ago, now by the learned made rigid, mechanical and inane in the books he was pursuing, wherein they were stultified, for lack of common sense and human feeling. . . . He began to feel a vacancy in himself, the need of something more nutritious to the mind than a play of marionettes. He felt the need and the lack of a red-blooded explanation, of a valiant idea that should bring life to arouse this cemetery of orders and of styles. . . . Moreover, as the time passed he began to discover that this school was but a pale reflection of the Ecole des Beaux Arts; and he thought it high time that he go to headquarters to learn if what was preached there as a gospel really signified glad tidings."

Louis made up his mind that he would leave M.I.T. at the end of his first year. He was aggressive and impatient; he knew what he wanted. He determined at that time to go to the Ecole, but before this he wanted a year or so of actual experience in an architect's office—to investigate the practice as well as the theory of architecture. This decision was a very important one, as it gave him a certain hard-headed knowledge of building that stood him in good stead when he later encountered the glamour and the superficial brilliance of the Ecole training.

Louis said good-bye to "Tech" at the end of his first year, and headed for Philadelphia to live with his grandfather and uncle. On his way he stopped off in New York for a few days. He met Richard Morris Hunt, then in his middle forties but already successful. Hunt, first of American architects to study in Paris, told Louis stories of life at the Ecole in the good old days of 1845, and of his work in the *atelier libre* of Hector Lefuel, and later of the great work on the New Louvre in which he had assisted Lefuel. Hunt patted the enterprising youth of sixteen on the back, and encouraged him in his aspirations. Louis went on to Philadelphia.

Once established at his grandfather's, he went out to look for work in his own way. It was not his method to comb the architects' offices to see which one would take him. Rather he combed the streets looking at the work of architects to see which office he would take. It was characteristic of his taste that the building which most appealed to him—a large residence being completed on South Broad Street—was by one of the freest and most original architects of Philadelphia in that day, Frank Furness. Louis accordingly presented himself at the office the next day, and informed Mr. Furness that he had come to enter his employ. Mr. Furness inquired as to his experience, and when informed that Louis had just come from the Massachusetts Institute of Technology, exploded, blowing up in fragments all the schools in the land and scattering the professors headless and limbless to the four quarters of earth and hell. Louis, he said, was a fool; a fool and an idiot to have wasted his time in a place where one was filled with sawdust, like a doll, and became a prig, a snob, and an ass. Louis was warmed by this fire; to hear his own sentiments so eloquently expressed reinforced his determination to work for this Frank Furness. He agreed that he knew little or nothing, but said that he was capable of learning, told of his discovery of the house on Broad Street and how he had followed "from the nugget to the solid vein," said that here he could learn, that here he was, and that here he would remain. By this time Louis was capable of something of a Celtic eloquence himself, and it ended in his being taken on at ten dollars a week. "Come tomorrow morning for a trial," said Furness, "but I prophesy you won't outlast a week." Louis entered the office. At the end of the week Furness said, "You may stay another week," and at the end of that week he said, "You may stay as long as you like." His first job was to retrace a set of plans for a Savings Institution to be erected on Chestnut Street.

"Frank Furness was a curious character. He affected the English in fashion. He wore loud plaids, and a scowl, and from his face depended fan-like a marvellous red beard, beautiful in tone with each separate hair delicately crinkled from beginning to end. Moreover, his face was snarled and homely as an English bull-dog's. . . . The other member of the firm was George Hewitt, a slender, mustached person, pale and reserved, who seldom relaxed from his pose. It was he who did the Victorian Gothic in its pantalettes, when a church building or something of the sort was on the boards. With precision, as though he held his elements by pincers, he worked out these decorous sublimities of inanity, as per the English current magazines and other English sources. . . . Louis regarded him with admiration as a draftsman, and with mild contempt as a man who kept his nose in the books. Frank Furness 'made buildings out of his head.' That suited Louis better. And Furness as a freehand draftsman was extraordinary. He had Louis hypnotized, especially when he drew and swore at the same time."

John Hewitt, George's younger brother, helped Louis a great deal with his draftsmanship. Louis worked hard day and night. At first he lived with his grandfather and uncle in West Philadelphia, but soon moved into town to be nearer the office. The summer was hot, and he frequently walked through Fairmount Park (before it was landscaped for the Centennial Exhibition) and up the small valley of the Wissahickon of a Sunday. The offices of Furness & Hewitt were on the top floor of a four-story brick building at the corner of Third Street and Chestnut. From this vantage point, on a hot September day, Louis looked down into the streets on the mob scenes attendant on the closing of Jay Cooke & Company's office, a few doors down the street, that inaugurated the bank runs and historic panic of 1873. His first architectural experience was to be short-lived. Furness & Hewitt, like every other firm, was hit by the depression. They finished up commissions already undertaken, but in November work was running dry, and since Louis had been the last to be taken on, he was the first to be released. He left the office with the regrets and warm best wishes of Frank Furness.

Within a week Louis took the train for Chicago to join his parents. He arrived through miles of disheartening shanties and the dirty ruins of the Great Fire. It was the day before Thanksgiving, 1873. The city was still largely in ashes, but the ambition of recovery was in the air. Building was extremely active. In the first years after the fire, 1872 and 1873, the output of the more important architects' offices was actually measured by the mile. John M. Van Osdel designed over 8,000 feet of "first class" front during the eighteen months after the fire; Carter, Drake & Wight did five miles; W. W. Boyington over three. Less important then, but to become big names in the world of architecture during the next generation, were the firms of Jenney, Schermerhorn & Bogart (William LeBaron Jenney began practice in Chicago in 1868); Burling & Adler (established 1871); and the promising young firm of Burnham & Root (established 1873).

The seventeen-year-old youth was fascinated by the city. "Louis thought it all magnificent and wild: a crude extravaganza, an intoxicating rawness, a sense of big things to be done. . . . The elevated wooden sidewalks in the business district, with steps at each street corner, seemed shabby and grotesque; but when Louis learned that this meant that the city had determined to raise itself three feet more out of the mud, his soul declared that this resolve meant high courage; that the idea was big; that there must be big men here. The shabby walks now became a symbol of stout hearts. . . . The pavements were vile, because hastily laid; they erupted here and there and everywhere in ooze. Most of the buildings, too, were paltry. . . . But in spite of the panic, there was stir; an energy that made him tingle to be in the game."

Louis followed his Philadelphia procedure in looking for a job. In the course of his explorations, he especially admired the Portland Block, a new building at the southeast corner of Dearborn and Washington Streets. He inquired as to the architect, and was given the name of Major William LeBaron Jenney. He forthwith applied at the Major's office, and was taken on immediately, as more help was needed. During his six months in Major Jenney's office, Louis formed his first acquaintance with the many interesting personalities of the architectural world in Chicago. Major Jenney was the first of these, and Louis has left a classic description of him. "The Major was a free-and-easy cultured gentleman, but not an architect except by courtesy of terms. His true profession was that of engineer. He received his training at the Ecole Polytechnique in France, and had served through the Civil War as Major of Engineers. He had been with Sherman on the march to the sea. He spoke French with an accent so atrocious that it jarred Louis' teeth, while his English speech jerked about as though it had St. Vitus' dance. He was monstrously pop-eyed, with hanging mobile features, sensuous lips, and he disposed of matters easily in the manner of a war veteran who believed he knew what was what. Louis soon found out that the Major was not, really, in his heart, an engineer at all, but by nature and in toto, a *bon vivant*, a *gourmet*. He lived at Riverside, a suburb, and Louis often smiled to see him carry home by their naked feet, with all plumage, a brace or two of choice wild ducks, or other game birds, or a rare and odorous cheese from abroad. And the Major knew his vintages, every one, and his sauces, every one; he was also a master of the chafing dish and the charcoal grille. All in all the Major was effusive; a hail fellow well met, an officer of the Loyal Legion, a welcome guest anywhere, but by preference a host. He was also an excellent *raconteur*, with a lively sense of humor and a certain

piquancy of fancy that seemed Gallic. In his stories or his mono-
logues, his unique vocal mannerisms or gyrations or gymnastics
were a rich asset, as he squeaked or blew, or lost his voice, or ran
in arpeggio from deep bass to harmonics, or took octaves, or fifths,
or sevenths, or ninths in spasmodic splendor. His audience roared,
for his stories were choice, and his voice as one caught bits of it,
was plastic, rich and sweet, and these bits, in sequence and collec-
tively had a warming effect."

Many stories attest to the kindliness and generosity of the Major,
and his abilities as a teacher are indicated by a list of some of
the men who got their start in his office. Besides Louis Sullivan,
there were, at one time or another, Martin Roche, William A.
Holabird, John Edelmann, Irving K. Pond, Howard Van Doren
Shaw, James Gamble Rogers, and Alfred Granger. If the Major
liked a student in his office, or a draftsman, he would stop his
work and spend an hour or two teaching, instructing, explaining.

At the time Louis entered the office John Edelmann was foreman. They became close friends, and Louis conceived an admiration for John which lasted the rest of his life. Edelmann was twenty-
four at the time, "brawny, bearded, unkempt, careless, his voice
rich, sonorous, modulant, his vocabulary an overflowing reser-
voir. . . . By nature indolent, by vanity and practice very rapid.
He was a profound thinker, a man of immense range of reading,
a brain of extraordinary keenness, strong, vivid, that ranged in
its operations from saturnine intelligence concerning men and their
motives to the highest transcendentalisms of German metaphysics.

"There was enough work in the office to keep five men and a
boy busy, provided they took intervals of rest, which they did.
In the Major's absences, which were frequent and long, bedlam
reigned. John Edelmann would mount a drawing table and make
a howling stump speech on greenback currency, or single tax,

while at the same time Louis, at the top of his voice, sang selections from oratorios, beginning with his favorite, 'Why Do the Nations So Furiously Rage Together?'; and so all the force furiously raged together in joyous deviltry and bang-bang-bang. . . . The office-rat suddenly appears: 'Cheese it, Cullies; the Boss!' . . . Sudden silence, sudden industry, intense concentration. The Major enters and announces his pleasure in something less than three octaves. Thus the day's work comes out fairly even. . . ."

With John Edelmann Louis went every Sunday afternoon through that winter to hear Hans Balatka and his orchestra play Wagner in Turner Hall, on the North Side. Wagner was the first of his great enthusiasms. He saw in him a mighty personality, a great free spirit, who had created a domain of his own out of his imagination and his will. He responded to the power in Wagner as he later responded to the unbounded power of Michelangelo. Louis and John Edelmann also frequented the gymnasium together, and in the spring lived for a time in the latter's boat-house in the preserves of the "Lotus Club," on the Calumet River.

As the spring months wore on Louis decided that his experience in the offices of Furness & Hewitt and of Jenney had given him that taste of architecture as it is practiced which he had desired as a part of his training, and that it was now time for him to fulfil his resolve to go to the fountain-head of architectural education— the Ecole des Beaux Arts. He took the train East, and on July 10, 1874, sailed from New York on the *Britannic*. The boat called at Queenstown, where Louis got a glimpse of the high hills of the coastline, his only view of Ireland, and landed at Liverpool. He remained in Liverpool a day or two, and in London two weeks, then took the Dover-Dieppe Channel boat for France. He arrived in Paris after nightfall, and went to the Hotel St. Honoré. After a few days there he found himself permanent quarters on the seventh floor of a rooming hotel at the corner of the Rue Monsieur le Prince and the Rue Racine, in the Latin Quarter.

Louis had six weeks in which to prepare himself for the searching entrance examinations of the Ecole. During this time he had to become proficient in spoken French, and brush up on a wide range of subjects, especially Mathematics and History. He was in good physical condition, and he planned to work eighteen hours a day, allotting one hour a day for gymnasium to keep himself in trim. His high-school French, he found, was woefully inadequate. He intended to work several hours a day and to learn colloquial French. He engaged a tutor to come every day, was not satisfied, and selected a second who was soon worn out. The third one stuck. "He saw into Louis' plan and it amused him greatly, so much so that he joined in jovially, and made a play of it. A *petit verre* started him off nicely. He possessed a rare art of conversation, was full of anecdote, personal incident and reminiscence, knew his Paris, had the sense of comedy to a degree, looked upon life as a huge joke, upon all persons as jokes, and upon Louis as such in particular—he would amuse himself with this frantic person. At once he spoke to Louis *en camarade, vieux copain*, as one Frenchman to another. He made running comments on the news of the day, explained all sorts of things Louis was beginning to note in Paris life, put him in the running. He had a gift of mimicry, would imitate the provincial dialects and peasant jargon, with fitting tone and gesture, and, taking a given topic or incident, would relate it in terms and impersonations ranging in series from gamin to Academician. . . . He was well built, well under middle age, seldom sat for long, but paced the floor, or lolled here and there by moments. His voice was suave, his manner frank and free. He had an air, was well bred. He was either an unconscious or a crafty teacher, a *rara avis*, he knew how to get results. The daily lesson lasted one hour, and Louis plowed on at high tension."

At the American Legation he was referred to a Monsieur Clopet as an excellent tutor in Mathematics. He lost no time in calling, and was greeted by a small dark man. The preliminaries over, M. Clopet asked: "And what are the books you have under your arm?" Louis replied, "Books I was told at the American Legation I would need." He took the books, selected a large work on Descriptive Geometry, and began to turn the pages. "Now observe: Here is a problem with five exceptions or special cases; here is a theorem, three special cases; another nine, and so on and on, a procession of exceptions and special cases. I suggest you place the book in the waste basket; we shall not have need of it here; for here our demonstrations shall be so broad as to admit of no exception." The phrase flashed through Louis' mind. Here, perhaps, was born his life's aim in the field of architecture: to make a "Clopet demonstration" for architecture—to formulate *a rule so broad as to admit of no exceptions.*

Louis joined the Mathematics class, consisting of some twenty young men, but no other English or Americans. "At M. Clopet's class all were hard put to it to keep up their notes as a lecture progressed. M. Clopet was gentle, polished, forceful. 'One must work; that is what one is here for.' As a drill master he was a potent driver, as an expounder he made good his word to Louis in a method and a manner, revealing, inspiriting, as he calmly unfolded, step by step, a well reasoned process in his demonstrations, which were so simple, so inclusive, so completely rounded as to preclude exception; and there was not a book in sight. . . . Louis was especially pleased at the novelty of saying *je dis*— 'I say'—at the beginning of a demonstration. It humanized matters, brought them home, close up, a sort of challenge. How much more intelligent and lively to begin: 'I say that the sum of the angles of any triangle equals two right angles' than the formal impersonal statement: 'The sum of the angles of any triangle equals two right angles.' The latter statement one may take or leave. The former is a personal assertion and implies 'I will show you.' In fact, it was this 'I say' and this 'I will show you' that made up the charm of M. Clopet's teaching method. . . . At the end of the first half-hour M. Clopet always called a recess. From his pocket he drew forth his pouch and his little book of rice papers; so did the others. There was sauntering, spectacular smoking and conversation. The cigarette finished, work was resumed. . . . After recess the students were put through their paces at the blackboard for the final half-hour."

At the earnest urging of his fellow students, Louis discarded his flannel suit and white canvas shoes, to appear in a tall silk hat, an infant beard, long tail coat, dark trousers, polished shoes, kid gloves, and a jaunty cane—a student among the students. Every night he studied by candle-light in his small room on the seventh floor—arranged his Mathematics notes, studied French vocabulary, read History by the hour. And so the six weeks passed; the examinations, early in October, had arrived.

The examinations were written, drawn, and oral, covering a period of three weeks. The free-hand drawing, the mechanical drawing, and a simple architectural project were easy for Louis. More difficult were the oral examinations, which were conducted in little amphitheatres, with a professor presiding, and all aspirants free to come and go as they wished. Louis faced his inquisitor in Mathematics for over an hour of steady questioning. The examination was designed to test, not his memory, but his ability to think in mathematical terms. At the end of the examination the professor shook his hand and said: "I felicitate you, Monsieur Sullivan; you have the mathematical imagination which is rather rare. I wish you well." The examination in History included only three questions, but each of these involved an hour and a half of constant talking. The three questions were: "Monsieur, will you be kind enough to tell me the story of the Hebrew people?"; "I would like an account of ten emperors of Rome"; and "Give me an intimate account of the times of Francis I." The latter question interested Louis especially, as he had studied the period carefully, and the time and its people, its manners and customs and thoughts stood out before him as a very present picture. He passed the examination with the highest rating. These examinations gave Louis an insight into the quality and reach of French thought—its richness, its solidity, and above all the severity of its discipline beneath so smooth a surface.

The examinations passed successfully, Louis was entered as a member of the Ecole des Beaux Arts, and elected to study in the *atelier libre* of M. Emil Vaudremer. M. Vaudremer was a practicing architect of middle age, considered a distinguished member of his profession. The first problem was a three-months' *projet*, for which the twenty-four-hour sketches were made *en loge* and filed as briefs. The *esquisse-en-loge* served as a kind of outline, a thesis, which must be adhered to closely in the development of the complete conception. This, it seemed to Louis, was discipline of an inspired sort, as it permitted free play to the individual creative imagination in establishing the essentials of a problem, then a firm adherence to those essentials in working out its ramifications and details. Once the *projet* was given out all the students in the atelier vanished, to work out the details wherever and however they wished. Many of them left the city. Louis felt the need of relaxation after the stress of preparing for the examinations, and decided to take a short trip to Italy.

He went first to Rome. He spent only three days there—two of them in the Sistine Chapel. Needless to say, it was Michelangelo's great ceiling paintings which held him. Michelangelo became for him another and a greater than Wagner. "Here Louis communed in silence with a Super-Man. Here he felt and saw a great Free Spirit. Here he was filled with the awe that stills. . . . Here was power as he had seen it in the mountains, here was power as he had seen it in the prairies, in the open sky, in the great lake stretching like a floor toward the horizon, here was the power of the forest primeval. Here was the power of the open—of the free spirit of man striding abroad in the open. Here was the living presence of a man who had done things in the beneficence of power." This enthusiasm for Michelangelo when a boy of eighteen remained with him the rest of his life, and he always kept as a prized possession a little folio of reproductions of the paintings of the Sistine Ceiling. Next, he journeyed to Florence, where he stayed six weeks, but nothing there seemed to have impressed him as much as did Michelangelo. He returned along the Riviera to Nice, and thence to Paris.

Louis went back to his old rooms at the corner of the Rue Monsieur le Prince and the Rue Racine, and took up again his work in the atelier. The quarters were not palatial. "The atelier . . . was at the ground level, a rough affair, like a carpenter's shop, large enough to accommodate about twenty young ruffians. Here it was the work was done amid a cross-fire of insults, and it was also here that Monsieur Emil Vaudremer came to make his 'criticisms.' He was one of the dark Frenchmen, of medium size, who carried a fine air of native distinction; a man toward whom one's heart instantly went out in respectful esteem bordering on pride and affection. His personality was calm, deliberate yet magnetic, a sustained, quiet dignity bespeaking a finished product. His 'criticisms' were, therefore, just what one might expect them to be, clear, clean-cut, constructive, and personal to each student—in each case with that peculiar sympathy with the young which comes from remembrance of one's own youth. Always, however, he was a disciplinarian, and one felt the steady pressure."

Louis went to work to carry out his *projet*, entering heart and soul into the serious yet occasionally tumultuous life of the atelier. At first, like all the *nouveaux*, the neophytes, he was required by the older students to carry wood for the stove, or clean the drawing boards. But his ready command of French and the sprinkling of thieves' slang which he had picked up from his tutor and used effectively on occasions soon raised his status to that of an *ancien*. The intimate contacts, the free commingling of younger and older students, the discussions about the work, seemed invaluable to him.

Louis remained in Paris about two years.[2] He studied carefully all the monuments and museums of Paris, followed all the architectural exhibitions at the Ecole, and thoroughly familiarized himself with the theory of its training. But like the architectural school at M.I.T., he soon found it merely academic. The problems it set were not the real problems of architecture. How could they teach creation in a vacuum? To Sullivan in his later years there could be no real creation in architecture without the stimulus of a definite and actual problem that had to be solved, a need that had to be filled. The problems set at the Ecole were not such as would be met with in actual architectural practice, and because they were not real problems they failed to achieve the general value and significance that they might have had. In Louis' mind, the theory of the school "settled down to a theory of *plan*, yielding results of extraordinary brilliancy, but which, after all, was not the reality he sought, but an abstraction, a method, a state of mind, that was local and specific; not universal. Intellectual and aesthetic, it beautifully set forth a sense of order, of function, of highly skilled manipulation. Yet there was for him a fatal residuum of artificiality, which gave him a secret sense of misery where he wished but too tenderly to be happy."

It was not that Louis disliked the history of architecture, which he studied intensively. It was the tendency of the Ecole to study the history of architecture as a series of crystallizations called "styles" that seemed artificial to him. He preferred to study the history of architecture "not merely as a fixation here and there in time and place, but as a continuous outpouring never to end, from the infinite fertility of man's imagination, evoked by his changing needs." There came to him the conviction that the Ecole, perfect as it was within the limits of its theory of education, lacked "the profound animus of a primal inspiration." "Thus crept over him the certitude that the book was about to close; that he was becoming solitary in his thoughts and heart-hungry, that he must go his way alone, that the Paris of his delight must and should remain the dream of his delight, that the pang of inevitable parting was at hand."

Louis returned to Chicago. When he arrived the effects of the panic of 1873 had not wholly passed, and the building industry was inactive. He found no immediate employment, and to put in his time he made a systematic reconnaissance of the city. Daily he made twenty miles or more on foot. Thus he discovered and knew the whole city. After a time he obtained a minor position in an architect's office, and after this a series of brief engagements in other offices, until he had nearly covered the field. Most of his employers were men of the older generation, of homely make-up and homely ways, who had little respect for Louis' new-fangled foreign education, and for whom he felt much sympathy. He found them very human, and enjoyed their shop-talk, which was that of the graduate carpenter. During the course of the year 1877 building conditions were improving and his engagements in offices grew longer. He came to have the reputation of a hard worker and a clever draftsman, and he increased his salary somewhat with each move. But still he was not satisfied to remain a draftsman. His intention was to enter the office of an older architect with an established practice, provided he could find the right man, and to work up as rapidly as his industry and his talents would permit to the position of a partner in the firm. But the desired opportunity did not appear at once. For some three years after his return from Paris Louis was a rolling stone.

Although not definitely located professionally, he used his evenings to try to locate himself intellectually. He was consciously trying to work out a "Clopet demonstration" for architecture. At first he swung to pure engineering. He often saw Frederick Baumann, an able engineer who had published a paper on *A Theory of Isolated Pier Foundations* in 1873, which was to become the basis for standard practice during the eighties and nineties. Together they discussed engineering problems. Louis made Trautwine's *Engineer's Pocket Book* his bible, and spent long hours with it. The engineering journals kept him in close touch with current doings; he followed every detail of the construction of the Eads Bridge over the Mississippi at St. Louis, and the Kentucky River Bridge. The chief engineers became his new heroes, and as he went into the subject he began to feel that the engineers of the day were the only builders who faced a problem squarely. He even dreamed for a while of becoming an engineer.

But his interest in the science of engineering soon developed into a larger interest in science in general. He read much of Darwin, Spencer, Huxley, and Tyndall. In them he found an enormous new world opening before him. The scientific method appealed to him as a weapon of thought for him to master and apply to the solution of his problems in architecture.

One day his old friend John Edelmann returned from Iowa, where he had had a spell of farming during the dull period, and found a position in the office of the firm of Burling & Adler. Louis met him in Kinsley's restaurant, where the draftsmen from various architects' offices habitually lunched and talked shop. Edelmann suggested that Louis go over to his office to meet Adler. This was the first meeting between Dankmar Adler and his future partner. Edelmann and Sullivan "entered the large bare room, drawing tables scattered about it; in the center were two plain desks . . . both partners were present and busy. Burling was slouched in a swivel chair, his long legs covering the desk top; he wiggled a chewed cigar as he talked to a caller, and spat into a square box. He was an incredible, long and bulky nosed Yankee, perceptibly aging fast, and of manifestly weakening will—one of the passing generation who had done a huge business after the fire but whom the panic had hit hard. . . . Further away stood Adler at a draftsman's table. . . . He was a heavy-set short-nosed Jew, well-bearded, with a magnificent domed forehead which stopped suddenly at a solid mass of black hair. (Fig. 2 is a photograph of Adler taken about 1880.) He was a picture of sturdy strength, physical and mental. . . . His broad, serious face, and kindly brown, efficient eyes joined in a rich smile of open welcome. It did not take many ticks of the clock to note that Adler's brain was intensely active and ambitious, his mind open, broad, receptive, and of an unusually high order. . . . The talk was brief and lively; Adler said nice things, questioned Louis as to his stay at the Beaux Arts. The little talk ended, Louis left; John remained in his preserve. This was the last Louis saw of Adler for many moons. He was pleased to have met him and to have reason heartily to respect his vigorous personality. But he was no part of Louis' program, hence he soon faded from view, and became almost completely forgotten."

It was not until about a year later that the two men came together again. John Edelmann had in the meantime established a partnership with George H. Johnson, a pioneer in the use of tile for fireproofing buildings, but he kept in touch with his former employers. One day early in 1879 Edelmann sought Louis out to tell him that Adler had dissolved his partnership with Burling, and had set up independently. Adler had put through the important new Central Music Hall, then under construction, and had other jobs in the office. Edelmann urged that this was Louis' opportunity. Adler, he knew, would welcome a competent designer.

"So they made a second call on Adler. There ensued a mutual sizing-up at close range, very friendly indeed. And it was then and there agreed that Louis was to take charge of Adler's office, was to have a free hand, and, if all went well for a period and they should get along well together, there was something tangible in the background. Louis took hold and made things hum. Soon there came into the office three large orders; a six-story high grade office building—the Borden Block; an up-to-date theatre, and a large substantial residence. Louis put through the work with the efficiency of combined Moses Woolson and Beaux Arts training. It was his first fine opportunity. He used it. He found in Adler a most congenial co-worker, open-minded, generous-minded, quick to perceive, thorough-going, warm in his enthusiasms, opening to Louis every opportunity to go ahead on his own responsibility, posting him on matters of building technique of which he had a complete grasp, and all in all treating Louis as a prize pet. . . . Thus they became warm friends. Adler said one day 'How would you like to take me into partnership?' Louis laughed. 'All right,' said Adler, 'draw up a contract for five years, beginning first of May. First year you one-third, after that even.' Louis drew up a brief memorandum on a sheet of office stationery, which Adler read over once and signed. On the first day of May, 1880, D. Adler and Co. moved into a fine suite of offices on the top floor of the Borden Block aforesaid. On the first day of May, 1881, the firm of Adler & Sullivan, Architects, had its name on the entrance door." Thus after architectural training and experience of nearly nine years, Sullivan became at the age of twenty-four a full partner in one of the important architectural firms of Chicago.

[1] This and subsequent quotations in this chapter are drawn from *The Autobiography of an Idea*.

[2] Sullivan does not state in *The Autobiography of an Idea* how long he remained at the Ecole, and no other definite source of information on this point has been uncovered. Mr. George Elmslie, who worked with him later for some twenty years, asserts that he was in Paris "short of two years," which would have meant that he came back to Chicago before July, 1876.

# II. EARLY WORKS

By 1880 architecture in Chicago and the Middle West generally had reached its nadir. The earlier Greek Revival tradition, which had produced a reasonably satisfactory vernacular architecture, died away shortly after the Civil War. In its place there was no tradition, only a clamor of discordant fashions ranging from what H. Stewart Leonard has termed "carpenter's frenzy," a St. Vitus' dance of spindly lathe-work and jig-saw scrolls, to the slightly recognizable "styles" of the professional architects; all were pretentious, all were romantically historical in intention, and all were completely and irremediably bad. Although architects and carpenter-builders professed to be designing in historical styles, there were none in Chicago with even the scholarship of Richard Morris Hunt, whose Vanderbilt House in New York (1879–81) in the Early French Renaissance manner at least set a new standard of imitation in the East. Nor was there such a powerful creative figure as H. H. Richardson. Richardson's "Romanesque" was by this time beginning to be a vogue in the East; his Trinity Church in Boston had been finished in 1877 and was proving a potent influence. But his style had not yet reached Chicago. To be sure, his American Merchants' Union Express Building in Chicago, built in 1872, had used some Romanesque forms, but it was by no means typical of his developed style, which did not reach Chicago until he built there in the middle eighties.

The popular "styles" in Chicago in 1880 were those which give the epithets "The Gilded Age" and "The Reign of Terror" their justification. Most fashionable, perhaps, was the mansarded French Second Empire, a style much corrupted in transmission from the Paris of Baron Haussmann. It was a comparatively recent importation to Chicago, its first important exemplar there (and one of the most elaborate in America) being the Palmer House, built after the fire by John M. Van Osdel, and famous throughout the Middle West for its sumptuous elegance and the silver dollars imbedded in the barber-shop floor. Van Osdel had not at that time been to Europe, but he easily found every last detail in the monumental tomes of César Daly's *Architecture privée du XIX^e siècle*, published in 1864. His position as the dean of Chicago architects (he had been the first professional architect in the city and had enjoyed a long and honorable practice there for thirty-five years) established the new style as fashionable, and in 1880 it was still the cachet of wealth and a position in society.

The only serious rival was the Victorian Gothic, inherited from Pugin's and Scott's revivals of the Gothic in England, confused by Butterfield's velleity for Italian polychromy, Italian Gothic arches, picturesque roof-lines, pinnacles, chimney-buttresses, and other "Gothic" paraphernalia. The Victorian Gothic was perhaps the most widespread of any single style, lending itself to all types of buildings, public and private. Another style, best known to Chicagoans in the Potter Palmer "castle" on the Lake Shore Drive (1884) and in the quaint old Water Tower (1869) rising in the middle of North Michigan Avenue, is commonly· referred to as "Castellated Gothic," and properly known as "pure Norman" according to the architects who employed it. With rough, quarry-faced masonry, rugged walls pierced by small and irregularly-placed windows, donjon-tower accents and battlemented parapets, the style was fairly popular, especially in penitentiary and armory architecture. Then there was a host of other "styles," such as the miraculous Byzantine of Boyington's gaudy Board of Trade Building, or the Flemish guild-hall effect of the old Dearborn Street Station. Perhaps the quintessence of romantic eclecticism had been reached in the previous generation in the Crosby Opera House (1865), which an account of 1891 describes as "an Italo-Byzantine French Venetian structure with Norman windows," adding that it was "the finest building in Chicago in its day." There was indeed a babel of tongues.

On the side of engineering, however, Chicago architecture was leading the country. The circumstances of the Great Fire of 1871 and the difficult soil-conditions combined to force experiments in new methods of fireproofing and foundation construction. George H. Johnson designed, in the Kendall Building in 1872, the first fireproof hollow tile floor construction in the country, and the Montauk Building, built by Burnham & Root in 1880–81, was the first office building entirely fireproofed in the modern manner, with all iron framework sheathed. The difficult problem of making foundations strong enough to support high buildings on a compressible soil was partially solved by Frederick Baumann's invention of isolated spread-footing foundations in 1873. Burnham & Root still further improved foundations for high buildings by devising the steel-grillage imbedded in concrete in 1884. Meantime, Major William LeBaron Jenney was making the series of experiments in the use of an iron frame which resulted in the epoch-making invention of skyscraper construction in the Home Insurance Building of 1884.[1]

Chicago had fully recovered from the depression of 1873, and the building industry was booming. The offices of Burnham & Root, Van Osdel, Jenney, and Boyington were full of commissions, and the Loop section of the city was being completely transformed.

There were still thousands of houses to be built to replace those destroyed in the fire, and to accommodate the expanding population of the city. The spirit of growth was in the air.

It was into this mélange of high ambition, practical sense, and aesthetic confusion that Sullivan stepped when he began practice with Adler in 1880. From the time of their first joint work to the undertaking of the Auditorium, they designed some sixty-five structures of various types—office buildings, factories, theatres, residences, etc.

It was in the office buildings that the most signal advances in construction and design were achieved. The engineering problems were more difficult than those of residential building, and the opportunities for improvement in design more apparent, to a man like Sullivan, than those of either residential or theatre architecture. The multi-story office building was new; it called for new functional arrangements of the interior and for new structural methods. What more stimulating than the problem of evolving a suitable design to express these new facts? Sullivan writes: "The building business was again under full swing, and a series of important mercantile structures came into the office, each one of which he (Sullivan) treated experimentally, feeling his way toward a basic process, a grammar of his own. The immediate problem was daylight, the maximum of daylight. This led him to use slender piers, tending toward a masonry and iron combination, the beginnings of a vertical system. . . . Into the work was slowly infiltrated a corresponding system of artistic expression, which appeared in these structures as novel, and, to some, repellent in its total disregard of accepted notions." [2]

The "accepted notions" of office-building design in 1880 may be briefly set forth, as it is only thus that the innovations made by Adler & Sullivan may be understood. Office buildings at that time were ordinarily three or four stories high. Their walls rested on a continuous foundation of considerable weight and depth—in Chicago, usually extending several feet down to hardpan. Above the street level, the wall at the base might be about two and a half feet thick for a three-story building, three feet thick for a four-story building, somewhat more for a five-story building, and so on. The wall of the tallest masonry building in Chicago, the sixteen-story Monadnock Block built as late as 1891, is about twelve feet thick at the base. Thus for buildings over six or seven stories, a great deal of the lot-area was taken up by thick walls, and potential space for renting was lost. The floors were usually supported inside the walls by a framework of cast-iron and wrought-iron posts, girders, and beams, carrying hollow tile floor arches. The outside ends of the floor beams were carried by the brick wall, which might be thickened into piers at the points of support. Cast-iron posts were sometimes used to reinforce these piers. This type of wall construction meant that only relatively small windows could be used, and even then the reveals were so deep that much light was lost.

Architecturally, the building was an envelope, the exterior of which was treated in any way that pleased the architect or his client. Since the multi-story building was a new problem in design, for which there were no satisfactory historical precedents, its height became an embarrassment rather than an advantage. Architects usually cut it up horizontally by string courses or cornices into units of one or two stories, using every device to make a high building look like a low one. At the top they capped it with a large cornice of galvanized iron of the cheapest construction compatible with aesthetic decency, or else a mansard or pitched roof such as might be found on a residence.

Adler & Sullivan did not solve all the problems of construction and design in the office building at once. In fact, their best solution of the problem did not come until ten years later. But it is interesting to see how far beyond the standard of the day they advanced in the first office building they put up—the Borden Block in Chicago. (Pl. 50) It was built 1879–80, completed before May 1, 1880, as on that date the firm of D. Adler & Co. moved into a suite of offices on its top floor. Adler doubtless accomplished the business arrangements and supervised the structural engineering, while Sullivan did the designing. He was chief draftsman in Adler's office at the time.

The Borden Block embodied several structural innovations. Adler & Sullivan realized that the primary need in office-building design was to lighten the walls and to open more window space. They accomplished this by strengthening the brick weight-bearing piers, thus dividing the wall into a series of bays, reducing the thickness of the wall in these bays. The two windows in each bay were separated by a cast-iron mullion, giving more light and strength than a masonry pier between them would have permitted. The lintels over the windows were cast-iron I-beams imbedded in the masonry of the piers, carrying spandrel panels of carved stone. The structural system of intermittent weight-bearing piers logically called for a departure from the old-fashioned continuous foundation, and the wall-piers were carried on isolated foundations of stone carried to a depth of about nine feet. This may have been the first example of the use of isolated spread-footings for wall support. The late Mr. Paul Mueller, structural engineer who worked for years in Adler & Sullivan's office, stated that the Borden Block was the first building in Chicago to break away from the solid-wall principle, although the first Leiter Building, built by William LeBaron Jenney in the same year, may be a rival claimant, as it is essentially of the same construction.

The exterior architectural treatment was quite novel in its day. The piers were faced by pilaster-strips [3] carried from bottom to top, which served to emphasize the vertical effect of the design. Each bay was topped by a semicircular lunette, richly carved, a common stylism in Sullivan's buildings of the eighties. The spandrels, the entablature over the second story, and panels under the top cornice were also carved. The details of Sullivan's early ornament can be better studied in later examples, but it will be observed that the disposition on non-structural parts, the clear bounding of the panels, and the flat surface quality of the ornament are entirely architectural in governance and feeling. Sullivan showed himself still influenced by conventional design in dividing the building horizontally into three groups of two stories each by the entablature over the second story and the cornice over the fourth. These detract from the feeling of vertical continuity that the building might have had. The top cornice was simple and of no great projection. In comparison with other "high grade" office buildings of the day, the Borden Block was dignified and reticent.

The next building was the Rothschild Store, (Pl. 1) on West Monroe Street, Chicago, built in 1880–81. There is a marked increase in the amount of window-space in the façade. In the whole width of fifty feet there are only three weight-bearing masonry piers, dividing the façade into two wide bays. Each bay has three large windows, and the slender mullions separating them, as well as the spandrels between floors, are of cast-iron. Except for the three piers, it is entirely a cast-iron front. The "beginnings of a vertical system" are here clearly apparent: the window mullions have unbroken vertical continuity from the second floor to the top. The floor-levels are marked on the piers, however, by applied ornament.

The efflorescence of cast-iron ornament at the top is arresting.

It is totally unlike Sullivan's later ornament in buildings from the Auditorium on, and rather difficult to analyze. It is not in any sense historical ornament, but it seems derived from the Egyptian style more closely than anything else. There are reminiscences of the lotus and the palmette, and small wheel-like projections resembling the seed-pod of the lotus. There are corrugated spirals not unlike certain sea-shells, and other shell-like and flower-like forms. The general appearance is rather brittle and spiky, and certain details project strongly. The growth of one motive into another at the top of the piers in a continuous development is worthy of note. This type of ornament occurs in most of Sullivan's buildings of the early eighties, dying out after 1884. Its origin may be sought in his friendship with John Edelmann, begun eight years before in Jenney's office, and ripened after his return from Paris. Sullivan was twenty-four now; Edelmann thirty-two. That Edelmann had a somewhat romantic flair for the Egyptian we can guess from his giving the name "Lotus Club" to his summer-outing retreat on the Calumet River; certainly his ornament, such as that on the stair rails and elevator grilles in the Pullman Building in Chicago (done when he was a draftsman in S. S. Beman's office) employs Egyptoid forms, and although it is less brittle than Sullivan's, there seems little doubt that Edelmann influenced Sullivan considerably during these early years.

From 1881 to 1886 Adler & Sullivan designed four office buildings in Chicago for Martin Ryerson. Three of these are still standing; the fourth, built in 1886, was demolished several years ago. The first of the series, at Wabash Avenue and Adams Street, was for years occupied by the Alexander H. Revell Furniture Company, and is commonly known as the Revell Building. (Pl. 2) It was begun in 1881 and finished in 1883. The two lower stories were completely modernized in 1929. It was a large, solidly built, fireproof structure, and the biggest commission obtained by the firm before the Auditorium, costing over $320,000. The interior construction was of iron columns and girders sheathed in a new fireproof building material obtained from Peter B. Wight. According to Sullivan, the fireproofing of the structure added between $60,000 and $75,000 to the cost.[4] The exterior design shows no marked changes from the scheme of the Rothschild Store. Since it has a wider frontage, it is divided into more units. Vertical lines of windows are embraced by projecting piers of brick and stone, and between them are bays of triple-windows, slightly recessed, the spandrels and mullions being of cast-iron, a partial anticipation of skyscraper construction. The south façade, being wider than the west, has a somewhat more complex division. The ornamental detail of the attic is similar to that of the Rothschild Store, but more clearly confined in panels. The small pediments and fan-like projections against the skyline are unusual features. The façade as a whole is original in its details, and the one-one-three-one disposition of the stories suggests the later development into a base-shaft-capital ordinance, but the vertical division into projecting pavilions and receding bays shows the influence of conventional design.

A second structure built for Martin Ryerson, in 1881–82, is known as the "Jewelers' Building." It is much smaller than the Revell Building, with five stories and a frontage of only sixty feet, but is essentially the same in its interior iron construction and its exterior design. The decorative panels of the attic and the top cornice are much more sober and restrained than in the Revell Building.

The third extant structure built for Martin Ryerson is a six-story office building on East Randolph Street, built in 1884. (Pl. 3) The front is divided into three bays by masonry piers, carrying an armature of iron and glass. Although the organization is logical, and a great deal of light is admitted into the interior by the expanse of glass, it is the least successful of Sullivan's attempts to evolve a new grammar of ornament. The forms are the Egyptoid motives employed on the Rothschild Store and other early buildings, but are unskilful and redundant. There is a curious exotic quality, notably in the heavy squat pillars of the lower story which suggest an Aztec origin, and in the flare of the masonry piers as they spread into the window-space of the fifth story. The decoration of the central piers and of the heavy flat lintel under the top story, the strange baluster-like mullions separating the top windows, and the corrugation of the façade through the projecting oriels all contribute to a flickering disruption of the surface which endows it with an impressionistic texture but robs it of surface continuity.

The Troescher Building in Chicago (now the Daily Times Building) is much more direct and successful. (Pl. 4) Built the same year as the Ryerson Building on Randolph Street, and of comparable size and cost, it offers an interesting contrast in treatment. Instead of the clumsy columns at the lower story, the façade is carried on small rectangular piers with simple capitals and four semi-elliptical arches of slightly rusticated brownstone. Rising from this as a base are five slender piers of brick, undecorated, and uninterrupted through the four middle stories. Their projection emphasizes the verticality. Three windows in each bay, separated only by iron mullions, admit the maximum amount of light, equivalent to the amount of window-space possible in metal-skeleton construction. In fact, the use of eight-inch iron I-beams as lintels resting from pier to pier to support the spandrels over these windows constitutes the essential element in skyscraper construction, here not complete because there are no iron supporting columns in the piers. Only the spandrels between the second and third stories are decorated with terra cotta panels. The top story is distinguished from the uniform treatment of the others by the use of colonet-forms as mullions, and lunettes embellished with terra cotta reliefs. It is noteworthy that although the same ornamental motives are employed, they are given less individual prominence and are woven into more geometrical compositions than in the Ryerson Building, and are more clearly subjected to the aim of architectonic clarity. The Troescher Building was the most concise solution of the office-building problem achieved by Adler & Sullivan through the middle eighties, and still has an air of unity and directness which contrasts strongly with its contemporary neighbors on Market Street. The transom windows at the top of the two middle bays increase the amount of available light in a top-story drafting-room, also lighted by skylights.

In 1886 two office buildings were erected by Adler & Sullivan: a small and inexpensive five-story structure built for Ferdinand W. Peck at the corner of LaSalle and Water Streets, demolished when the Wacker Drive development was put through; and a larger office building at 318 West Adams for Martin Ryerson, which for years served as the Martin Ryerson Charities Trust Building, but which was eventually demolished for the erection of a larger sky-scraper.

The next office building, and the last both chronologically and stylistically before the era of the Auditorium, was the Dexter Building on South Wabash Avenue. (Pl. 5) It was a six-story structure built in 1887. A logical outgrowth of the Troescher Building, with which it may be closely compared, the Dexter Building represents the end-point of the style-development of the early and middle eighties. Entirely different from the Auditorium, which was under way during the year in which this was completed, it shows no trace of Richardson's influence, nor of the characteristic leaf-ornament which Sullivan developed during the next decade.

On the other hand, it is an entirely mature work, rigorously thought through. Sullivan has here finally eliminated the Egyptoid ornamental forms of the earlier buildings, and attained a new simplicity and monumentality growing directly out of the problems of the commercial office building. Doubtless he was influenced toward simplicity by his experience in factory designing in the preceding years, but also by the clarification of his ideas and the beginnings of the formation of his architectural credo, which may be placed at about 1885 or 1886. The conflict between realistic structure and romantic ornament is here eliminated through the virtual abandonment of ornament, and the growth in its place of a purely structural monumentality. This represents a clear-cut step beyond which Sullivan, if he had possessed less creative fertility, might never have progressed, and indeed a step beyond which most of his lesser contemporaries never went. During the next decade, however, stimulated by the difference in structural nature between the masonry and the metal skeleton building, and by the growth of a new conception of ornament, Sullivan progressed toward new and entirely different achievements in his mature style. The Dexter Building represents both the culmination of the old and the wiping clean of the slate in preparation for the new, and is thus a significant monument in Sullivan's development.

Like other Chicago architects of the eighties, Adler & Sullivan were called upon to do almost as many factories and warehouses as office buildings. The expansion of the city was industrial as well as commercial, and although the usual practice was to hire an engineer to design an industrial building, commissions were often given to architects accustomed to a more polite practice. There was, perhaps, less distinction between the architect and the engineer in those days than at present, and this was especially true in the boom days after the fire in Chicago. Although the disparaging critic might point out that monumental architecture was often no better than industrial building, the comparison works both ways, and it is worth remarking that the distinguishing quality of Chicago architecture during the eighties and nineties was a forthright simplicity and bareness which may be attributed largely to its close relationship to industrial architecture. Structures such as the Monadnock Building, of 1891, mark the dawn of an "engineer's aesthetic" long before Le Corbusier thought of the phrase, and critics as different as Montgomery Schuyler and Paul Bourget were quick to remark on the superiority of Chicago's achievements over those of New York in advancing toward a truly modern architecture.

Of the ten or a dozen factory structures designed by Adler & Sullivan in the eighties, none is of especial note, with the single exception of the Walker Warehouse built in 1888–89, after the Auditorium. Their average cost was less than six cents a cubic foot, and although some of them have a dignified simplicity, it was doubtless a simplicity of necessity rather than of choice. They do not seem to have influenced the design of other types of buildings, with the possible exception of the Dexter Building, mentioned above. Although it is commonly believed that Sullivan's whole philosophy of architecture was a kind of mechanistic functionalism, he actually insisted on the infusion of a degree of emotional expression which was quite impossible in these factory buildings, and certainly his taste for ornament was incapable of satisfaction in brick boxes costing less than six cents a cubic foot. For these reasons the factory buildings and warehouses of Adler & Sullivan, although often impressive, do not seem of great significance in the formation of Sullivan's style.

The Kniseley Building in Chicago, built in 1884, may be taken

as an example. (Pl. 6) The plain brick wall is given variety and
vertical emphasis by the projecting piers between the windows, and
the recessing of the arched central bay creates an effective accent.
Without the exterior fire-escape and the partial top story, added
after the original construction, the façade must have been a very
satisfactory one.

The most impressive factory building designed by Adler &
Sullivan is the first unit of the large Selz, Schwab & Company Shoe
Factory in Chicago, built in 1886–87. (Pl. 7) Built at a cost of five
and a half cents a cubic foot, it is utterly simple, and achieves its
effectiveness through its very economy. The scheme followed is the
same as that of the Kniseley Building, with the bays widened to
include two windows each, and the piers between windows both
wider and deeper. The verticals of the piers dominate the composition, being carried unbroken from bottom to top, and there is not
even a projecting cornice. The horizontal floor lines are clearly
indicated by the white stone sills of the windows, but these are
suppressed behind the piers. The stark angularity of the building is
relieved by the graceful tapering of the piers. The structure of the
building calls for thicker walls at the base than at the top, and this
thickening is accomplished in the exterior piers rather than inside;
the projection of the piers is greatest at the bottom, and the reveals
are gradually diminished in the upper stories. The window-head-
ings, instead of being hard horizontal lines, are slightly curved
segmental arches. These features give the building a movement and
grace which somewhat mitigate its austerity, and the result is quite
comparable to the more lofty Monadnock Building built four years
later by Burnham & Root.

In the special field of theatre design Adler & Sullivan early acquired a reputation. Some ten theatres were designed during the

years from 1880 to 1891, the greatest of which was the Auditorium. The reputation of the firm was based largely on Adler's unique knowledge of acoustics, his talent in engineering, and his ability in planning an efficient complex of seats, corridors, and public spaces. The Central Music Hall, built by Adler in 1879, was a great success and it brought other commissions to the firm in the following years, several of which were for remodelling older theatres.

The first of these was the remodelling of the Grand Opera House for William Borden in 1880. The remodelling, which cost $55,000, was completed in September. Although Adler was responsible for the general lay-out, undoubtedly Sullivan did much of the designing. There is no available information on the appearance of the proscenium and stage after this remodelling, but an old photograph of the auditorium shows two curved balconies and a species of coved ceiling similar in general arrangement to that of the Central Music Hall. The sight-lines and acoustics of the building were much admired, and the general plan remained in effect through many later remodellings of entrances, stage boxes, and decorations. Sullivan writes: "The Grand Opéra House was immediately a great success. It was quite a luxurious theatre for that day, and quite a wonder in its architecture." [5]

Adler & Sullivan remodelled "Hooley's Theatre," Chicago, in 1884–85. Both the Grand Opera House and Hooley's Theatre have been known under several other names, and there has consequently been much confusion in accounts of these two buildings, but since the former was completely rebuilt in 1925, and the latter demolished in 1923, this need not concern us greatly. No photographs of Adler & Sullivan's work on Hooley's Theatre have been found, but from descriptions we know that the proscenium boxes were made of cast-iron, decorated in gold and bronze colors.

A third remodelling job was done by Adler & Sullivan on the McVicker's Theatre in 1885. The building dated from 1872, and this work, on which $95,000 was spent, was almost entirely destroyed in a serious fire in 1890, despite the supposedly fire-resistant construction. Sullivan wrote of it many years later. "At that time, I believe, was made the first decorative use of the electric lamp. It was a little innovation of my own, that of placing the lamps in a decoration instead of clustering them in fixtures, but even then the installation of an electric lighting system was primitive to the last degree. The wires were bedded in plaster; the lighting conduit not being known. The dynamos were run by little primitive engines." [6] The decorative use of the electric lamp is of interest, as Sullivan developed this motive very successfully in the Auditorium a few years later.

The great forerunner of the Auditorium, however, was the temporary opera house built within the huge barn-like Interstate Exposition Building in Grant Park. The Exposition Building, built in 1873 by W. W. Boyington, was used for fairs and exhibitions, and had housed the Republican Conventions in 1880 and 1884. It was standing empty, and in the winter of 1885 Messrs. N. K. Fairbank and Ferdinand W. Peck, two of the city's most influential citizens, conceived the idea of remodelling it for an opera festival. Ferdinand Peck approached Adler for assistance on the architectural problem. It was decided that a temporary structure of wood, housed within the extant building, could be built at a reasonable cost. But since the opera festival was scheduled to last only two weeks, an enormous number of seats had to be provided. A vast auditorium, to seat 6,200 persons, was planned to fit within the shell of the old building. Work was begun in February, with armies of men employed to shovel away huge banks of snow and to team in great quantities of lumber; carpenters and decorators swarmed through the noisy interior, and by April 1st the new Grand Opera House was ready. (Fig. 3)

The auditorium was fan-shaped in plan, with aisles radiating out from the proscenium. Nearest the stage was the parquet, seating 2,238 persons; back of this and elevated slightly above it was the dress-circle, seating 1,486, curving backward in the center. Projecting over it some twenty-five feet was the main balcony, for 1,824 persons, with a rise of thirty feet toward the rear. From the proscenium two lines of boxes on each side, with bowed-out fronts, and each with its own entrance from a lobby, extended outward to meet small dress balconies extending back to the main balcony; boxes and dress balconies seating 652 persons. This made a total of 6,200 seats, about 2,000 more than were later provided for in the permanent structure of the Auditorium Theatre.

The stage at the north end of the building, eighty feet deep and one hundred and twenty feet wide, was one of the largest in the country. It was completely fitted out for scene-shifting, with a rigging-loft sixty feet above the floor, numerous fly-galleries and traps. Dressing-rooms were provided on each side, a musicians' room beneath it, and rooms for the chorus in the rear. The stage opening was sixty feet wide, topped by an arch curving up to a height of forty feet. The stage floor projected twenty feet in front of the curtain line, and above it a sloping ceiling, expanding outward and extending eighty feet over the auditorium, formed an immense sounding-board, which afforded such perfect acoustic properties that the singing could be heard in full volume and purity from every seat in the immense house. "The effect was thrilling. An audience of 6,200 persons saw and heard; saw in a clear line of vision; heard, even to the faintest pianissimo. No reverberation, no echo—the clear untarnished tone, of voice and instrument, reached all." [7]

Figure 3. Chicago Opera Festival Auditorium in the Interstate Exposition Building, Grant Park. 1885. (From the *Inland Architect & Builder*, March, 1885.)

In addition to the stage and auditorium, the necessary lobbies, corridors, dressing-rooms, promenades, salons, and carriage entrances were provided for. The auditorium and stage were brilliantly lighted by seven thousand gas jets. An article in the Chicago *Tribune* of March 1st, 1885, says: "The grand promenade will be beautifully adorned with evergreens, plants, pictures, statuary, mirrors, etc. The grand salon will be elegantly arranged, and the audience will be privileged to leave the seats between acts and enjoy the relief of promenading, refreshments, and social intercourse." The advertisements of the opera festival are amusing reflections of the era: "April 6—Two Weeks Only! First Chicago Grand Opera Festival. Under the Auspices of the Chicago Opera Festival Association. The Greatest Musical Event in the History of Chicago! Special Notice: The Grand Opera Hall will be thoroughly warmed by Steam, furnished with Elegant Opera Chairs by the American Store Stool Company, and brilliantly lighted. Madame Adelina Patti's Farewell Appearance in America, with many other notables, including tenori, baritoni, and bassi. The repertoire will include the following favorite operas, presenting a pleasing variety from the German, Italian, and French Masters to gratify all tastes: Lohengrin, Der Freischutz, Aïda, Mirella (first time), Luida di Chamouni, l'Africaine, Semiramide, Faust, Martha, I Puritani, Lucia di Lammermoor, and La Traviata."

The opera festival was a great success. It demonstrated that the Chicago public was interested in grand opera, that it was possible to seat a huge audience so that all might see and hear, and it gave birth to Ferdinand Peck's dream of a great permanent opera house for Chicago. The very great similarity in the general lay-out of the Exposition Opera Hall and the later Auditorium Theatre indicates that the experience of Adler & Sullivan in designing the temporary structure stood them in good stead in their greatest commission, and undoubtedly was the chief reason for their selection as the architects of the Auditorium. The old Exposition Building was demolished in 1892, and the present Art Institute erected on the site.

Almost half the total number of buildings designed by Adler & Sullivan between 1880 and 1887 were residences. The building list given in the appendix names thirty. On the whole, the residences show less difference from the contemporary average than do the office buildings. Perhaps this may be explained by the fact that they offered a less novel problem, a problem in which functional and structural articulations were traditionally established, and therefore afforded less striking need for changes in design. Of course the style of Adler & Sullivan houses is readily distinguishable from that of other contemporary architects, as the ornamental motives are quite unique. But the use of ornament and the general composition is entirely in accord with the aesthetic of the early eighties. The picturesque is increasingly the dominant quality. Façades are broken by oriels and bays, roofs have pavilions or cupolas, and the skyline silhouette is often quite fantastic. Ornament in cast-iron or terra cotta is freely used in panels or along cornice lines. The general effect is of broken surfaces, rich texture, and irregular outline, impressionistic in character.

The first residence by the firm was built for John Borden on Lake Park Avenue in Chicago in 1880. (Pl. 8) This is probably the "large substantial residence" mentioned by Sullivan [8] as one of the three commissions which came into the office shortly after his arrival. The house is a three-story structure, soundly built, and is still standing. It might be almost any solid residence of the day, with the tall, narrow windows, the prominent chimneys, the color contrast of red brick and white stone trim, and the mansard roof popular in Chicago in 1880. But the inset panels above the second-story windows, and an astonishing efflorescence of Sullivanesque ornament on a pavilion roof in the middle of the south side, betray the individuality of the architect. The slight projection and simple treatment of the dormers, and the subtly tapered tops of the high chimneys do much to create a feeling of compact density in the mass as a whole.

Quite in contrast to the dignified solidity of the Borden house, a very small house on West Chicago Avenue (Pl. 9) shows the only instance of an apparent effort on Sullivan's part to carry over the open construction and vertical design of the early office buildings into domestic architecture. It is highly original, and without the "Cozy Hand Laundry" now installed in a basement addition, must have been highly effective. The wall-surface is plaster, grooved to simulate masonry. This smooth surface is broken by incised ornamental patterns and the projecting piers topped by spreading lotus-flower caps. The lunettes of the top-story windows are left bare. The most arresting feature of the façade is the triple window bay extending through the two lower stories. The windows are separated by slender iron mullions like double reeds, and recessed spandrel panels, also of iron. This is clearly an adaptation of the scheme of the Rothschild Store to a smaller building, and its success makes one wonder why Sullivan never attempted it in another residence. The calculated asymmetry of the façade is worthy of note.

Adler & Sullivan did several small and inexpensive residences and flat-buildings for Mr. Max M. Rothschild during the early eighties. Of these, the most interesting is a three-family house on Indiana Avenue, Chicago, built in 1883. (Pl. 10) Although certainly not distinguished, its effect is gained solely through architectural forms rather than ornamental details. The grouping of three stories of windows under large arches reminds one of the later Walker Warehouse, except that here there is no suggestion of a structural articulation of the façade: it is merely a flat surface pattern. The smooth surface, the proportions of the openings, and the cornice all suggest a carry-over into Sullivan's work of the Greek Revival tradition of a few decades earlier, but this is reduced to a composition of the elementary architectural forms, the pier, the lintel, and the arch.

In the latter part of 1883 and in 1884 the style of Adler & Sullivan residences reaches the apogee of its impressionistic disintegration of volume and emphasis on brilliant, not to say florid surface ornament. The houses of these years are almost identical in feeling to the Ryerson Building on Randolph Street. Late in 1883 came two adjacent residences built for Morris Selz and Charles H. Schwab on Michigan Avenue. They have since been remodelled and most of the ornate roof-cresting removed, but originally they must have presented a most elaborate aspect, with the mass much broken by bay-windows, mansards and dormers, and adorned by brittle fans and wheels, conventionalized lotus-flowers, and heavy forms like grotesque masks along the roof-cresting. They seem to represent a conscious, if unsuccessful, striving for originality.

Much the same quality can be found in the Barbe residence on Prairie Avenue and the Strauss residence on Wabash Avenue, both built in 1884. One new decorative motive popular in residences of the eighties occurs in the Barbe residence: a kind of stylized half-timber work in the gable of a projecting bay. This was often executed in cast-iron or terra cotta, rather than in wood. The Strauss residence has in its largest and clearest form a decorative motive of which Sullivan seems to have been very fond: what may be termed, for lack of a better name, a caduceus-motive, as its curious form suggests more than anything else the snakes curling around the wand of Hermes. Sullivan used it repeatedly in the buildings of the eighties.

A marked sobering down of the style becomes apparent in the houses of 1885 and 1886. This is notably true of the Lindauer residence on Wabash Avenue, built in 1885. This has a façade of rusticated masonry, a bold mass, and very little ornamental detail. A large tower projects from one corner of the façade, is carried above it to three full stories, and is capped by a pyramidal roof. The main roof slopes inward more than a typical mansard, and the large dormer with segmental pediment is unique for Adler & Sullivan. In mass, it has much the quality of large solidity that characterized the Borden residence; in detail it represents the same sobering down from the ornateness of 1883 and 1884 that is found in the Troescher Building and the Dexter Building. The Goodman residence on Wabash Avenue, built in 1885–86, shows the same trend toward simplification and elimination of ornament. The brick wall with angle quoins regains an effect of integrated mass, and the mansard roof, although retaining some ornamental features, is less picturesquely conceived.

In the year 1885–86, Dankmar Adler built three small houses on Ellis Avenue as residences for himself, his mother-in-law Mrs. Abraham Kohn, and Mr. Eli B. Felsenthal. (Fig. 4) Although somewhat remodelled, they are still standing. Smaller and less pretentious, these houses are still picturesquely conceived but are far more successful than those of the previous years. The other houses of the eighties do not merit individual mention.

Brief mention, however, should be made of two of the miscellaneous structures of the period 1880–87, which include a library, a schoolhouse, a synagogue, a clubhouse, and two small railroad stations. One of these was the Zion Temple, at Washington Street

Figure 4. Residences of Dila Kohn, Dankmar Adler, and Eli B.
Felsenthal, Chicago. 1885–86. (From *Building Budget*.)

and Ogden Avenue, Chicago, built in 1884–85. A brief account of this building, published in 1891, describes it as follows: "The Moresque style was adopted for this building, and the contractor, with the aid of Adler & Sullivan and of the pressed-brick and terra cotta manufacturers, gave to that section of the city its best specimen of Spanish architecture, as it was known in the days of the occupation of Spain by the Moors." [9] One is curious to know what the other "specimens" may have looked like; judging from a drawing made before the building was destroyed that section of the city must have presented a gala appearance. One is also curious to know just how much of the design of the building was due to the pressed-brick and terra cotta manufacturers and the clients, and how much to Adler & Sullivan. If they indeed had any important part in it, it is the only example in their work of an intent to design in an historical style. That style, needless to remark, was only remotely Islamic, and rather more directly an expression of American popular taste in the 1880's. The building was destroyed by fire in 1930.

The West Chicago Club, on Throop Street, was built in 1886. (Pl. 11) It is of brick, with stone and terra cotta trim, and similar to the residences in general appearance. The projecting bay over the entrance is a striking feature, with its central mullion like three attenuated lotus-stems bearing seed-pods, its flat spandrel panel decorated by interlaced circles, and the "half-timber" motive in the gable.

All told, it must be admitted that Sullivan's buildings of the eighties (at least, all those prior to the Auditorium and the Walker Warehouse) have more interest to the historian than to the critic of modern architecture. In their picturesqueness, their use of elaborate ornament, their striving for individuality, they represent their generation; they seem to bear little if any relation to modern architecture. Yet certain things about them are worthy of note. The office buildings and theatres and factories, especially, reveal not only an advanced knowledge of such technical matters as foundations, iron construction, and fireproofing, but a disposition to regard these things as of architectural importance. As Sullivan himself wrote, he was treating these new problems experimentally, "feeling his way toward a basic process, a grammar of his own." In the use of a masonry-and-iron combination to admit the maximum amount of light to the interiors of office buildings he was not only recognizing the importance of function—putting first things first—but recognizing that his architectural expression must depend on and grow out of the structural form rather than deny it. This was a kind of hard realism, of architectural common-sense, that was rare indeed in the decade of the eighties.

Sullivan's early ornament does not carry through his basic architectural expression with complete success, but at least it was aimed in the right direction. In attempting to endow his buildings with beauty he was not content to borrow past forms of beauty, such as historical ornament, but attempted to devise a new vocabulary of ornamental forms. The Egyptoid forms (if so they can be described) which he employed were by no means imitative, nor, it must be admitted, were they entirely successful. But this is not surprising; for many generations there had been little or no development of a modern architectural ornament, and one man could hardly be expected to do the creative work of a century overnight. Sullivan's use of ornament was very largely conditioned by the aesthetic of his generation; his whole experience of architecture had been that ornament was something applied to a building rather lavishly to make it look picturesque and expensive. This he could not at once forget. The extent of his originality was limited, and for a time he used new ornament in old ways. But already in 1886 he was feeling his way toward wiping clean the slate, and in such structures as the Dexter Building he was beginning, like Cézanne, to return to fundamentals and to become the primitive of his own way.

The years from 1880 to 1886 were the formative period in Sullivan's development. But even though he had not yet arrived at his most productive years, his influence was being felt. Few American architects were known in Europe at that time, but as early as 1883, when Sullivan was only twenty-six, some of his designs for an exhibition of silver work in Chicago were commented on favorably in the Parisian journal *Arts Décoratifs*,[10] and in 1885 his first essay, an address on "Characteristics and Tendencies of American Architecture," read before a convention of the Western Association of Architects in St. Louis, was published in full, with laudatory comments, in "The Builders' Weekly Reporter" of London.[11] By 1886, Sullivan's thirtieth year, his ideas concerning architecture were clearly formulated, and destined to become the strongest single factor in the development of a modern system of thinking about architecture. The first public exposition of these ideas in this country occurred in the famous "Inspiration" address, read before the Third Annual Convention of the Western Association of Architects in Chicago on November 17, 1886. Sullivan was ready to enter the period of his greatest achievements.

[1] A recent article by E. M. Upjohn makes an admirable analysis of Leroy S. Buffington's claim to the invention of the skyscraper. This demonstrates conclusively that Buffington antedated Jenney in theory, having a clear conception of the principle of skyscraper construction and many of its practical potentialities as early as 1882. Since he did not build one, Jenney still has the distinction of the first application of the idea. See

E. M. Upjohn: "Buffington and the Skyscraper," *Art Bulletin*, vol. XVII, no. 1, March, 1935.

[2] *Autobiography*, p. 258.

[3] From the very beginning, Sullivan modified traditional elements of design so that such terms as "pilaster," "entablature," "cornice," etc., are not strictly applicable. His forms are not historical, and they vary from building to building. But since we have no other vocabulary to apply to them, the terms will be used with the understanding that they only loosely describe these forms.

[4] Sullivan: "Development of Construction," *The Economist*, vol. 55, no. 26, p. 1252, June 24, 1916.

[5] Sullivan: "Development of Construction," *The Economist*, vol. 55, no. 26, p. 1252, June 24, 1916.

[6] Sullivan: "Development of Construction," *The Economist*, vol. 55, no. 26, p. 1252, June 24, 1916.

[7] *Autobiography*, p. 293.

[8] *Autobiography*, p. 256.

[9] *Industrial Chicago*, p. 267.

[10] A. D. F. Hamlin: "L'Art Nouveau," *The Craftsman*, vol. III, p. 129.

[11] *Inland Architect and Builder*, vol. 7, p. 6, February, 1886.

# III. THE AUDITORIUM

When the Auditorium commission came into the office, Dankmar Adler was forty-two years old, Louis Sullivan was thirty. Both men were at the height of their powers. It is interesting to attempt a description of how they looked and worked, their personal characteristics, and their relations with each other. For this we must draw largely on the writings of their contemporaries and pupils. One of the most vivid pictures is contained in the pages of Frank Lloyd Wright's *Autobiography*, from which I quote *ad lib*.

"What was Dankmar Adler like? Just before noon he opened the same door from which Mr. Sullivan had entered. A personality, short-built and heavy, like an old Byzantine church . . . one to inspire others with confidence in his power at once. I felt comforted. He walked with deliberate, heavy-legged, flat-footed steps over to Mueller's desk, talking to him. The while his deep bass voice rumbled, he went about with his hands stuck under his coattails, looking at drawings, a word of greeting occasionally. He would sit and make suggestions in a fatherly sort of way. He got to me. Looked at me pleasantly from his deep-set eyes under the bushy brows. 'Hello! Sullivan's new man?' 'Yes, sir!' He sat down on the stool I had vacated to stand up to him. As he put one leg over the other I noticed his enormous mannish feet. They spread flat like the foundations for some heavy building. 'Sullivan needs help, Wright. It's difficult to find anyone to catch on to what he wants. I hope you will succeed!' He got up abruptly almost as soon

as he had sat down and, as though suddenly remembering something, he went heavily out among the draughting tables like a barge
making its way between river craft. . . . Dankmar Adler had
been an Army engineer. He commanded the confidence of contractor and client alike. His handling of both was masterful. . . .
He was a good planner, a good critic, but all for Sullivan. He always
called him 'Sullivan,' never 'Louis.' In Sullivan's genius Adler had
implicit confidence." It may be remarked that all the office staff—
from Sullivan, Wright, Elmslie, and Mueller down to the lowest
office cub—always referred to Adler with respect and affection as
the "Big Chief."

Louis Sullivan was different. Decided and unyielding, he could
be extremely arrogant toward some, affable and pleasant toward
others. Wright's first morning in the office gives us a good picture:
"About 10: 30 the door opened. Mr. Sullivan walked slowly in
with a haughty air, a handkerchief to his nose. Paying no attention
to anyone. No 'good mornings.' No words of greeting as he went
from desk to desk. Saw me waiting for him. Came forward at once
with a pleasant 'Ah! Wright, there you are,' and the office had my
name. And evidently, in Sullivan's unusually pleasant address,
also my 'number.' 'Here,' lifting a board by my table, 'Take this
drawing of mine, a duffer I fired Saturday spoiled it. Redraw it
and ink it in.' And they all knew what I was there for. He wandered
about some more in a haughty sort of way. . . . The Master's
very walk at this time bore dangerous resemblance to a strut.[1] He
had no respect whatever for a draughtsman, as he more than once
confided to me in later years. Nor, so far as I could see, respect
for anyone else except the Big Chief—Dankmar Adler—whom he
trusted and loved. And also Paul Mueller. . . . But I had from
the first seen a different side of him, as I felt I would. He always
loved to talk and I would often stay after dark in the offices in the

upper stories of the great tower of the Auditorium looking out over Lake Michigan, or over the lighted City. Sometimes he would keep on talking, seeming to have forgotten me—keep on until late at night. . . . I believe the Master used to talk to me to express his own feelings and thoughts, regardless, forgetting me often. . . . He was absorbed in what seemed extravagant worship of Wagner at the time, which I could not share, but which I could understand. . . . He would often try to sing the leitmotifs for me and describe the scenes to which they belonged as he sat at my drawing board. He adored Whitman, as I did. And, explain it as you can, was deep in Herbert Spencer. Spencer's 'Synthetic Philosophy' he gave me to take home and read. . . . The deep quiet of his temper had great charm for me. The rich humor that was lurking in the deeps within him and that sat in his eyes whatever his mouth might be saying, however earnest the moment might be, was rich and rare in human quality."

George Elmslie, the most faithful friend of Sullivan, and one of his most talented disciples, entered the office in 1889, and remained with him for twenty years. Elmslie writes of him: "Sullivan was a faithful worker, a tireless thinker, an extraordinary talker; wherever he sat was the head of the table. That was easy to see at the Cliff Dwellers. He could be arrogant and unnecessarily decisive at times, and a bit prone to give advice where not needed to good clients. Of course he lost many jobs because he would not compromise his ideals or play fast and loose with vital conceptions of what was fitting for the purpose intended. Sullivan was a bit of a recluse. He liked to be alone, to think and write. He was a solitary man in most ways and constitutionally averse to social display of any kind. He lived alone most of his life, and when he drank, he drank alone. Yet he was the most interesting, fascinating, inspiriting and encouraging companion anyone could have. He believed in himself and had reason to do so. He had a true message to deliver and delivered it with eloquence, virility and great power. Sullivan started from scratch in a semi-wilderness of cultural values to follow a path he never, essentially, departed from."

In general Adler directed the business and engineering side of the office work, Sullivan directed the designing. The relationship between the two men seems to have been a perfect partnership in the best sense of the word. Many persons, however, basing their opinions on an incomplete knowledge of the causes of the break-up of the partnership in 1895, or on some personal prejudice in favor of the one man or the other, still aver that there was considerable friction and even enmity between them, and that one was the guiding genius and the other merely the pedestrian businessman or the eccentric visionary, depending on the point of view. The truth seems to be that Adler was the guider and Sullivan the genius, and that they got along very well together. It was Adler's vision and generosity that opened for Sullivan his great opportunity, and at the same time made possible his own greatest contributions to architecture. From a study of the work which each did independently before and after the partnership there can be no question that Sullivan did his greatest work while he was with Adler, and that Adler reached the height of his achievement while with Sullivan. Sullivan himself writes of Adler in the *Autobiography* as follows: "Adler was essentially a technician, an engineer, a conscientious administrator, a large progressive judicial and judicious mind securing alike the confidence of conservative and radical. . . . He was a man whose reputation was solidly secured in utter honesty, fine intelligence and a fund of that sort of wisdom which attracts and holds. Between the two there existed a fine confidence, and the handling of the work was divided and adjusted on a temperamental basis—each to have initiative and final authority in his own field, without a sharp arbitrary line being drawn that might lead to dissension. What was particularly fine, as we consider human nature, was Adler's open frank way of pushing his young partner to the front." [2]

Nevertheless, from the point of view of the historian of architecture, Sullivan must remain the more interesting figure. Both as designing artist and as thinker he stands out as Adler's master. Montgomery Schuyler, writing in 1895, said: "It is of the essence of every work of art that it should be done by an individual and embody an individual conception. This does not prevent the taking of counsel in an architectural work, and the modification of it accordingly. But it is always necessary that there should be a single mind behind the work. . . . In the biographical notes with which he has favored me, Mr. Adler writes that since the formation of the firm 'the preëminence in the artistic field of Mr. Sullivan' has relieved the senior partner from that branch of professional work, and left him free to devote himself to the engineering problems involved in the modern office building. . . . It is especially gratifying to be relieved by Mr. Adler's frankness and magnanimity from all embarrassment, and to be at liberty to treat the very marked artistic individuality in the work of Adler & Sullivan as the individuality of Mr. Sullivan." [3] All available information points to the justness of this estimate, and in discussing the artistic achievement of the firm of Adler & Sullivan we shall be concerned with the architecture of Louis Sullivan.

The office of Adler & Sullivan occupied most of the top floor of the Borden Block. There were about twenty men on the staff. Chief among these was Paul Mueller, faithful, competent, German; the man whom Sullivan respected. Mueller had been in the office for a short time in 1883; then he had gone to Sillsbee's office as an engineer for three years. In 1886 Adler needed an intelligent and resourceful assistant in engineering and construction to study through the Auditorium problem, and Mueller came back as office foreman. He was young, tall, with black hair and beard, and piercing dark eyes. Mueller directed the construction of the Auditorium, the Schiller Building in Chicago, the Union Trust Building in St. Louis, and many other large structures designed by Adler & Sullivan, finally continuing with Frank Lloyd Wright and achieving with him the engineering triumph of the Imperial Hotel in Tokyo.

Sullivan also needed help on the Auditorium job. On a Tuesday late in 1887, Frank Lloyd Wright, then eighteen years of age, appeared in the office with some drawings. He had been working a few months in Sillsbee's office since his arrival from Madison, Wisconsin. Sullivan was very busy, with a convention in St. Louis to attend. He asked Wright to do some drawings of ornamental details and to bring them in the following Friday. Wright worked the following evenings, and on Friday morning arrived at the office with quite a sheaf. Sullivan was interested; already he could see the mark of genius in this youth. His comments were reserved, but he took Wright on at twenty-five dollars a week. Wright very soon caught on to Sullivan's style of ornament, and he detailed most of the ornament of the Auditorium, although the pencil sketches and essential conception were Sullivan's. When the building was done Wright was made foreman of the designers, and in the office in the Auditorium Tower had thirty draftsmen under him. Wright stayed with Adler & Sullivan until 1893, when he began independent practice.

The story of the Auditorium Building goes back to the temporary opera hall in the Old Exposition Building. The great success of the Opera Festival in the spring of 1885 fired its sponsor, Ferdinand W. Peck, with the idea of a great permanent opera house. He conceived of it as a civic center for the highest development of the opera, the symphony, the dance, and musical festivals, as well as for glittering society balls and political conventions. As the idea grew, it became apparent that these functions would require a building on such a scale and of such great cost that it could not be expected to maintain itself financially. Commodore Peck hit upon the idea of adding to the "cultural" part of the building a "commercial" part which should afford the necessary revenue for the maintenance of the whole. Thus the concept was enlarged to include a hotel and business offices, arranged as a shell around the theatres, all to be controlled by a single organization. The idea, already well-formulated, was presented in an address to the Commercial Club on May 29, 1886. Other supporters were found, and the Chicago Auditorium Association was organized; stock was issued to the amount of $2,000,000, and bonds to $900,000; eventually there were about three hundred stockholders.

The architectural commission for such a great structure was sought by every architect in the city, but Peck's confidence in Adler, and the previous success of the Exposition Opera Hall, brought the commission to Adler & Sullivan. This was in the late summer of 1886. At that time only two-thirds of the ground and less than one-half of the money finally absorbed by the work were placed at Adler & Sullivan's disposal. As the months went on the project grew: the Board of Directors of the Auditorium Association amplified its ideas; all kinds of technical improvements in theatre mechanism were incorporated; the building grew in height; a banquet hall was added to the hotel; the estimated cost jumped to well over $3,000,000. Even after the foundations were built the plans changed, and the architects were working on uncertainties because conditions changed so rapidly. The plans were drawn and redrawn; over $60,000 was spent by Adler & Sullivan on preliminary studies.

Two of the early renderings for the exterior may be studied in

Pls. 12 and 13. Sullivan's first conceptions were more ornate than the final design. The first one shows a building with a two-story base of stone, brick walls and elaborate terra cotta decoration to a height of eight stories, and a ninth story included under a gable roof with numerous dormers and corner pinnacles. Several large three-story oriels, carried on iron frames, break the wall surface. The tower signalizing the theatre entrance does not rise far above the main roof level, but is capped by a steep-pitched roof rather Gothic in feeling. Although generally far inferior to the executed design, certain features, such as the relative height of the base to the main group of five stories under arches, and the recessed (rather than projecting) balcony over the Michigan Avenue entrances, are better than in the finished work. As the work progressed (Pl. 13) a tenth story was added, the gable roof omitted in favor of a flat one, and the silhouette pruned of its picturesque excrescences. The façade, however, was broken up by even more incredible oriels than in the first scheme, especially the one on the Congress Street side, which was six bays wide, four stories high, and recessed in the middle of the upper three stories to form a species of arched loggia—a Gargantuan conceit which was fortunately omitted in the final design. Other features began to take their final form. The two lower stories are almost identical with those of the finished building, and the tower is nearly the same. Professor Ware, Sullivan's old teacher at M.I.T., criticized the squatness of the tower in the first designs, and at his instance Sullivan added to its height and gave it a simple pyramidal roof.

But even with these previous modifications, a decisive change took place in the final design. This was chiefly due to the influence of H. H. Richardson. Richardson went to Chicago in the early part of 1885 to design residences for John J. Glessner and Franklin McVeagh, and a large wholesale block for Marshall Field & Company. The Marshall Field Wholesale Building was begun late in 1885 and was nearing completion early in 1887, just as the final designs for the Auditorium were under way. Richardson's work was a new and elemental force in American architecture, and moreover a force which achieved clear-cut maturity not in Trinity Church, Boston, nor even in the Allegheny County Court House at Pittsburgh, but in the Field Building in Chicago. (Pl. 28) Here was a building stripped of all sentimentalities and trivialities, all but free from historical preconceptions, large and simple in its units, bold and starkly geometric in its mass, vibrant in its surface, powerfully monumental. Sullivan's admiration for the Field Building is evident in his chapter called "The Oasis" in *Kindergarten Chats*, one of the finest tributes ever given by one architect to another. A comparison of the exteriors of the Field Building and the Auditorium (Pl. 14) can leave no doubt of their close relationship. Of course Sullivan built creatively on what Richardson gave him, never merely imitating but assimilating and going beyond Richardson; this can be seen even more clearly in later buildings such as the Walker Warehouse in Chicago and the Dooly Block in Salt Lake City.

Other factors doubtless played a part in the modification of the preliminary designs of the Auditorium. There is an anecdote that John Root, on seeing some of the early designs, made some disparaging comments to the effect that Sullivan was going to "smear another façade with ornament," and that Sullivan, piqued, determined to show him that he was capable of a large simplicity. There may have been some influence from George B. Post's New York Produce Exchange Building, which in general form is strongly similar to the Auditorium Building. It is certain that Ferdinand Peck so admired the Field Building that he urged a close adaptation of its design on Adler & Sullivan, and that the Board of Directors of the Auditorium Association advocated the omission of a great deal of the exterior ornament as a measure of economy. Adler deplored this latter course: "It is to be regretted that the severe simplicity of treatment rendered necessary by the financial policy of the earlier days of the enterprise, the deep impression made by Richardson's Marshall Field Building upon the Directors of the Auditorium Association, and a reaction from a course of indulgence in the creation of highly decorative effects on the part of its architects, should have happened to coincide as to time and object, and thereby deprive the exterior of the building of those graces of plastic surface decoration which are so characteristic of its internal treatment." [4] Be that as it may, the final designs called for a much-simplified exterior, along the lines of the Field Building, and executed entirely of masonry.

The construction of the Auditorium took three years. The site finally acquired was an irregular plot on the south half of the block bounded by Michigan, Congress, Wabash, and Van Buren Streets, with a total area of 63,500 square feet, or about an acre and a half. Excavation was begun on January 28, 1887, and the work was rushed. Two hundred men and thirty teams were on the job, and sometimes work was carried on at night by electric flood-lights. Construction began on June 1, 1887, although the cornerstone ceremony did not take place until October 6.

Since the exterior walls and the two main partition walls separating the theatre from the hotel and the business offices (see longitudinal section, Fig. 5) were of solid masonry, the load on the foundations was continuous rather than intermittent, and the old-fashioned type of continuous-abutment foundations was called for. These foundations had to carry exceptionally heavy loads—over two tons per square foot—and were made of concrete reinforced by huge timbers and a steel grillage. To offset possible excess settlement all pipe connections coming into the building were fitted with lead insertions to afford flexibility. In the course of years the foundations did settle considerably—in some parts as much as eighteen inches—and during his last years Adler worried considerably about the soundness of the building. But beyond some irregularities in the floors no damage was effected, and the building stands solid today. Foundations of the same type were later used for the eighteen-story Monadnock Building, also of solid masonry wall construction.

Cast-iron columns were used as interior supports between the main structural walls, and these were carried in accordance with customary practice on isolated spread-footings: small pyramids of concrete reinforced by steel rails, placed just below the level of the cellar floor.

The great foundation problem was the support of the immense seventeen-story tower, weighing about fifteen thousand tons. This called for a special foundation and a special mode of construction. The actual area of the tower was 2,870 square feet, but its foundation was much larger, spreading the load over 6,700 square feet. It might be described as a kind of platform composed of a five-foot thickness of concrete reinforced by two layers of heavy timbers, three layers of criss-crossed steel rails, and three layers of iron I-beams, the whole forming an integral foundation supporting the tower like a single solid pier or stack.

But still the necessary settlement had to be allowed for, and this introduced one of the most baffling problems, and one of the most ingenious solutions in the entire structure of the Auditorium. As Sullivan remarked, Adler's handling of the problem was a "regular Columbus egg stunt." Under normal conditions, the settlement of the foundations would have progressed uniformly as the building

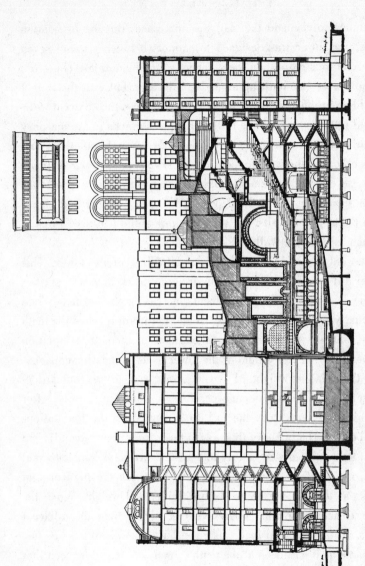

Figure 5. Auditorium Building, Chicago. Longitudinal section. (From the *Inland Architect & News Record*, July, 1888.)

continued to rise and the load was increased. But the foundation under the tower was designed to support between six and seven thousand tons more than the adjacent wall foundations. Therefore if the tower were built up along with the adjacent wall the weight would be insufficient to compress its foundations, the adjacent walls would settle more than the tower walls, and cracks in the masonry would ensue. The problem was to load the tower foundations concurrently with the wall foundations *in proportion to their ultimate loads* so that the settlement would be even throughout. The tower might have been built up independently, always higher and higher than the adjacent walls, but this was impossible because it was to be bonded into the walls.

The only solution was an artificial loading of the tower. This Adler did by means of adding pig-iron and brick in vast quantities to the lower stories and basement, increasing the artificial load gradually as the height of the walls and tower approached the tenth story, but always maintaining a constant mathematical equation between the relative weight of the tower to its foundation-capacity, and the relative weight of the adjacent wall to *its* foundation-capacity. Thus the settlement proceeded absolutely uniformly. After reaching the tenth story the full settlement of all the foundations had been reached. Above this, as the tower rose above the adjacent wall, the problem was merely to translate artificial load into real load, and this was done by gradually removing the pig-iron and bricks as the tower grew to its full height and weight. When the tower reached the top, ninety-five feet higher than the adjacent walls, all the artificial load was gone, but the total weight was just the same as it had been at the tenth-story level. It can be seen that modern building operations are enormously simplified by the caisson foundation going down to bed-rock, where no settlement has to be allowed for, and inequalities of loading on foundations are of no great moment. The first caisson foundations were to be used by Adler & Sullivan only a few years later.

Another pioneer solution of a problem in construction was embodied in the basement floor deep below the stage of the theatre. There was a great deal of mechanical equipment below the stage— pumps and hydraulic rams for the operation of the traps and bridges in the stage floor, engines for the curtains and cyclorama, ventilating machinery, a sewage ejector, etc. All of this required a basement floor eighteen feet below the stage and seven feet below the water-level of Lake Michigan, which meant a difficult problem in waterproofing. The problem was solved by the use of a laminated floor built up of several layers of concrete, Trinidad asphalt, and asphalt-saturated felt, counterweighted by concrete and steel rails to offset the upward pressure of ground-water beneath the floor. This treatment proved to be entirely waterproof.

Above the foundations, the construction embodied no important innovations. The walls were of solid masonry (the Auditorium was not of skyscraper construction), consisting of brick faced by cut stone. The rusticated facing of the three lower stories was of granite; the ashlar facing of the remaining stories was of gray-buff Indiana limestone. Although iron was not used as a supporting framework in the walls, many of the larger interior spaces were spanned by iron girders bearing on the masonry walls. Several thousand tons of metal, chiefly cast- and wrought-iron, were used in the building, enough to tax the capacity of the Carnegie Company in Pittsburgh, so that delayed shipments impeded construction a great deal. The entire building had a volume of 8,737,000 cubic feet, and its cost was $3,145,291, or about thirty-six cents a cubic foot. This was three times as expensive as previous first-class buildings by the

firm, the average cost of the office buildings before the Auditorium
being very slightly over twelve cents a cubic foot.

By March, 1888, the theatre was sufficiently completed to be
used for the Republican National Convention of that year, and
underneath the flags entwined in the rafters and scaffolding of the
unfinished ceiling, Benjamin Harrison and Levi P. Morton were
nominated as Republican candidates for President and Vice-
President. Eleven thousand persons were present. Twenty-one
months later President Harrison and Vice-President Morton were
among the dignitaries present for the dedication of the completed
Auditorium, on December 9, 1889.

The building is so large and complex that a description of the
entire edifice is apt to be confusing; for the sake of clarity the
exterior as a whole will be examined first. (Pls. 14 and 15) The
theatre itself at no point penetrates to the street fronts, being surrounded and surmounted by a shell of hotel rooms and business
offices, the fenestration of these being dominant in the general design of the exterior. The main entrance to the theatre is a triple
arch on the Congress Street façade, about three-quarters of the
way down the side. Since this was the natural approach, it does not
seem that the main entrance was signalized emphatically enough;
possibly a bolder projection from the wall would have made it
more evident, or a wider and more lofty arch. The three arched
entrances to the hotel on Michigan Avenue are more decisive, but
the projecting balcony carried over them on huge corbels is an
elephantine accent. Apart from these features the wall is a severe
and cliff-like mass, proclaiming the solidity of its construction.

The design is very similar to that of Richardson's Marshall Field
Building, especially in the grouping of the four middle stories under high arches, the grouping of the next two stories under smaller
arches, two arches over each one below, and the use of small

rectangular windows in the top story. Being a higher building, the base is increased to three stories, the rusticated granite very heavily treated to give a sense of solid support. The heavy squat columns between the display windows, the mammoth size of the granite blocks, the narrow windows with heavy lintels and small transoms, all give an effect of Richardsonian force. The base is in itself a very impressive unit, but in relation to the upper part of the building it seems too high. The main horizontal divisions give a 3–4–3 grouping of stories, and it seems that the design might have been more effective if the central group had been more decisive. Both the bottom and top stories are set off from the others by minor horizontal divisions, and counting these the grouping of stories is 1–2–4–2–1, still a symmetrical division. The disposition of the elements of the façade is thus in a measure a formal and artificial one, and it certainly does not correspond with the internal functional divisions which vary on the three sides of the building. On the other hand, the exterior design admirably expresses the heavy masonry construction, and in its large simplicity, its abstinence from merely trivial or "picturesque" outbreaks of surface ornament or irregularities of silhouette, it goes far beyond the buildings of its era in achieving a truly monumental form.

The great tower, like a heavy campanile, rises on the Congress Street side of the building. The main mass, seventeen stories in height, is surmounted by a small lantern housing various instruments of a U.S. Signal Service station and affording a stairway for access to the roof of the tower as a sightseeing platform. When built, it was the highest point in Chicago. The design of the tower as a unit is highly effective, but its relationship to the rest of the building may be criticized in certain details. Below the main cornice, it takes its scheme from the adjacent wall, being marked only by a slight projection. The main cornice cuts across it and tends to give the upper section of the tower the effect of a separate superimposed mass. The tower would probably have been more effective if it had been more decisively detached from the lower wall and allowed more vertical continuity by the suppression of the main cornice. Nevertheless, the broad corner piers give it a very satisfactory solidity, and the increased weight at the top affords a proper crown to a proud building; as Sullivan said, "the tower holds its head in the air, as a tower should."

Above the tall arches of the upper section of the tower the wall is solid for the height of a full story; inside at this level are several large tanks holding water for the hydraulic machinery of the stage. Above this a rectangular panel frames a long opening set with small columns resting on a broad overhanging ledge, the whole having the effect of an open loggia. Windows are set within these columns and a great deal of light is admitted to the rooms inside. This entire story was designed for the offices of Adler & Sullivan, and for more than twenty years Sullivan did his work in this spacious and well-lighted office overlooking the city. The copestone on top of the tower was laid with appropriate ceremonies on October 2, 1889.

The Auditorium Hotel occupies a kind of shell, surrounding two sides of the theatre: the Michigan Avenue side, and the Congress Street side as far as the line of the tower. The plan is very ingenious. The average depth is only forty-five feet, yet the hotel includes a large lobby, men's smoking-room, parlor, restaurant, dining-room, banquet hall, four hundred large guest rooms, and the necessary kitchens and service rooms. The three entrance arches on Michigan Avenue open into a spacious lobby (Pl. 16) with a marble mosaic floor, and a six-foot dado of Mexican onyx. A row of piers supports the ceiling, divided into panels by beams and stencilled with geometric patterns. The decoration of the archivolts and soffits of the arches, the frieze at the top of the wall, and the corbels and pier capitals is all of gilded plaster relief made from Sullivan's designs. This work, together with the richly colored ceiling and the fine marbles, has the sumptuous effect deemed proper for hotel lobbies in the eighties, without the vulgarity of other fashionable hostelries of that era.

The decoration of the long bar in the restaurant (Pl. 17) is noteworthy: the forms executed in carved wood and moulded plaster are entirely new architectural ornament, revealing Sullivan's rebellion against traditional forms and proportions, and his extraordinary fertility in the invention of a new vocabulary. On the second floor, above the lobby, is the main parlor of the hotel, reached by a grand staircase rich in onyx panelling and gilded plaster relief, and with fine wrought-iron stair-rails. The mosaic floors of the landings were especially designed by Sullivan, and show an amazing power in the proper use of the material, originality of motive, delicacy of treatment and wealth of color. The execution was largely by Italian and French craftsmen. The larger part of the ten-story building is taken up by guest rooms. The Auditorium Hotel was considered the last word in luxury and had large rooms and many fine suites.

Indubitably the finest public room in the hotel was the great dining hall on the tenth floor (Pls. 18 and 19), running the whole length of the Michigan Avenue front, and with a magnificent view from the large windows overlooking the lake-front park. The main room was covered by a curved vault, the curve beginning at the floor level. Five arched trusses divided the ceiling into bays, and each arch was decorated by soffit panels of ornamental plaster reliefs centering on electric lights. There were also electric flood-lights over the skylights, so that the room was extremely effective at night. The ceiling was originally decorated by a rich stencilled pattern, now painted over. At the ends were two smaller dining-rooms separated from the main room by columns carrying a very rich frieze. The segmental arches above the frieze were adorned by mural paintings. In the conception of the whole and in detail this was not only entirely novel, but one of the most beautiful rooms which Sullivan designed. The kitchens for this dining-room were located in a structurally independent building, four stories high, carried by trusses over the theatre stage, and reached from the dining-room by bridges.

Finally, the hotel possessed a special banquet hall located directly over the auditorium of the theatre, and carried by two huge iron trusses.[5] Entirely different from the main dining-room, the banquet hall was no less original in conception or refined in detail. In it another novel decorative use of electric lighting demonstrates Sullivan's resource in utilizing every practical necessity as an integral element in the architectural whole. These two rooms alone, if nothing else remained of his work, would establish Sullivan as a great architect. It is regrettable that the present use of the banquet hall as a Masonic lodge has effected some unfortunate changes in the decorative scheme.

The business portion of the Auditorium Building consisted of a number of stores on the Wabash Avenue side, and 136 offices on the floors above these and in the tower. Although this section of the building was independent of the theatre and separated from it by a thick masonry bearing-wall, it was used as an auxiliary entrance to the two upper galleries of the theatre which were connected by bridges and doors to the sixth-floor office corridor; the small recital hall above the upper galleries was also entered from the seventh-floor office corridor. The business offices in the tower were reached by elevators rising from the theatre entrance on Congress Street.

The hotel and the business offices were, when all is said and done, merely incidentals. The *raison d'être* of the Auditorium Building, and its most striking architectural achievement, was the great theatre. Physically and spiritually it was the heart of the building, and to more than a generation of Chicago opera-lovers the name "Auditorium" has meant, not the building as a whole, but the theatre itself.

The ten-story building containing hotel rooms and offices formed three sides of a rectangle measuring 118 feet by 246 feet; within this rectangle was built the theatre. The Auditorium Theatre was the largest permanent theatre (excluding open-air theatres) erected up to that time, with seating capacity for 4,237 persons. Including its vestibules, foyers, cloak-rooms, etc., it occupied more than half of the total area of the building, and about a third of its total volume.

The triple-arched entrance under the tower led into a large box-office vestibule, from which six pairs of doors afforded ample entrance to the ground-story foyer of the theatre. Due to the unusually great rise of the main floor of the theatre from front to back, entrances to it were provided from foyers on two different levels, the ground-story foyer leading by means of tunnels underneath the rear half of the floor to the front seats, and the second-story foyer connecting directly with the rear seats of the floor, from which it was originally separated only by an iron trellis. The main balcony was also entered from foyers on two different levels, tunnel entrances connecting the lower foyer with the front half of the balcony and the upper foyer with the rear half. All of the foyers were equipped with ample cloak-rooms, dressing-rooms, smoking-rooms, etc.

The parquet, or main floor of the theatre, originally measured 112 feet from the footlights to the last row of seats, and it seated 1,442 persons. The rise of the floor from orchestra pit to the back was determined by acoustic principles rather than sight-lines, the

total rise of seventeen feet being more than is actually necessary
for clear vision. Adler designed the gradually rising curve on the
basis of Scott Russell's "isocoustic curve," so that the direct outward movement of the sound waves from the stage would encounter
every part of the floor. This, together with the disposition of the
reflecting arches above, is responsible for the nearly perfect acoustic properties.

There were originally forty boxes at the sides, a lower range
of eight and an upper range of twelve, on each side, the lower range
forming a decorative arcade for the support of the upper. The
fronts were made of cast-iron, slightly curved out, decorated in
the prevailing color scheme of the house, ivory and gold. The
plush draperies of the upper boxes were of an ivory color slightly
darker than that of the box-fronts, and the chairs were upholstered
in yellow satin. Several years after the completion of the Auditorium new building laws called for the construction of a fireproof
partition between the parquet seats and the main foyer, and at this
time the last eight rows of seats in the parquet were removed and
the double range of boxes carried around the back in a continuous
curve. This reduced the capacity of the parquet by 412 seats, but
added to the number of places in the boxes.

The main balcony was even larger than the parquet, having
1,632 seats. The curve of the balcony was determined by the same
acoustic principles which were applied to the parquet, and the total
rise was forty feet. Above the balcony were two galleries, both
entered from the same floor-level, since one is not above but in
front of the other. (Fig. 5) This floor was reached by narrow staircases from the top of the balcony, but also, and more usually, by
the elevators in the adjacent office section, the gallery floor connecting with the sixth-floor office corridor. From the gallery floor, three
aisles led directly downward into the first gallery, containing 526

seats. The second gallery was carried slightly above and in front of the lower one on iron columns and trusses in such a way that it did not interfere with the sight-lines of the latter. It was reached by horizontal bridges and tunnel entrances, and had 437 seats. The total seating capacity of the theatre was thus 4,237, almost 1,200 more seats than were provided in the Metropolitan Opera House in New York, the largest theatre in America up to that time. More remarkable than the size, however, was the acoustic perfection and the ease of vision from every seat in the house. Music-lovers assert that there is not another theatre of comparable size in the country that matches the Auditorium in these essential respects, and Frank Lloyd Wright says of it: "It was acknowledged to be the greatest building achievement of the period: and to this day, probably, is the best room for opera, all things considered, yet built in the world." [6]

Looking toward the stage (Pl. 20) the architectural effect is strikingly beautiful. The proscenium arch rises in a graceful curve bordered by a mural painting by Charles Holloway using as its theme the sentence: "The utterance of life is a song, the symphony of Nature," the figures forming a frieze against a gold background. The reducing curtain is richly ornamented by gilded plaster reliefs inscribed with the names of great composers, and the drop-curtain is made of silk embroidered with gold. The proscenium wings spread out from the curtain at an angle and are decorated by graceful fan-like trellises and gilded plaster reliefs, with an organ grille at the left. The organ itself was placed in an auxiliary building to the north, and when built was the most complete instrument in the world. The stage-apron projects six feet in front of the curtain, with the prompter's box in the middle, and the orchestra pit below it.

The general form of the ceiling was determined by acoustic

principles.[7] It consists of a series of four expanding elliptical
arches, becoming successively wider and higher until the outermost
one attains the full width of the theatre. Between these arches the
ceiling panels are smooth, to act as sound reflectors. Sound waves
meeting a reflecting surface act like water waves or light waves:
the angle of reflection is equal to the angle of incidence. The spacing of these sections of ceiling is so calculated that sound waves
from the stage are reflected downward to every part of the main
floor and to part of the balcony. A perfect semicircular reflecting
arch would have focused all reflected waves on one spot in the
middle of the floor; the flat elliptical arches prevent focusing of
reflected sound, and the vertical breaks between the arches throw
the reflected waves farther and farther back, diffusing them over
the entire area.

Other important acoustic factors entered into the design of these
arches. If the path difference between direct and reflected sound is
so great that a sound originating on the stage reaches an auditor
more than one-sixth of a second later from a reflecting surface than
it does by direct outward movement of sound waves, the result is
an annoying echo; if the time-difference is less than this, the result
is reinforcement which is an aid to hearing. This factor determined
the height of the arches; the one nearest the stage had to be the
lowest, and is actually only forty-five feet above the floor. Most
important of all is the reverberation time. Reverberation is the
prolongation of sound in a room after the source has ceased to
operate; if it is too great, the overlapping of successive sounds
blurs the fine effects of music; if it is too small, loss of volume and
dullness of tone result. Reverberation is directly proportional to
the total volume of a room and inversely proportional to its absorption capacity. Thus in a very large theatre either the total volume must be reduced as much as possible or the absorption must

be increased by the use of sound-absorbing surfaces. The great arches in the Auditorium serve to reduce the total volume of the room very considerably, and thus to diminish reverberation time. It is interesting to note that in the design of the new Chicago Civic Opera House built in 1928 the old Auditorium was taken as the most desirable acoustic standard, and that despite the advancement in the science of acoustics and the variety of new sound-absorbing materials available today, the new theatre proved to have a longer reverberation time than the Auditorium, which being considerably larger was a more difficult problem. This event, coming forty years after the construction of the old building, indicates how far ahead of his time Dankmar Adler was in the science of acoustics.

The great arches also serve as ventilating ducts, carrying conditioned air, washed and humidified, heated in winter and cooled in summer, to the numerous air outlets on the front faces of the arches. These are treated decoratively as patterned bosses, like small bee-hives, and it is probable that few spectators realize their humble utilitarian function. It is worth remarking that the main structural supports of the ceiling are not housed within the arches, as might appear, but are huge horizontal iron trusses 118 feet in length and carrying a load of 660 tons, spanning the whole theatre above the topmost arch; the arches are light frameworks hung from the trusses, shaped almost entirely by acoustical needs.

The use of these arches as an architectural and decorative motive is admirable. Sullivan made them the dominant theme of the interior and the repeated curves have a grand sweep over the hall. They are decorated by plaster reliefs, chevron mouldings dividing the faces into hexagons enclosing foliage designs, diamonds enclosing the grilled bosses, and smaller triangles enclosing other foliage designs. The whole surface is covered by gold leaf and studded with electric lights, gleaming like dull, mellow gold. Even the borders of the arched ceiling panels are enriched by relief bands and an inner lace-like pattern delicately stencilled in gold. Rarely has there been such a wedding of large and majestic simplicity with refined and subtle detail. The effect is superb.

Above and outside of the golden arches, a coved ceiling rises many feet, and an immense rectangular skylight is filled by stained glass. (Pl. 21) On the sidewalls under this ceiling are two large arches framing mural paintings by Fleury. On one side is a scene at dawn with a wooded meadow and a running stream, the whole in tender shades of green and silver. A solitary poet is inspired by the sunrise and the awakening of life, and below is inscribed a line from Sullivan's "Inspiration": "O soft melodious springtime, first-born of life and love." On the other side is a scene of pathless wilds, in gray, subsiding autumn, with brown leaves settling through the air in a deep twilight. The poet is inspired to an autumn reverie, and below is the line: "A great life has passed into the tomb and there awaits the requiem of winter's snows."

One of the most ingenious devices in the Auditorium is a means for reducing the seating capacity of the theatre. Concert artists with whom Adler conferred impressed upon him the disturbing effects of singing or playing solo programs to a half-empty theatre, since only symphony concerts and operatic productions were expected to fill all of the four thousand-odd seats. Acting on the advice of Augustin Daly, Adler devised means for closing off completely the first and second galleries, and the rear third of the balcony. The curved section of ceiling leading up to the central skylight is in reality a hinged panel which can be lifted to reveal the second gallery, and in that position it forms part of an upper coved ceiling. Similarly, the slanting ceiling below this is a panel cutting off the first gallery, and it can be lifted up to fit flat underneath the floor of the second gallery. These two hinged ceilings are built on iron frames and weigh twenty tons, but are counterbalanced so that one man at each of six windlasses can raise or lower them in a few minutes. The rear third of the balcony can also be closed off by means of curtains drawn across the row of columns supporting the gallery. These various devices made possible the reduction of the total seating capacity to 2,574. As a matter of actual practice, concert singers soon found that even with both galleries open there was a much greater feeling of intimacy with the audience than in many smaller theatres, and the acoustics were so perfect that they felt their voices carrying clearly to the most distant parts of the house. This was so frequently expressed that after a few years the gallery mechanism was no longer used, although it is said to be in perfect condition today.

The Auditorium theatre was planned not only for symphonic and operatic programs, but also for great choral concerts, occasional conventions, and society balls. For such events the reducing curtain of the stage opening could be lifted, the whole stage floor could be stepped up from front to back by means of the hydraulic mechanism lifting the floor in sections, and thus afford room for more than five hundred seats on the stage. Choral concerts with a full symphony orchestra and several hundred singers on the stage were frequently given. Since the stage floor was normally level rather than inclined, its full extent could be used for dancing, and a hardwood floor, kept in sections in the storerooms, could be laid directly over the whole front half of the parquet seats. In this way a ballroom capable of accommodating eight thousand persons could be made. The numerous entrances and exits made it possible for this number to leave the theatre in about four and a half minutes.

The mechanical equipment of the stage was the most complete installed in any theatre to that date. While the Auditorium designs were under way, Adler made a trip to Europe to study the latest improvements in stage design, especially in the opera houses at Halle, Prague, and Budapest. All three of these used movable stage floors, elevated or depressed by hydraulic apparatus; and those at Halle and Budapest used a panoramic horizon in place of the "sky-borders" customary for stage back-drops in this country. The machinery employed was designed and built by the *Asphalia Gesellschaft* in Vienna. Adler requested them to prepare designs for similar apparatus for the Auditorium, but when the plans arrived in Chicago so many divergences between Continental and American mechanical practice became apparent that the plans had to be largely redrawn by Paul Mueller, and many alterations and improvements were made by the Crane Company engineers who installed the hydraulic apparatus.

The stage of the Auditorium is still one of the largest in the country, measuring sixty-two feet from curtain line to back wall, and ninety-eight feet clear across, with the side walls one hundred and ten feet apart. This gave ample space for the production of the largest operatic scenes. The stage floor is level, and is constructed with a large number of sections that can be moved up or down, to create a base for scenery simulating steps, terraces, hills, pits, etc.; to provide for appearing or disappearing objects or persons; to produce wave-like or rocking motions up and down or obliquely; and to afford multitudinous other "effects" in the spectacular stage realism of the day. Above the stage the mechanism is no less elaborate. The rigging-loft, or grid-iron, is high enough above the stage to lift the highest drops above the proscenium opening, and it carries eighty tons of miscellaneous apparatus: fly-galleries, scene bridges, a paint-frame, paint-bridge, property galleries, all with the necessary counter-weights and controlling cables. One of the most interesting innovations was a panoramic "horizon," an endless canvas roll which ran on a steel-linked belt and track carried around the three sides of the stage, on which was painted in various sections the sky of every season of the year in every weather condition. Thus a change of mood in the dramatic action could be easily reflected in the sky of the background—all moods, from sunny and cheerful to lowering and somber, were provided. This must have been a great asset to the Wagnerian operas. On the right side-stage is the electrical screen, bristling with polished brass levers controlling the 5,000 house lights, 150 footlights, 6 borders with 165 lights each, and the artificial moon, stars, and lightning flashes used in conjunction with the panoramic horizon. There are also transparent moving clouds for use on the sky. On the same side are three levers controlling the hydraulic hoisting apparatus of the three curtains, which weigh sixteen tons.

The intermediate basement below the stage is a perfect powerhouse of machinery: hydraulic engines for lifting all the drops, frames, galleries, bridges, curtains, border-drops, and the panorama; ventilating machinery; the twenty hydraulic rams of the stage floor; sewage ejector; pumps; levers, and other intricate mechanical equipment. Along its south wall are iron racks for rolled scene drops. Other scenery and property storerooms are located at the back and sides, and over the top of the proscenium arch. When the Auditorium opened, the management possessed a stock of 125 drops, 300 set pieces, and other complete equipment for the production of thirty different operas.

Operatic production also requires suitable accommodations for the performers, and these were studiously considered. There is a musicians' room for a hundred-piece symphony orchestra, located back of the orchestra pit at the level of the intermediate basement; thirty dressing-rooms furnished with make-up tables, electric and gas light, and ventilating ducts, and connected with the prompter's box by electric bells; six large and handsomely appointed dressing-rooms for the principals, and a stage reception-room connecting with the box-corridor. In short, no provision for the comfort of the performers or the smooth functioning of the mechanics of a grand opera was omitted. The mechanical advantages at hand were so complete that only twenty-five stage-hands were required for the production of the heaviest operas.

The difficulty of designing the complete structural and mechanical layout of such a building, involving as it did not merely unprecedented size but a large number of new principles and practices, can be imagined. The responsibility for all of it fell on Adler's shoulders. Sullivan said, years later: "The problems that Mr. Adler had to meet in that building were simply heart-breaking. In those days there were very few consulting engineers, and these few were employed mostly by the railroads, iron companies, and mines. There was one man who gave some attention to sanitary and heating matters, but that was almost all the professional advice Mr. Adler could call to his aid. He practically had to dig out his information for himself, and it was a tremendous proposition." [8]

The ceremonial dedication of the Auditorium Theatre took place on Monday evening, December 9, 1889. More than a thousand persons were seated on the stage, and the house was crowded to capacity. Two temporary boxes were constructed at the sides of the stage; one of them for Governor Fifer and his suite, the other for President Harrison and Mrs. Harrison, Vice-President Morton, and Commodore Peck. After several addresses of felicitation and the prolonged applause of the audience, the President made a few brief remarks. There followed a cantata composed by Frederick Grant Gleason with words by Harriet Monroe, sung by the chorus of the Apollo Club. Then came the *pièce de résistance* of the evening, Adelina Patti, America's opera idol, singing "Home Sweet Home"! The success of this was so emphatic that she granted an encore,

Eckert's "Swiss Echo Song." The evening closed amid general rejoicing. The next evening the opera season was inaugurated by the Abbey and Grau Opera Company singing "Romeo and Juliet," with Patti as prima donna.

The opera was for years under the management of Milward Adams; then in 1910 the Chicago Civic Opera Company was formed. In 1928 this organization transferred its productions to the new Chicago Civic Opera House, much to the regret of a great many music-lovers who avowed a preference for the architectural beauty and the associations of the old building. For forty years it had served its purpose; it was more than a building, it was an institution, and its passing was deplored. For four years it was used only for occasional plays, and was practically forgotten. Recently the Chicago Civic Opera Company was forced to abandon its new building, and hope for the return of the opera to its former home was revived. Late in 1932 the great theatre was once more restored to its original luster in a very careful and praiseworthy cleaning and restoration directed by Holabird & Root. Admirable discretion was used in attempting to regain as nearly as possible the original appearance.

The Auditorium was the chief monument upon which the later success of Adler & Sullivan was built. In point of cost, it was the largest building enterprise in the city of Chicago at that time, and ten times greater than any previous commission of the firm. As an engineering achievement it was outstanding, being the heaviest structure yet carried on floating foundations, and embodying extremely ingenious solutions of many other complex problems of planning, construction, and mechanical equipment. Its historical importance as a turning-point in Sullivan's style and as a great institution in the civic life of Chicago, not to speak of its architectural excellence, make it a building which should be preserved to future generations as one of the great monuments of American architecture.

[1] Actually, Sullivan had a somewhat malformed hip which gave a slight limp to his walk.

[2] *Autobiography*, pp. 257, 288.

[3] Montgomery Schuyler: "A Critique of the Works of Adler & Sullivan," *Architectural Record*, Great American Architects Series, no. 2, Dec. 1895.

[4] Dankmar Adler: "The Chicago Auditorium," *Architectural Record*, vol. 1, no. 4, p. 415, April–June, 1892.

[5] This is not shown in the longitudinal section, Fig. 5, which was made early in 1888, before the banquet hall had been planned.

[6] Frank Lloyd Wright: *Autobiography*, pp. 105–106.

[7] For an admirable brief analysis see Dr. Paul E. Sabine: "The Acoustics of the Chicago Civic Opera House," *Architectural Forum*, vol. 52, no. 4, pp. 599–604, April, 1930.

[8] Sullivan: "Development of Construction," *The Economist*, vol. 56, no. 1, p. 39, July 1, 1916.

# IV. YEARS OF EXPANSION

THE building of the Auditorium marked the beginning of the great era of the firm of Adler & Sullivan. From the time of its completion until the dissolution of the partnership in 1895 the firm was deluged by commissions and its practice was one of the largest in the country. Office buildings, theatres, hotels, clubs, warehouses, railroad stations, residences and numerous other structures were designed not only for Chicago and its suburbs, but for cities as far afield as Buffalo, St. Louis, New Orleans, Salt Lake City and Seattle.

The long strain of the Auditorium work had wearied Sullivan, and for several weeks he was in poor health. As soon as it was completed, he decided to leave the raw winter climate of Chicago for a trip to the West Coast, combining a necessary business visit to Pueblo and Salt Lake City with a rest in California. Since Adler disliked leaving home, Sullivan usually made the necessary trips to supervise out-of-town operations; he enjoyed travel, and in time had visited almost every state in the Union. He spent most of January and February, 1890, in San Francisco and San Diego, but was still in poor health and the climate did not suit him. From San Diego he went to New Orleans in February, and there met friends from Chicago, Mr. and Mrs. James Charnley, who persuaded him to go with them to Ocean Springs, Mississippi. Ocean Springs was at that time a small rustic hamlet, about eighty miles east of New Orleans on the eastern shore of Biloxi Bay. Sullivan fell in love with the place at once, and after two quiet weeks he was restored to good health. He decided to buy land and build a vacation cottage a few miles east on the shore of the bay. It was a stretch of utterly wild forest: "immense rugged short-leaved pines, sheer eighty feet to their stiff gnarled crowns, graceful swamp pines, very tall, delicately plumed; slender vertical Loblolly pines in dense masses; patriarchal sweet gums and black gums with their younger broods; maples, hickories, myrtles; in the undergrowth, dogwoods, halesias, sloe plums, buckeyes and azaleas, all in a riot of bloom; a giant magnolia and grandiflora near the front—all grouped and arranged as though by the hand of an unseen poet." [1] There was one marvellous wistaria vine dropping in great waves from a tree. The owner of the property, Colonel Newcomb Clark, sold a large plot running a hundred yards along the beach and about a third of a mile inland, and Sullivan designed two bungalows, one for himself and one for the Charnleys, about a hundred yards apart, with stables and servants' quarters set far back in the woods. (Pls. 22, 23) The design of all the buildings was very simple, Sullivan's aim being to make them as inconspicuous as possible in their forest surroundings. The construction was left to a local carpenter. The cottages at Ocean Springs became Sullivan's most-loved home, and for eighteen years he visited them frequently for recreation and the inspiration which he found in a close communion with nature. During the years he cultivated over a hundred species of roses in his garden. In March, 1890, he returned to Chicago and set to work with renewed energy.

From the beginning of the Auditorium to the end of the partnership in 1895 Adler & Sullivan designed about forty buildings. Only two of these, the Stock Exchange in Chicago and the Guaranty Building in Buffalo, were finished after 1893, as the panic of that year was reflected in an almost complete cessation of building activity. Seven others were never constructed. The great achievements of these years were the skyscrapers erected in Chicago, St. Louis, and Buffalo, which are discussed in the following chapter. The other buildings erected between 1888 and 1893 form a miscellaneous group which may well be discussed together.

That Richardson exerted a strong influence on Sullivan in the late eighties is apparent not only in the Auditorium but in the Standard Club and the Heath residence, both built before the Auditorium was finished. The Standard Club, one of Chicago's oldest Jewish organizations, commissioned a new building in the summer of 1887 which was virtually completed by the end of the following year, although the interiors were not finished and the building occupied until February, 1889. The exterior (Pl. 24) was faced by rusticated limestone, the window sills and lintels being large single blocks. The division of the façade into base, two stories grouped under arches, and top story with small rectangular windows recalls Richardson, as does also the general severity of treatment. The buff-colored terra cotta panels under the third-story windows are Richardsonian in disposition, but the detail is spikier and the curves of the foliage more brittle than in his work. Doubtless Richardson's ornament influenced Sullivan, as there is certainly an immense difference between this and Sullivan's earlier ornament otherwise difficult to account for, but Sullivan very readily developed it into a characteristic vocabulary of his own. The building as a whole seems adequate but not at all impressive, and we feel that although Sullivan is searching for a new architectural form he is not at home in the idiom of another man. An addition, somewhat higher than the main building, was built at the south in 1893. The inside of this, facing an inner court, is illustrated in Pl. 26. The Standard Club was demolished in 1931.

The Ira Heath residence, built in 1889, is much more Richardsonian and much better architecture, although totally unlike any other residence designed by Adler & Sullivan. (Pl. 25) Here the extravagant depth of voussoirs over doors and windows and the vibrant surface texture of random-coursed and quarry-face masonry endow the façade with much greater richness and force. Richardson himself could not have done better in a similar program.

The most interesting aspect of Richardson's influence on Sullivan is the rapidity with which Sullivan assimilated it and developed it into something entirely new. It is hard to overestimate the importance of the Walker Warehouse (Pl. 27) in this respect. Architecturally, the Walker Warehouse is far more significant than the Auditorium, and it takes its place with the Wainwright Building as one of Sullivan's great achievements. Being a commercial structure in the inner part of Chicago's Loop, it is not well known, and the present obliteration of the building by advertising signs prevents the casual observer from gaining an idea of its quality. It was built for Martin A. Ryerson, Jr., begun in July, 1888, and finished in October, 1889. Thus it was begun about a year and a half after the Auditorium, and finished nearly at the same time. Since the general design was obviously inspired by Richardson's Marshall Field Building (Pl. 28), and the programs of the two buildings were very similar, they offer a more instructive comparison than do the Field Building and the Auditorium.

Each building is a seven-story warehouse structure occupying a full block; the mass in both cases is cubic, with only a slightly projecting cornice and a clean-cut silhouette; ornamental detail is virtually omitted, so that the architectural effect depends almost solely on the plastic articulation of the larger forms. The difference between the two buildings lies in the arrangement and treatment of these forms. Richardson's building, although a great advance over previous structures, represents the persistence in a slight degree of conventional design, in that, although grown away from the historical styles, it is not yet entirely free from them. The rustication of the masonry and the emphasis of the voussoirs of the arches betray Richardson's insistence on traditional masonry construction. The division of the façade into four groups of stories also reveals the conventional embarrassment, not acute in this instance, of the nineteenth-century architect faced with the design of a high building: its height appeared a liability rather than an asset, and he sought to divide it up into as many horizontal units of familiar size and proportion as were required. This accounts for the 1–3–2–1 division of stories, and the dominance of the horizontals separating basement and attic stories from the intervening ones.

The Walker Building goes beyond the Field Building in two essential respects: the greater freedom from historical or conventional forms, and the more precise statement of its elements of design in a firmly articulated whole. It is a sort of pure architecture, using the fundamental elements of the pier, the lintel, and the arch in an abstract composition, dissociated from the expression of specifically masonry effects. The omission of heavy rustication on the arches signifies that Sullivan is using a geometrical shape, not a traditional form. The use of smooth ashlar masonry instead of rustication signifies an emphasis on the wall plane rather than on the surface of the wall as solid mass. In every detail, Sullivan develops toward an abstract architecture. The individual elements are both more clearly stated and more simply organized than in Richardson's building. The corner masses of the piers rise unbroken from pavement to cornice; the middle group of four stories is unchallenged by other and lesser groups. Every element is clean-cut, smooth, rectilinear, positive. In composition, the relationship of the two-story base to the main unit is happier than is the one-story base of the Field Building. Even the scale of the building is an abstract one, since the ground-story arches are larger than required for entrance doors and do not in fact serve for them; they are determined by the size of the building as a whole, like the stylobate of the Parthenon which being scaled to the temple as a whole has steps too high for convenient human use.

Another building demonstrating Sullivan's assimilation of Richardson's influence and his development toward a more abstract form is the Dooly Block in Salt Lake City (Pl. 29), built in 1890–91. It is clearly allied to the Walker Warehouse in its use of the pier, the lintel, and the arch as an elementary vocabulary, and since its commercial purpose is similar to that of the Walker Building, the form is also similar in general effect. The treatment of the four upper stories under arches is virtually identical, but the inclusion of stores in the ground story necessitated a reduction of wall area for the opening of display windows. The small windows in the attic open into a top floor of mechanical equipment lighted chiefly by skylights, so that they are not functionally necessary. The projecting cornice faced by a band of rich decoration represents the first appearance of a characteristic feature which is discussed in connection with the Wainwright Building.

If it is permissible for the critic to judge an architect by his best achievements, it is also incumbent on the historian to include such as are of admittedly inferior quality. Many of Sullivan's buildings between the Walker Warehouse and the Transportation Building of 1893 seem to fall within this latter group. Inspiration is a variable quality, and even a genius cannot always measure up to a uniform standard of excellence, but it is nevertheless hard to account for the great discrepancy in style between the best and the worst buildings of this period. Doubtless since there were about forty jobs in the office within five years, some of them large, Sullivan was able to give less personal attention to detailing the ornament and minor features of some than of others, but on the other hand there can be no question that the general design of all of them was his.

Ten of the buildings of this period were hotels and theatres, sometimes separate structures but often combined in one building as in the Auditorium. For this reason they will be discussed as a single group. Five of them were ill-fated projects destined never to be constructed, but since they existed as completed designs they are perhaps as significant as the executed structures in a consideration of Sullivan's stylistic development.

The first of these, the Opera House Block in Pueblo, Colorado (Pl. 30), was designed while the Auditorium was under way and finished in 1890. The building was later somewhat remodelled, and finally destroyed by fire in 1922. It occupied a street corner and consisted of a theatre enclosed by a shell of offices on the two street façades. The main entrance to the theatre consisted of recessed arches resting on short piers, with terra cotta decoration and portrait medallions in the spandrels and a recessed loggia in a rich frame above. There were separate entrances to the office portion of the building. The form of the main entrance arch was repeated in thirteen smaller arches fronting the ground-story offices, forming an arcaded base for the wall. Four of these and the two corner entrances were later removed for the construction of a large corner store, but fortunately no other remodellings were made. The wall was of rusticated masonry, with simple rectangular windows. The top story had a long recessed balcony on both façades, interrupted only by supporting colonets and the broad corner piers faced by terra cotta ornament. The roof was of low pitch and projected about six feet to form a protecting cornice for this balcony. The heavy square tower was open at the top to form an observation platform, and was also topped by an extravagantly projecting cornice. The roof was broken by two clerestory-like houses, carrying sharp-roofed lanterns, and a curious turret with a steep roof and stepped gables; these features were used for air exhaust vents. The general effect is as gay as the Italian quattrocento style—indeed the loggias beneath the eaves recall those of Cronaca's Palazzo Guadagni.

The Seattle Opera House Block was one of the office tragedies. The commission came in 1890 as a result of the Pueblo building, and complete designs and working drawings were prepared but the project failed of construction because of financial difficulties. The completed design (Fig. 6) shows a six-story structure dominated by a great tower twelve stories high. The twelfth story was evidently to be used as an observation platform, and has a richly ornamented balcony projecting on all four sides, surmounted by a steep-pitched roof. This overhanging balcony motive is found in two or three other designs of this period, with much the same picturesque but top-heavy effect. The Hotel Ontario at Salt Lake City was also designed in 1890, and although the office work was completely finished the construction was never carried above the foundations.

The most famous of Adler & Sullivan's theatres after the Auditorium was McVicker's in Chicago. Mention has already been made of their remodelling of this theatre in 1885. On August 26, 1890, it was largely destroyed by fire. Mr. McVicker engaged Adler & Sullivan to rebuild the interior, preserving the orchestra, balcony, and gallery pitches that had afforded such excellent sight-lines and acoustics in the old building, but redesigning the proscenium opening and redecorating the entire interior. The cost of the remodelling was $106,000, and the theatre was reopened March 30, 1891. The new McVicker's was undoubtedly one of Sullivan's masterpieces, the proscenium in particular being in its architectural form and decorative enrichment perhaps the finest single feature in all his work. (Pl. 32)

Figure 6. Design for Seattle Opera House. 1890.

The semicircular proscenium arch formed a rich frame to the stage opening, and its broad unmoulded face was decorated by intricate plaster reliefs sheathed in gold leaf. The design consisted of overlapping shields or medallions, alternating a brittle star-shaped pattern with a free-flowing foliage pattern. The proscenium arch was framed by strictly rectangular panels successively wider and higher until the outermost one, over the middle of the floor, achieved the full width and height of the auditorium. The delicate and intricate surface ornament on these panels was colored in tones ranging from deep salmon to cream white, touched with gold, and softly illuminated by the diffused light of electric lamps set in foliage clusters on the front faces of the panels. The front faces were also perforated by grilles to permit the sound of the organ (the pipes of which were located above) to enter the theatre. The long rectangular relief panels over the boxes were by Johannes Gelert. The decoration of the house was carried out in colors ranging from dark brown and mahogany red to the salmon pink and cream of the proscenium, all given brilliance by gold leaf bands. In theatre architecture, more than in any other, an effect of joyful richness in decoration is desirable, and in the McVicker's Theatre the perfect harmonies of color and the exuberant efflorescence of Sullivan's foliate and geometric designs combined to effect an enchanting beauty, controlled and balanced by the masculine positiveness of the broad and simple architectural lines. Sullivan is at his best here, in a kind of design most appropriate to his temperament, and at a time when he had achieved a consummate mastery of his art.

The structural engineering in the McVicker's Theatre is also worthy of note. At Adler's suggestion, Mr. McVicker decided to have two stories of offices constructed over the auditorium of the theatre. These were carried by latticed steel columns resting on new foundations independent of the old walls, and six heavy steel trusses spanning the auditorium. This construction was fireproofed by encasing all steel in porous terra cotta tile, and by using fireproof tile in all floors, ceilings, roofs, and partitions. Electric wiring was carried in conduits. Twenty-four new offices were added and connected with the older office building in front of the theatre, where an additional elevator was installed to serve them. The arrangements for heating, lighting, and ventilating were very complete, as was also the reconstruction of the stage. Many of the mechanical devices introduced in the Auditorium were used here. This McVicker's Theatre lasted almost in its original state from 1891 to 1925, when it was demolished and supplanted by a cinema theatre.

Numerous hotels were projected in Chicago during the years just prior to the World's Fair. Adler & Sullivan designed three, but only one of these, the Victoria Hotel in Chicago Heights, was actually erected. The other two exist as designs only, dating from the year 1891. One design (Fig. 7) is clearly allied to the Dooly Block and the Hotel Ontario in Salt Lake City. Two wings project in front of a recessed court in the middle, screened by an entrance arch, and an eleven-story tower of octagonal shape with a pyramidal roof dominates the whole. The design of the wings, with rectilinear ground-story openings and four stories above grouped under arches, and a top story of rectangular windows, is eminently simple and pleasing. The octagonal tower, although an interesting feature, seems impracticable for hotel rooms, and does not seem to justify its existence through connection with other features of the design.

The St. Nicholas Hotel, St. Louis (Pl. 33), was built in 1892–93. Although it has many picturesque features and is graced with rich decoration, Montgomery Schuyler rated its success as "purely architectonic." There is a base of two stories, treated as a simple arcade in finely jointed brown sandstone ashlar. Above, the next five stories are of plain buff-colored brick. Four of these stories are enriched by projecting oriels, with buff terra cotta spandrels moulded in intricate designs. The entire top story of the front block of the building was given over to a dining hall with high trussed ceiling, which accounts for the long exterior balconies and the gabled roof. The balcony fronts are richly ornamented in terra cotta, and the great arched windows in the gable ends filled by stained glass. The kitchens and service rooms are in the top story of the rear wing. The steep-pitched roof is not only a picturesque feature, but it clearly defines the major axis of the building which might otherwise be doubtful. The break of the balconies revealing the corner pier is another device to secure architectonic clarity. Unfortunately the top story was destroyed by fire in 1903 and at that time the entire building was taken over for purely commercial purposes, three stories of offices being added above the line of the former balconies. The remodelling was done by a St. Louis firm, and although "Sullivanesque" ornament was employed, the present appearance with four severely plain stories above the oriels and a flat box-roof is curiously mixed, like a gentleman in full dress wearing a battered felt hat.

The Victoria Hotel at Chicago Heights (Pl. 31) was built in 1892–93 and opened for the World's Fair business. It was an inexpensive building and of no great distinction. The two lower stories were of red brick, forming a series of large arches in the ground story, and the third story was faced by stucco in relief painted a buff-yellow. The stucco was protected by a widely projecting wooden cornice. The general effect is similar to that of the Pueblo Opera House. The building has since been twice remodelled, the arches of the ground story being obliterated by large store windows and signs, the main dining-room and the lobby altered. In the most

Figure 7. Design for a hotel, Chicago. 1891.

recent remodelling, however, some attempt was made to regain the original aspect. The Victoria Hotel was the last hotel building designed by Adler & Sullivan.

At this time the firm was called on to do a synagogue for the Kehilath Anshe Ma'ariv in Chicago. The building is of especial interest because of its close personal connection with Dankmar Adler. The Kehilath Anshe Ma'ariv (Congregation of the Men of the West) was founded by Abraham Kohn, Adler's father-in-law, and his own father, Liebman Adler, became its first rabbi on his arrival in Chicago in 1861. Dankmar Adler was always a faithful member of the congregation, and on his death the funeral services were held in the synagogue. The building was begun in 1890 and dedicated on June 11, 1891. As originally contemplated, the structure was to be entirely of ashlar masonry, far more monumental in appearance than the executed design. One of the early renderings, made in water color by Paul Lautrup, may be seen in Pl. 34. With battered walls, extremely heavy window mullions and transoms, large arches, and a dense mass pruned of picturesque projections, it has a lithic solidity and force far surpassing that of the finished building. Lack of funds prevented the execution of this impressive conception, and the reduction of cost through the use of cheaper Joliet stone and pressed sheet metal made the finished building a lamentable compromise. The south and east walls, since they faced inside the block, were made of brick, and the interior constructed as economically as possible of wood and terra cotta.

The exterior of the present building (Pl. 35) has a rusticated wall three stories high, capped by a slight cornice. The use of arches is reminiscent of Richardson, but the effect is hard and cold. This rectangular block is covered by a flat roof, out of which arises a clerestory with steep-pitched roof. The transition from the lower mass to the upper is abrupt, and the steep-pitched roof loses its proper effect through the omission of the lower-pitched roof around the outside shown in the earlier design. The decorative treatment of the sheet metal walls of the clerestory, although by itself as beautiful as the pattern of an Oriental rug, is hard to reconcile with the bolder texture of the wall below. The decorated cornice and parapet, made as cheaply as possible, are also poor substitutes for the masculine vigor and simplicity of these features in the early design. However, it must be recognized that in view of the limitations imposed on the architects they achieved a reasonable success.

The interior of the synagogue (Pl. 36) is considerably more effective. The ground floor is used for school and social rooms, and the large hall for the congregation rises from the second floor to a high vaulted roof in the clerestory. The pews on the floor are arranged in concentric segmental curves facing the pulpit, and there is a gallery curving around sides and back. Above the hall rises a species of tunnel vault, panelled in wood, with two large transverse ribs, toward which curved panels at the ends converge. The clerestory windows in groups of three arched lights penetrate the sides and back of this vault. At the east end is a semi-dome, and the curve of this is bordered by a broad and richly decorated arch above. The decorative designs in the bands of terra cotta facing the gallery and at the base of the clerestory are among the richest examples of Sullivan's work. Although the structure of this auditorium is completely different from that of the theatres, the acoustic properties are outstanding—another evidence of Adler's mastery of the science. Altogether the interior is admirably suited to its purpose, novel, and quite effective, although the gold of the decoration and the rich colors of the woods are necessary to a full realization of its beauty.

Adler & Sullivan designed several factory and warehouse structures during this period, but all of them have since been demolished.

By far the largest and most impressive of these was the great warehouse built for the Chicago Cold Storage Exchange in 1891, covering a whole block in the industrial section along the Chicago River.
(Pl. 37) It consisted of two eight-story buildings, connected by
arcades and bridges, and served by both rail and water traffic from
the basement and sub-basement. The first two stories above the
street level were used for stores and offices, having large windows.
The upper floors, used for storage purposes, have very small windows grouped vertically to give the effect of narrow slits. The for-
tress-like appearance created by the solid walls and narrow windows
is further enhanced by a machicolated cornice. But the building
does not pretend to be medieval; there are no medieval decorative
details, nor does the wall-surface suggest a massive thickness. It is
in reality architecture reduced to the most elemental terms of
volumes and plane surfaces, and suggests, a generation ahead of
its time, *"Die neue Sächlichkeit"* of modern German architecture.
The warehouse was demolished in 1902. Another more or less plain
and utilitarian structure was the New Orleans Passenger Station of
the Illinois Central Railroad, built in 1892. (Fig. 8) It is a long,
low, two-story structure built on an L-shaped plan with baggage and
express rooms in one wing and the waiting rooms, ticket-offices, etc.,
in the other. A colonnade carries a projecting roof to form a covered platform across the front, and the corners are emphasized by
round-arched structures like porte-cochères. The building is of
brick, and practically devoid of decoration.

To turn from the utilitarian to the purely monumental, three
tombs designed by Sullivan during these years are among the finest
of all his works. Sepulchral architecture in America has been in
general a field of conspicuous failure. Such monuments as pretend
to architectural distinction too often achieve merely an expensive
notoriety—the pretension without the distinction. The word "fash-

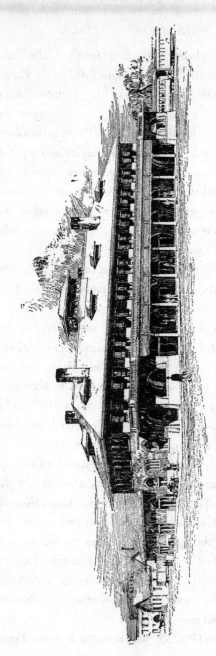

Figure 8. Illinois Central Railroad Station, New Orleans. 1892.

ionable" is nowhere better applied: evidences of the Gothic fashion, the Romanesque fashion, the Egyptian fashion, the Classic fashion, and all other fashions, abound, as if the architects hoped to celebrate the permanence of death through borrowing styles that have been dead for many hundreds of years. Worse, they have not been able to borrow styles, but merely fragments and tags of styles, so that sepulchral monuments are *disjecta membra*—a Gothic pinnacle here, a detached colonnade there—a cemetery resembles a kind of architectural morgue. The sentiment expressed in the majority of monuments is the preoccupation with death, its awfulness, its inevitability, its utter permanence.

A different spirit animates Sullivan's tombs. They celebrate, not the permanence of death, but the permanence of life; they express in terms of lyric beauty that a man or a woman has *lived*, not merely that he or she has died. They are individual in form and they speak unmistakably of a personality, a personality that is immortal if only because it is enshrined in a living architecture.

Sullivan's first tomb was the monument to Martin Ryerson in Graceland Cemetery, Chicago, completed in 1889. (Pl. 38) Massively constructed of huge blocks of polished blue-black Quincy granite, this has a compact density and force which is arresting. The form is Egyptian in feeling, with battered walls and a severely rectangular entrance recalling a mastaba door; but the detail is entirely original. The prime purpose of a tomb, duration, is thoroughly expressed in the form and treatment of the architectural composition. But the feeling is far from the somberness of death. The battered walls flare out at the base in a graceful and springing curve instinct with life, and on a clear day the polished black walls form a dark mirror in which one sees ethereal reflections of green trees, blue sky, and moving clouds.

The Getty Tomb (Pls. 39, 40), near the Ryerson Tomb in Graceland Cemetery, was built as a monument to Carrie Eliza Getty in 1890. It is appropriately more graceful and feminine than the Ryerson Tomb, and enriched with delicately carved decoration. The construction is of blocks of gray Bedford limestone, with bronze gates and inner door. The rectangular block of the monument rests on a stylobate of four single stones, and the lower half of the wall is of smooth ashlar masonry. The upper half of the wall has an all-over incised pattern of octagonal panels enclosing eight-pointed stars, and above this is an enriched cornice with three scallops on the sides indicating the divisions between the large stone slabs constituting the roof. On the front and two sides are large arches springing from the ashlar base to cover the door and the side lunettes. The wedge-shaped voussoirs extend through the whole depth of these arches, but the faces are incised with four bands and lines of ornament alternating with plain surfaces. This treatment recalls Richardson's entrances to the Austin Law School at Harvard, but is flatter and more delicate. The outer gates and the entrance door have superb designs, one in pierced bronze and the other in low relief.

The Wainwright Tomb (Pl. 41) in Bellefontaine Cemetery, St. Louis, is the monument of Charlotte Dickson Wainwright, and was completed in 1892. A memorial to a very beautiful woman, it is the most sensitive and the most graceful of Sullivan's tombs, distinguished alike in its architectural form and its decorative enrichment. In the writer's opinion, at least, it is unmatched in quality by any other known tomb. The construction is of gray limestone, finely jointed. The four sides are decorated by bands of rich and delicate carving, beautifully precise and clear, following the top and side borders and carried across the wall at the level of the projecting parapet. The ornamental motives are varied on each of the four sides. Above the main rectangular block rises a stepped circular base for the low dome. The interior of this dome is faced by a very dark blue mosaic with a gold star at the crown. On the floor are two tomb slabs, with inscriptions to Charlotte A. Dickson, who died April 15, 1891, and her husband Ellis Wainwright, who died November 6, 1924. There is an unmistakable Oriental quality in this tomb, but it resides more in the contrast of rich bands of ornament with plane surfaces than in the adoption of any specific forms or decorative motives. Altogether it is one of Sullivan's masterpieces.

Adler & Sullivan did only a few residences during these years. Some were imperative due to social obligations or the desires of clients of larger buildings, but in general the firm busied itself only with larger commissions. The Heath residence of 1889 has already been mentioned, and in the same year the firm made a large addition to the residence of Mr. Wirt Dexter, owner of the Dexter Building on Wabash Avenue. The cottages for the Charnleys and Sullivan at Ocean Springs, mentioned above, were built in 1890. In the same year Mr. Victor Falkenau commissioned a block of three houses, still standing on Wabash Avenue. An office rendering of this building (Fig. 9) bears the legend "F.L.W. del.," and Wright tells us in his *Autobiography* [2] that he made drawings for some of the houses at his own home evenings and Sundays. It seems likely, however, that his work was confined to detailing Sullivan's sketches for all of the houses except the Charnley residence, which is the finest of the group and shows evidence of Wright's own personal conception. The Falkenau houses are far removed from the style of Sullivan's residences of the late eighties, but the changes are of the same kind that we have observed in the Auditorium and the Walker Warehouse, and are easily explicable as due to Richardson's influence. The use of heavy transoms in the lower windows, the round-arched windows, the grouping of small rectangular windows in the top story, and the almost entire omission

Figure 9. Three residences built for Victor Falkenau, Chicago. 1890.

of the cornice, are all Richardsonian in derivation; but the smooth ashlar masonry and the clear separation and articulation of the parts display Sullivan's characteristic development out of Richardson as already seen in the Walker Warehouse. The use of projecting oriel windows and the cessation of the upper string-course and applied cornice inside the corners seem to be inappropriate, and it must be admitted that the design as a whole lacks distinction.

The James Charnley residence (Pl. 42), at the corner of Astor and Schiller Streets, Chicago, was built in 1892. Frank Lloyd Wright is probably responsible for the general form, and certainly for detailing the working drawings, although the latter were traced and printed in the office of Adler & Sullivan. It is broader in conception than any of Sullivan's other residences, with more feeling for the organization of plane surfaces, skilfully punctuated by the window voids. The severely cubic volumes suggest the beginnings of Wright's later horizontalism. Certain features, such as the balcony and the cornice, are indeed Sullivanesque, but although Wright had completely mastered Sullivan's ornament, he tended when left free to organize it in a tighter geometric fashion, eliminating much of the free-flowing efflorescence of Sullivan's leaf ornament and reducing it to a flatter plane; the difference between the detail of this balcony and Sullivan's own work is striking. The base of the building is of limestone ashlar, extending upward to form a horizontal panel around the door and two flanking windows. This is a composition of great simplicity and distinction. The walls are of long, narrow ("Roman") brick, yellow in color, the balcony is stained wood, and the cornices are a light green copper. Students familiar with Wright's developed "prairie style" of the early 1900's find it hard to believe that this is one of his designs, since it has so many qualities of formal symmetry, monumentality, and sheer height that are completely lacking in his later work, together with

1. Rothschild Store, Chicago. 1880–81. (*Fuermann*)

2. Revell Building, Chicago. 1881–83.

(*Barnum & Barnum*)

GRAY, KINGMAN & COLLINS. WHOLESALE GROCERS.

3. Ryerson Building, Chicago. 1884.          (*Fuermann*)

4. Troescher Building, Chicago. 1884.
(Barnum & Barnum)

5. Dexter Building, Chicago. 1887.
(Fuermann)

7. Selz Schwab & Company Factory, Chicago. 1886–87. (*Barron*)

6. Knisely Building, Chicago. 1884. (*Barron*)

8. Borden Residence, Chicago. 1880.

(*Barron*)

9. Bloomenfeld Residence, Chicago. 1883.
(*Barron*)

10. Three Residences, Chicago. 1883. (*Barron*) 11. West Chicago Club, Chicago. 1886. (*Barron*)

**12.** Auditorium, Chicago. Preliminary design, 1886.   (*Fuermann*)

**13.** Auditorium, Chicago. Preliminary design, 1886.   (*Fuermann*)

14. Auditorium, Chicago. Exterior from East.     (*Fuermann*)

15. Auditorium, Chicago. Exterior from Southwest. (*Barnum & Barnum*)

16. Auditorium Hotel, Chicago. Lobby. (*Fuermann*)

17. Auditorium Hotel, Chicago. Restaurant and bar. (*Fuermann*)

18. Auditorium Hotel, Chicago. Main dining-room.
(*Chicago Architectural Photograph Co.*)

19. Auditorium Hotel, Chicago. Main dining-room, detail. (*Fuermann*)

20. Auditorium Theatre, Chicago. View toward stage.

(*Fuermann*)

21. Auditorium Theatre, Chicago. Orchestra and balcony.

(*Fuermann*)

22. Cottage, Ocean Springs, Mississippi. 1890.    (*Fuermann*)

23. Stables, Ocean Springs, Mississippi. 1890.    (*Fuermann*)

25. Heath Residence, Chicago. 1889.
(*Barron*)

(*Fuermann*)

24. Standard Club, Chicago. 1887–89.

26. Standard Club, Chicago. Addition, 1893.
(From the *Inland Architect & News Record*, vol. 22, no. 4, Nov. 1893.)

27. Walker Warehouse, Chicago. 1888–89.

(*Chicago Architectural Photograph Co.*)

28. Marshall Field Wholesale Building, Chicago, by H. H. Richardson. 1885–87. (*Chicago Architectural Photograph Co.*)

29. Dooly Block, Salt Lake City. 1890–91. (*Harry Shipler*)

30. Opera House Block, Pueblo, Colorado. 1890.

31. Victoria Hotel, Chicago Heights, Illinois. 1892–93.     (*Fuermann*)

32. McVicker's Theatre, Chicago. Proscenium wing and boxes. 1890–91.
(*Barnum & Barnum*)

33. St. Nicholas Hotel, St. Louis. 1892–93. (*St. Louis Historical Society*)

34. Anshe Ma'ariv Synagogue, Chicago. Preliminary design. (*Fuermann*)

35. Anshe Ma'ariv Synagogue, Chicago. Exterior. 1890–91. (*Barron*)

36. Anshe Ma'ariv Synagogue, Chicago. Interior.

(*Chicago Architectural Photograph Co.*)

37. Chicago Cold Storage Exchange Warehouse. 1891.
(From the *Inland Architect & News Record*, vol. 16, no. 3, Oct. 1890.)

38. Ryerson Tomb, Graceland Cemetery, Chicago. 1889. (*Fuermann*)

39. Getty Tomb, Graceland Cemetery, Chicago, 1890. (*Fuermann*)

40. Getty Tomb, Chicago. Door. (*Fuermann*)

41. Wainwright Tomb, Bellefontaine Cemetery, St. Louis. 1892.

42. Charnley Residence, Chicago. 1892.

(*Fuermann*)

43. Albert Sullivan Residence, Chicago. 1892.     (*Fuermann*)

44. Transportation Building, World's Columbian Exposition, Chicago. 1893.

(*Fuermann*)

45. The "Golden Door" of the Transportation Building.

(*Fuermann*)

47. New York Life Insurance Building, Kansas City, by McKim, Mead & White. 1890.
(*Photographic & View Co. Kansas City*)

46. New York World Building, New York, by George B. Post. 1890.

48. Woman's Temple, Chicago, by Burnham & Root. 1891.
(*Chicago Architectural Photograph Co.*)

49. Wainwright Building, St. Louis. 1890–91. (*Keystone-Underwood*)

50. Schiller Building, Chicago. 1891–92. Borden Block (1879–80) in foreground.                    (*Chicago Architectural Photograph Co.*)

51. Design for Fraternity Temple, Chicago. 1891.

52. Design for Trust & Savings Bank Building, St. Louis. 1893.

(*Fuermann*)

53. Meyer Building, Chicago. 1893.

54.  Stock Exchange Building, Chicago. 1893–94.    (*Barnum & Barnum*)

55. Guaranty Building, Buffalo. 1894–95. *(Fuermann)*

56. Guaranty Building, Buffalo. Lower stories and corner.

(*Fuermann*)

57. Guaranty Building, Buffalo. Elevator lobby.

(*Fuermann*)

58. Bayard Building, New York. 1897–98.

(*Wurts Bros.*)

59. Gage Building, Chicago (at right). 1898–99.

(*Chicago Architectural Photograph Co.*)

60. Carson Pirie Scott Store, Chicago. 1899–1904.
*(Chicago Architectural Photograph Co.)*

61. Carson Pirie Scott Store, Chicago. Detail of façade.

62. Carson Pirie Scott Store, Chicago. Entrance on Madison Street.

63. Crane Company Building, Chicago. 1903–04.

64. Felsenthal Store, Chicago. 1905. *(Barron)*

65. Babson Residence, Riverside, Illinois. 1907.  (*Fuermann*)

66. Babson Residence, Riverside, Illinois. Garden façade. (*Fuermann*)

67. Bradley Residence, Madison, Wisconsin. 1909.

68. Bradley Residence, Madison, Wisconsin. Balcony.　　　　(*Barron*)

69. Bradley Residence, Madison, Wisconsin. Entrance hall.

(*Chicago Architectural Photograph Co.*)

70. National Farmers' Bank, Owatonna, Minn. 1907–08.

71. National Farmers' Bank, Owatonna, Minn. Detail of cornice.
*(Fuermann)*

72. National Farmers' Bank, Owatonna, Minn. Interior.

(*Fuermann*)

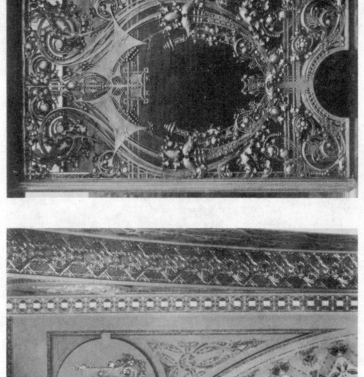

73. National Farmers' Bank, Owatonna, Minn.
Detail of arches. (*Fuermann*)

74. National Farmers' Bank, Owatonna,
Minn. Teller's wicket. (*Fuermann*)

75. People's Savings Bank, Cedar Rapids, Iowa. 1911.

*(Wm. Baldridge, Cedar Rapids)*

76. St. Paul's Church, Cedar Rapids, Iowa. 1913–14.

*(Wm. Baldridge, Cedar Rapids)*

77. Van Allen Store, Clinton, Iowa. 1913–15.    (*Beil Studio, Clinton*)

78. Adams Building, Algona, Iowa. 1913.                (*Barron*)

79. Merchants' National Bank, Grinnell, Iowa. 1914.

(*Fuermann*)

80. Merchants' National Bank, Grinnell, Iowa. Interior.    (*Fuermann*)

81. Home Building Association Bank, Newark, Ohio. (*Fuermann*) 1914.

82. Home Building Association Bank, Newark, Ohio. (*Fuermann*) Interior.

83. People's Savings & Loan Association Bank, Sidney, Ohio. 1917–18.

*(Fuermann)*

84. People's Savings & Loan Association Bank, Sidney, Ohio. Interior.　　(*Fuermann*)

85. People's Savings & Loan Association Bank, Sidney, Ohio. Lounge.    (*Fuermann*)

86.  Farmers' and Merchants' Union Bank, Columbus, Wisconsin. 1919.

(*Fuermann*)

87.  Farmers' and Merchants' Union Bank, Columbus, Wisconsin. Interior.

(*Fuermann*)

certain undeniable Sullivanesque features. But a comparison of the entrance bay with that of the Winslow residence in River Forest (1893), or better, of the whole building with the unpublished and little known Francis Apartments, at 43rd Street and Forestville Avenue, Chicago (1896), leaves little doubt that the Charnley residence may be considered as essentially a very early work of Frank Lloyd Wright.

The Albert Sullivan residence, Chicago (Pl. 43), was also built in 1892. This was commissioned by Louis' older brother, Albert W. Sullivan, who was for several years connected with the Illinois Central Railroad offices in Chicago. Louis himself lived in it from 1892 to 1896, after which his older brother occupied it until 1905, when it passed into other hands. Wright also mentions having worked on this house,[3] but his original designing must have been confined to certain details, as the general conception seems to be Sullivan's. It is perhaps the best small urban residence designed by the firm.

Many millions of persons who never even heard of Sullivan saw and remembered the Transportation Building of the World's Columbian Exposition in 1893. (Pls. 44, 45) And every student and critic of American architecture today knows of this building, if of few others by Sullivan. It has through this familiarity achieved a somewhat spurious reputation as his masterpiece and as a turning-point in his career. It came only a few years before the break-up of the partnership of Adler & Sullivan, and lent itself conveniently to the romantic notion that "Sullivan's sun set in the golden glow of the door of the Transportation Building." It was in truth an achievement, and in a sense it marked the end of an era; but it was by no means Sullivan's greatest work, nor did it indicate the passing of his greatness as an architect. In the same year that this was built at least one more significant monument was under erection and two other great skyscrapers followed it before Adler & Sullivan parted; and even after that occurred, the twenty-odd buildings designed by Sullivan independently constitute a record of superb achievement. Thus the Transportation Building is not of such great import as the widespread familiarity with it and the popular notions of its place in Sullivan's career would suggest.

The story of the World's Fair has been told too often to need repetition here.[4] Suffice it to say that Adler & Sullivan were among the six firms of Chicago architects represented by buildings at the Fair, and were given the largest single commission of any of these with the exception of the Fine Arts Palace, which Charles B. Atwood designed for D. H. Burnham & Company. The Transportation Building was located not far from the Administration Building, which was at the west end of the Court of Honor and in a direction southeast from it. The main façade looked east along the lagoon surrounding the informal "Wooded Island," and was on a line with the Horticultural Building, the next building adjacent to it at the north. It was one of the largest buildings: the front block covered five and a half acres, and four great train-sheds forming an annex at the back extending westward to Stony Island Avenue covered nine acres; a total of fourteen and a half acres.

The height of the main cornice line on all the major buildings of the Fair was arbitrarily fixed at sixty feet. Of course the building had to be as cheap as possible and capable of rapid construction and decoration. In view of these conditions, it demands a different kind of critical consideration from that applied to more familiar types. It was essentially a piece of show architecture. It needed to cover a certain area and to enclose a vast amount of space, and it needed to be impressive to look at. With definite limitations as to area, cornice height, and cost, it did not offer perfect freedom in plastic treatment. On the other hand, its purpose of housing displays was so simply satisfied by the form of a huge shed that the function was not sufficiently complex, anomalous as this sounds, to serve as a controlling force in the disposition and articulation of the architectural forms. Thus at neither end of the scale did the building problem "contain and suggest" its architectural solution, and it was a thing utterly foreign to Sullivan's creative method. This may explain both its good and its bad features.

It was, in fact, a great shed, attempting to atone for its lack of architectural variety through rather brilliantly painted walls. The cornice line was fixed; the rhythm of the openings was determined by the Roman arcades of all the other great buildings at the Fair: thus the essential form of the wall was set. Within this formula, the building differs from the other buildings of the Fair simply in an honest recognition of the temporary nature of its materials—it does not attempt to look like a white marble building—and in its effort to create new forms to fit within an established rhythm rather than to copy old ones. Even with the indifferent success of these efforts, the building must be recognized as the nearest approach to architecture in the Fair. The material of the wall was plaster. Instead of attempting to give it architectural authority by moulding it into the traditional forms of a masonry style of the past, Sullivan decided to leave it in the form in which it was most cheaply used, that is, the flat surface, and to enliven this necessarily dead surface by ornament moulded in low relief or by color, or both. Either technique was economical, effective, and appropriate to the material. The polychrome decoration of the long walls was brilliant in ultramarine blue, red, orange, yellow, and dark green, and satisfactory enough with the exception of the glaring white figures of exhibition angels in alternate spandrels, each bearing a scroll with the name of a famous inventor. The modification of the Roman forms is illuminating. The main arches are simply half circles; they lack

the Roman mouldings and keystones, and their soffits are aggres-
sively brilliant in color. The Roman screen colonnades and entablatures under the arches become simplified to such a point that
they are no longer Roman. The main cornice lacks the traditional
elements of the classical entablature and is simply a projecting
band. It is the same kind of reduction to abstract elements which we
have seen in the Walker Warehouse; except that here Sullivan was
bound to a somewhat more traditional disposition.

The sculpture adorning the building was done by John L. Boyle,
of Philadelphia, and consisted of four pairs of groups against the
base of the façade representing (*in toto*) the "Ship of State"; five
bas-reliefs around the base and in the tympanum of the main entrance, representing the Progress of Transportation; and three
figures on the cowcatcher of a locomotive, the location and significance of which the writer, to his regret, has not been able to discover.

Undoubtedly the most successful feature of the building was
the "Golden Door." Although an isolated fragment, entirely unrelated to the general scheme, it was a majestic conception. It
projected boldly to form a large flat panel within which five receding orders spanned the main entrance. A simple block cornice forcefully topped the whole. There is here the same combination of large
and simple architectural form and intricate detail which may be
seen in the Auditorium, and the adjustment of the one to the other
is perfect. The detail itself is admirable in its spirit and inventive-
ness, unmistakably a moulded and colored plaster technique with
no attempt at masonry forms, used in broad flat surfaces. There
was much gold leaf, and colors in warm shades of red, orange, and
yellow. The zigzag scrolls in the spandrels detract considerably
from the repose of the whole; they were required in the program
for inscriptions on the subject of transportation taken from resound-

ing sentences of Bacon and Macaulay. The decoration of the Golden Door was certainly the finest in the Fair, and it is interesting to note that of all the great architects who designed its buildings, Sullivan was the only one who received a foreign testimonial: he was awarded three medals by the *Union Centrale des Arts Décoratifs* in 1894.

Because of the unexampled richness of his decoration, Sullivan was immediately recognized as a great ornamentalist, but along with this went a superstition, alive in many minds today, that he was more of a decorator than an architect. This is patently untrue when one calls to mind the Auditorium, the Walker Warehouse, the McVicker's Theatre, the Wainwright Building, the three tombs, or the Golden Door; yet it may be well to attest the opinion of Montgomery Schuyler, who in an essay in 1895 criticized this attitude so justly and so forcefully that the passage bears repeating: "I have already protested against the narrowness of the appreciation which finds Mr. Sullivan only the first of our decorators, though that he so clearly is. This limitation ignores the structural instinct, or the reasoned engineering knowledge of mechanical relations, whichever you please, which presides over the placing, the magnitude, and the forms of his masses. I should be at a loss to name any other American architect whose perception of these things is more unerring. And surely it is this perception of the importance of the masses, this appreciation of the essential facts of structure, that makes the architect in contradistinction to the architectural decorator. No other buildings are more effectively blocked out on the one hand, none so admirably decorated on the other; and, as has been said already, the placing and adjustment, if not also the design of ornament itself, requires the faculty of the designer who is first of all a builder. Thus at each end of the scale Mr. Sullivan's work stands the strictest test. . . . He has a power of design that makes him one of the most striking and interesting individualities among living architects." [5]

The interior of the Transportation Building consisted of a central hall, rising into an arcaded clerestory, and separated from side aisles by rich colonnades. The central cupola rose to a height of 165 feet, and was reached by eight elevators, which themselves formed a part of the transportation exhibit. These elevators made access to the galleries over the side aisles easy. The exhibits included everything connected with transportation, as one account puts it, "ranging from a baby carriage to a mogul engine, from a cash conveyor to a carrier pigeon." The main hall was lined by scores of locomotives facing each other to form a long and novel vista; there was a balloon (but no airplane); and the four immense sheds at the back had whole trains drawn up for inspection. Especially interesting was the Pullman Palace Car exhibit, with examples just growing out of the gasolier and early-Pullman-plush period into the Louis XIV salon cars of a more sophisticated era.

The Transportation Building did represent the end of an era for Adler & Sullivan, insofar as the Panic of 1893 led to the almost complete cessation of building activity during the middle nineties. The firm had built over thirty structures between 1888 and 1893; from this time until 1895 it completed only two buildings, and after 1895 Sullivan finished only two others before 1900. This paucity of commissions was the chief factor leading to the dissolution of the partnership, as will be brought out later. But in the meantime we must turn to the eight great skyscraper designs done between 1890 and 1895, representing Sullivan's greatest contribution to American architecture.

[1] *Autobiography*, p. 297.
[2] Wright: *Autobiography*, p. 106.

[3] Wright: *Autobiography*, p. 106.

[4] The reader is referred to the chapter on the World's Columbian Exposition in T. E. Tallmadge's *The Story of Architecture in America* for a brief and readable account, and to Charles H. Moore's two-volume biography of Daniel H. Burnham for a more detailed history.

[5] Montgomery Schuyler: "A Critique of the Works of Adler & Sullivan," *Architectural Record*, Great American Architects Series, no. 2, December, 1895.

# V. GIVING FORM TO THE
## SKYSCRAPER

In the foreword to *The Autobiography of an Idea* Claude Bragdon says: "Louis Sullivan has the distinction of having been, perhaps, the first squarely to face the expressional problem of the steel-framed skyscraper and to deal with it honestly and logically." Avoiding for the time being the controversial element in this statement as to what constitutes honesty and logic in expressing a steel frame, it does set forth with fundamental truth Sullivan's greatest achievement in architectural practice. He gave definitive artistic form, for the first time, to the high building.

The high building was a comparatively new arrival in American architecture. It may be said to date from 1874, when Richard Morris Hunt erected the ten-story New York Tribune Building, one of the first of the "elevator buildings." Prior to that time six stories was the general height limit, due to a universal human disinclination to walk up more than five flights of stairs. The steam passenger elevator had been gradually developed from 1850 on, but was not used in an office building until 1871, and the hydraulic elevator was not patented until 1872.[1] During the decades of the seventies and eighties the height of the tallest commercial structures did not in general exceed twelve stories. The skyscraper in the technical sense of skeleton construction was an even more recent development, dating from 1884. The principle of supporting the exterior wall on a metal frame was first used by William LeBaron Jenney in the Home Insurance Building in Chicago, built in 1884–85. The second

skyscraper was the Tacoma Building in Chicago, designed by Holabird & Roche and built in 1887–88. The Tower Building, by Brad-
ford Gilbert, built in 1889, was the first skyscraper in New York.
Steel was first consistently used in skyscraper frames in 1889, in
the Leiter and Rand McNally Buildings in Chicago by Jenney and
Burnham & Root, respectively. In spite of these advances, the logic
of skyscraper construction was not immediately recognized. So far
as is known no other skyscrapers than the Home Insurance and
Tacoma Buildings had been erected by 1888, and in the year 1889
the number was probably less than half a dozen, most of which
were in Chicago. The Wainwright Building, Adler & Sullivan's
first skyscraper, was begun in 1890, and was thus one of the early
examples. In the year 1890, to be sure, the number increased by
leaps and bounds, the demand for structural steel in that year ex-
ceeding the ready supply. At that time the new building method
became generally known as the "Chicago construction." Solid
masonry-walled buildings continued to be built into the middle
nineties, and iron for frames was not entirely abandoned until 1904.

From this brief review it may be seen that in 1890 the high
building of "masonry" construction was about fifteen years old,
and that the skyscraper was still in an experimental stage, although
the fundamental structural principle had been applied. What was
the nature of the architectural treatment of the high building at
that time? The problem had not yet been solved successfully, even
by the country's greatest architects. To realize the tremendous
advance achieved by Sullivan in the Wainwright Building some
familiarity with the appearance of other high buildings of that
time is necessary. The Wainwright Building is a fine building even
in comparison with the best structures of today, but it becomes
far more impressive when placed beside its contemporaries. One
may fairly suggest comparison with works by the most highly

reputed firms designing high buildings in those years: McKim, Mead & White and George B. Post in New York, and Burnham & Root in Chicago. I have chosen three examples for illustration: the Pulitzer (New York World) Building in New York by George B. Post (Pl. 46); the New York Life Insurance Building in Kansas City by McKim, Mead & White (Pl. 47); and the Woman's Temple in Chicago by Burnham & Root. (Pl. 48) All three were built in 1890 and 1891, the years during which the Wainwright Building was under construction.

The primary characteristics of these large office buildings, in contrast to the other architectural types of the day, were their commercial purpose, their height, their volume, and the uniformity of their plan, story by story. These characteristics might logically be expected to have determined their architectural treatment. Actually, they did not. Utilitarianism was not yet accepted as a valid source of artistic inspiration; great height and great volume were considered artistic liabilities rather than assets; and uniformity was considered monotony. Critical writings in the architectural journals of the time are full of discussions as to what might be done to the new giants to make them architecturally respectable, and the general conclusion arrived at was a confession of failure: that the skyscraper was an artistically intractable problem which could best be solved by a series of compromises endeavoring to make it look like something else. The following devices were almost universally resorted to: the use of elaborate decoration to exalt the mere office building into a "mercantile palace"; the use of single stories or groups of stories as units of design, dividing the building horizontally so that through suggesting traditional modes of composition in lower buildings the effect of height might be diminished; the division of façades vertically by oriels, projecting or receding bays, pilaster strips, or other means, to disrupt the continuity of the bounding surfaces and thereby reduce the effect of great volume. In common with all other buildings of the time, skyscrapers were decorated by ornamental details derived from past styles, generally accenting the picturesque and romantic qualities conceived as attributes of the "mercantile palace." These ornamental details were greatly enlarged in scale to conform to the size of the building, and since they had been traditionally limited to a certain size, the effect was to diminish the apparent size of the whole building. Finally, no architectural distinction was made between tall buildings of skyscraper structure and of solid masonry structure; both types were treated with the time-honored masonry aesthetic. This summary of style applies to all high buildings from the time of their appearance down to 1890, and, of course, to many buildings erected after that date.

Specifically, the Pulitzer Building demonstrates these characteristics very clearly. It is obviously adorned in such a fashion as to belie its primary commercial purpose; it is divided vertically into three bays by a projecting pavilion in the middle of the façade; it is divided horizontally into groups of two stories under classic entablatures so that although its real height, exclusive of the dome, is thirteen stories, its architectural height is seven stories; and it employs Italian Renaissance decorative detail—columns and entablatures, Palladian motives, a pediment, and an elevated dome. It differs from the other two in being a masonry-walled structure, the great height (375 feet) necessitating a wall nine feet thick at the base. Although this distinguishes it practically, it does not distinguish it aesthetically from the others, since they are also conceived in terms of masonry construction.

The New York Life Insurance Building in Kansas City affords a more specific comparison with the Wainwright Building, since it has the same number of stories and almost the same plan. Moreover its architects, like Sullivan, had come under Richardson's influence and in this building used a Richardsonian composition of the wall. But instead of progressing from Richardson's example toward a more modern form, they retreated into an academic formalism lacking even Richardson's vigor. Dressed in Italian Renaissance detail and evading every essential problem, the building is merely a polite pretense of architecture.

The Woman's Temple in Chicago, demolished several years ago, was undoubtedly a more dignified monument than the other two, but the same mode of design is evident. The recessed court in the middle of the façade broke up the volume in the desired manner, and the reduction of apparent height was achieved by the 2–2–5–1 grouping of the stories in the façade and the inclusion of three stories in the roof. One would not think of this, on a cursory glance, as three stories higher than the Wainwright Building. The persistence of the feeling of a solid masonry wall is indicated in the massiveness of the two lower stories and the depth of the reveals in the tall embracing arches; the structure looked heavy, although it was in reality a steel-framed building. The ornamental detail was a mélange of Romanesque and Queen Anne, while the steep-pitched roof with its small dormers was Gothic, and it is interesting to know that a tall flèche which John Root contemplated for the middle of the roof was omitted only for financial reasons. The Woman's Temple was hailed on its completion as the finest of Burnham & Root's buildings, but in justice to the firm it may be recorded that both the Mills Building in San Francisco (1890) and the Monadnock Building in Chicago (1891) are now considered superior to it.

After this cursory survey of contemporary architectural style in high buildings, we may now more profitably examine the Wainwright Building. (Pl. 49) It was the first true skyscraper built by

Adler & Sullivan, and the surety, the justness, the completeness of this first attempt at solving a new architectural problem are astounding evidences of Sullivan's creative imagination and power of design. In the architectural world it was like an Athena sprung full-fledged from the brow of Zeus; the problem had been solved, a new need had called forth a new form.

The Wainwright Building was designed in 1890, and construction completed in 1891. It is still standing today. The exterior is faced by materials which give a rich harmony of reds and browns. The base of the building to a height of two feet above the sidewalk is of red Missouri granite; the lower two stories are of finely-jointed brown sandstone ashlar; the continuous piers from the third to the tenth floor are of red brick; the spandrel panels set back between the piers and the top story and cornice are of red terra cotta. The architectural design of the exterior displays the same combination of simplicity in the major lines with richness of detail which we have observed in the Auditorium and the McVicker's Theatre. The two lower stories form a simple and substantial base, penetrated by severely rectangular and unadorned openings. The only touches of ornament in this base are the narrow carved bands framing the main doors entering the building. Above the second story is an emphatic string-course clearly separating the base of the building from the shaft. This string-course is broken at the corners, however, to permit the uninterrupted sweep of the vertical masses of the corner piers from sidewalk to top story.

The treatment of the main group of stories is emphatically vertical. At the corners are broad piers, over seven feet wide; and on the sides narrow piers two and a half feet wide, each alternate pier enclosing a steel column. The narrow piers rest on a very small base and have a slight face ornament at the bottom and a terminal of terra cotta ornament some four feet high at the top. Thus the piers resemble pilasters, although the proportions and detail are entirely non-traditional. The "capitals" are similar in form to those employed by Frank Lloyd Wright on the tall piers of the interior light-court in the Larkin Building in Buffalo (1903). Apart from the slender brick piers, the only solids of the wall surface are the spandrel panels between the windows. Since these are carried on the steel spandrel beams they serve no other structural purpose than that of thin screens to keep out the elements, and are thus subordinated to the piers by being recessed behind them, and serve as appropriate fields for decoration. They have rich decorative patterns in low relief, varying in design and scale with each story.

The top story and cornice division is marked off from the shaft by a string-course carried all the way around the building, even across the corner piers. The most striking enrichment of the exterior occurs in the opulent foliate designs facing the entire tenth story. This forms a luxuriant frieze penetrated by small round windows. Above it a simple block cornice with a wide face and considerable projection terminates the façade in a decisive fashion. Such a cornice is manifestly useless, but it expresses vigorously the upper termination of the composition.

The construction of the building embodied the most advanced practice of the day. The foundations were of the isolated footing type, made of reinforced concrete, and carried to a depth of sixteen feet. The framework was entirely of steel, with riveted columns and girders, and spandrel beams carrying the exterior wall on shelves at every floor. All steel work was encased in fireproof tile, and all interior partitions were constructed of fireproof material. Interior partitions on the office floors were so constructed that any or all of them might be moved or eliminated, according to the needs of the clients. The ten stories total 135 feet in height, and the cost of the building was $561,255—slightly over thirty cents a cubic foot.

The plan and arrangement of the interior are of particular interest in attempting to interpret the exterior design as an expression of the interior functions. The basement floor, containing boiler, pump, and dynamo rooms, lavatories, and storage space, utilizes the entire plot. From the ground story up the plan is U-shaped, with an open light-court to the north, assuring outside light to every office; this light-court occupies almost 20 per cent of the total lot area. (See plan Fig. 10) The ground floor has nine stores of different sizes on the street fronts, and a large office in the northwest corner. The second floor is divided up into twenty-five offices and the necessary corridors. This is exactly the same as the typical plan of the office floors from the third to the ninth. (See plan Fig. 10) In the typical office floor the alternate wall piers (the ones containing no steel columns) serve no structural purpose other than the support of window frames, since in no case do they serve even as the terminus of interior office partitions. All told, there are two hundred offices, and the net rental area of the typical office floor amounts to 53 per cent of the total lot area, representing an efficiency in planning which is seldom exceeded today. The tenth story is used for large lavatories and a barber shop, lighted by skylights, but chiefly for the great steam mains employed in an overhead heating system and for other mechanical utilities. Its function is thus quite distinct from that of the floors below.

Returning to the exterior, how may we account for the radical innovation in architectural form which the Wainwright Building represents? Here we have a very illuminating explanation from Sullivan himself, in an article entitled "The Tall Office Building Artistically Considered." This was first published in March, 1896,[2] and Sullivan probably wrote it with the recently completed Guaranty Building in Buffalo more directly in mind than the Wainwright Building, but it presents so lucidly his method of approach to the general problem of the tall office building that it is of special interest in connection with his first attempt to solve it. The article formulates briefly and clearly his whole philosophy of art, but we may concern ourselves for the moment only with those parts of it which deal specifically with the tall office building.

In a brief introduction Sullivan proposes, with far more than ordinary perception, the baffling architectural problem which the tall building presents, and then says: "It is my belief that it is of the very essence of every problem that it contains and suggests its own solution. This I believe to be natural law. Let us examine, then, carefully the elements, let us search out this contained suggestion, this essence of the problem.

"The practical conditions are, broadly speaking, these:

"Wanted: first, a story below ground, containing boilers, engines of various sorts, etc.,—in short, the plant for power, heating, lighting, etc.; second, a ground floor, so called, devoted to stores, banks, or other establishments requiring large areas, ample spacing, ample light, and great freedom of access; third, a second story readily accessible by stairways, this space usually in large subdivisions, with corresponding liberality in structural spacing and expanse of glass and breadth of external openings; fourth, above this an indefinite number of stories of offices piled tier upon tier, one tier just like another tier, one office just like all the other offices, an office being similar to a cell in a honeycomb, merely a compartment, nothing more; fifth and last, at the top of this pile is placed a space or story that, as related to the life and usefulness of the structure, is purely physiological in its nature, namely the attic. In this the circulatory system completes itself and makes its grand turn, ascending and descending. The space is filled with tanks, pipes, valves, sheaves, and mechanical etcetera that supplement and complement the force-originating plant hidden below-ground in the

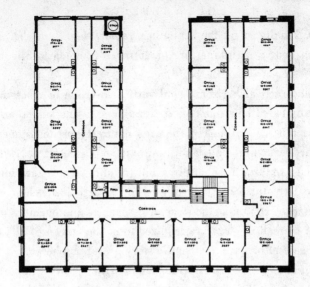

SIXTH FLOOR PLAN

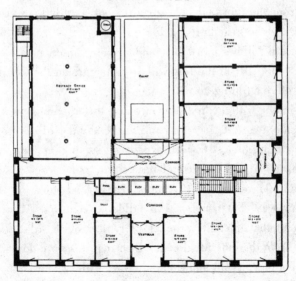

FIRST FLOOR PLAN

Figure 10. Wainwright Building, St. Louis. Plans of the first and sixth floors.

cellar. Finally, or at the beginning, rather, there must be on the ground floor a main aperture or entrance common to all the occupants or patrons of the building.

"The practical horizontal and vertical division or office unit is naturally based on a room of comfortable area and height, and the size of this standard office room as naturally predetermines the standard structural unit, and, approximately, the size of window openings. In turn, these purely arbitrary units of structure form in an equally natural way the true basis of the artistic development of the exterior. Of course the structural spacings and openings of the first or mercantile story are required to be the largest of all; those in the second or quasi-mercantile story are of a somewhat similar nature. The spacings and openings in the attic are of no importance whatsoever (the windows have no actual value), for light may be taken from the top, and no recognition of a cellular division is necessary in the structural spacing.

"Hence it follows inevitably, and in the simplest possible way, that . . . we will in the following manner design the exterior of our tall office building, to wit:

"Beginning with the first story, we give this a main entrance that attracts the eye to its location, and the remainder of the story we treat in a more or less liberal, expansive, sumptuous way—a way based exactly on the practical necessities, but expressed with a sentiment of largeness and freedom. The second story we treat in a similar way, but usually with milder pretension. Above this, throughout the indefinite number of typical office tiers, we take our cue from the individual cell, which requires a window with its separating pier, its sill and lintel, and we, without more ado, make them all look alike because they all are alike. This brings us to the attic, which, having no division into office cells, and no special requirement for lighting, gives us the power to show by means of its broad expanse of wall, and its dominating weight and character, that which is the fact, namely that the series of office tiers has come definitely to an end . . . the attic, specific and conclusive as it is in its very nature, its function shall equally be so in force, in significance, in continuity, in conclusiveness of outward expression.

"This may seem a bald result . . . but even so we certainly have advanced a most characteristic stage beyond the building of the speculator-engineer-builder. For the hand of the architect is now definitely felt in the decisive position at once taken, and the suggestion of a thoroughly sound, logical, coherent expression of the conditions is becoming apparent.

"However, thus far the results are only partial and tentative at best; . . . our building may have all this in a considerable degree and yet be far from that adequate solution of the problem I am attempting to define. We must now heed the imperative voice of emotion.

"It demands of us, What is the chief characteristic of the tall office building? And at once we answer, it is lofty. This loftiness is to the artist-nature its thrilling aspect. It is the very open organ-tone of its appeal. It must be in turn the dominant chord in his expression of it, the true excitant of his imagination. It must be tall. The force and power of altitude must be in it, the glory and pride of exaltation must be in it. It must be every inch a proud and soaring thing, rising in sheer exultation that from bottom to top it is a unit without a single dissenting line. . . ."

It is clear that a new spirit animated Sullivan's approach to the design of the tall office building. He saw it as a new problem in architectural design, a problem which contained and suggested its own solution, and therefore one which could not possibly be solved by established architectural rules, conventions, or habits. In facing this new problem, he attempted to eliminate all artificial precon-

ceptions and to think through to fundamentals. Having stated the
essential elements of a "true normal type," the first step in the
solution of the problem was to accept the practical conditions and
make these the basis of the design. But he went beyond the merely
practical. He conceived it as the task of the architect, through the
working of his creative imagination, to make beauty a part of
practicality, depending on it and growing out of it as the originating impulse. To accomplish this, the emotional force of the problem itself had first to be found—which in the case of the isolated
tall office building was its height in relation to surrounding buildings—and satisfactory *expression* be given to it. It is through expression that the diversity of practical facts is given unity and meaning; in fact, one sense of the word "expression" is "That which
expresses or symbolizes a thought, feeling, or quality." Sullivan insisted on architecture as an "art of expression"—he wrote a whole
essay by that title in the *Kindergarten Chats*—and indeed insofar
as it is art rather than engineering, it must be accepted as such. The
importance of the "emotional" element in Sullivan's mode of design
cannot be overstressed, as it completely dissociates him from the
mere mechanical and utilitarian functionalism with which he is so
often connected. "Functionalism" may mean merely the honest,
direct, and detailed recognition of the practical facts of a building;
in short, the revelation of function and structure. To Sullivan it
meant the expression of an emotional synthesis of practical conditions.

From the point of view of mechanical and utilitarian functionalism, the Wainwright Building offers many anomalies of design.
Does it, for instance, strictly reveal its structure? In detail it does
not. The structure of the lower two stories is similar to that of the
office floors above as far as the steel frame goes; why should there
be a thickening and strengthening of the wall of these lower stories,

as if it afforded a base for the support of the superstructure? The corner column in the steel frame does not carry as much weight as the adjacent lateral columns (in modern construction it is often lighter and sometimes eliminated entirely); why should the corners of the building be emphasized by broad masonry walls? The alternate piers of the façades enclose no steel columns and do not serve as the abutment of permanent interior partitions; why should they be the same in size and exterior treatment as the steel-bearing piers? The piers themselves are markedly vertical in emphasis, whereas the steel frame inside is a recticulated cage in which neither verticals nor horizontals particularly dominate. Is, then, the vertical emphasis in the design a revelation of structure? The projecting cornice does not serve either to shelter the sides of the building from rain, or to convey roof water beyond the line of the façade and discharge it by means of gutter scuppers; can it be said to have any structural purpose at all?

Or does the design reveal the functional articulation of the building? Again, no. For instance, the second story is an office floor identical in plan and arrangement and purpose to the superior stories; why should it be included, aesthetically, in the base? The top story is strictly utilitarian and mechanical in purpose; is there any reason why it should receive the most luxuriant and sumptuous adornment of the whole building if this purpose be revealed?

The answers to these questions are inherent in Sullivan's whole conception of architectural design as the symbolic expression of an emotion aroused by practical conditions. Such a theory rests on no purely mechanical basis. The judgment of the success of a work of architecture, according to Sullivan, should be made subjectively and synthetically rather than objectively and analytically. The interpretation of the specific features of a design need not depend on the intimacy of their correlation with specific constructive or functional facts, but on the intimacy of their correlation with the expressional quality of the whole. With this in mind, we can readily accept that as a whole the Wainwright Building expresses positively and successfully the feeling of its commercial purpose, its light steel frame, its height and its volume; every detail is a necessary and integral part of the unity of the whole, and the whole is eloquent of the physical and spiritual facts of its existence. In detail, the proper interpretation of the continuous vertical piers might be, not that they reveal the nature of the steel skeleton, which they do not, but that they contribute to the effect of height which Sullivan so eloquently sets forth as the primary quality of the building—a quality made possible by that particular type of construction. Or, in the case of the uniformity of the vertical piers, here the evident failure to reveal the steel structure (since only alternate piers contain steel) is of no necessary consequence; the primary aim is to express the volume of the whole, and this is most effectively achieved by a uniform rhythm along the façades. The matter is essentially one of creative expression, and this rests in turn on emotional validity and practical validity together.

The Wainwright Building was the first successful solution of the architectural problem of the high building. Sullivan himself wrote in the *Autobiography* with pardonable pride: "The steel-frame form of construction had come into use . . . it was first given authentic recognition and expression in the exterior of the Wainwright Building, a nine-story office structure by Louis Sullivan's own hand. He felt at once that the new form of engineering was revolutionary, demanding an equally revolutionary architectural mode. That masonry construction, insofar as tall buildings were concerned, was a thing of the past, to be forgotten, that the mind might be free to face and solve new problems in new functional forms. That the old ideas of superimposition must give way before the sense of vertical continuity." [3]

The influence of the Wainwright Building on contemporary architecture was immediate and extensive. Almost without exception, tall buildings for the next twenty-five years followed its scheme of accenting vertical lines, of recognizing volume through undifferentiated façades, of leaving the shaft of the building between a base and an enriched top sheer and uninterrupted. To be sure, architects crystallized the example of the Wainwright Building into a formula, considering the tall building as an analogue of the classic column, with base, shaft, and capital, and employing almost any form of historical ornament; so that Sullivan's creative method of approach was completely lost while the superficials of his results were being most widely copied.

Sullivan's own criticism of the old-fashioned method is of interest: "All of these critics and theorists agree, however, positively, unequivocally, in this: that the tall office building should not, must not, be made a field for the display of architectural knowledge in the encyclopaedic sense; that too much learning in this instance is fully as dangerous, as obnoxious, as too little learning; that miscellany is abhorrent to their sense; that the sixteen-story building must not consist of sixteen separate, distinct and unrelated buildings piled-one upon the other until the top of the pile is reached. To this latter folly I would not refer were it not the fact that nine out of every ten tall office buildings are designed in precisely this way in effect, not by the ignorant but by the educated. It would seem indeed as though the 'trained' architect, when facing this problem, were beset at every story, or at most, every third or fourth story, by the hysterical dread lest he be in 'bad form'; lest he be not bedecking his building with sufficiency of quotation from this, that or the other 'correct' building in some other land and some other time; lest he be not copious enough in the display of his wares; lest he betray, in short, a lack of resource. To loosen up the touch of this cramped and fidgety hand, to allow the nerves to calm, the brain to cool, to reflect equably, to reason naturally, seems beyond him; he lives, as it were, in a waking nightmare filled with the *disjecta membra* of architecture. The spectacle is not inspiriting." [4]

Sullivan's second skyscraper was the Schiller Building, in Chicago, a larger building than the Wainwright, containing a theatre, 342 offices, and club rooms. The impetus for the undertaking came from A. C. Hesing, owner of the *Illinois Staatszeitung*, who enlisted the aid of a large number of German-Americans in Chicago in the formation of a German opera company. The office portion of the building was added to the theatre as a means of giving the latter financial support. The commission for the design of the building was given to Adler & Sullivan early in 1891, and contracts for construction were awarded in June of that year. The theatre was opened on October 17, 1892, and the offices were completed and ready for occupancy on January 2, 1893.

The construction of the Schiller Building offers little of novelty except in the matter of the foundations. The construction of these was made especially difficult by the concentration of the heavy loads of a high building on a relatively small lot, and by the fact that the party walls of the adjacent building rested on foundations of insufficient strength to carry an additional load. Cantilevered foundations for the independent support of walls adjacent to existing walls had been used before, and Adler adopted this method. Isolated spread footings had given some dissatisfaction on Chicago soils, and Adler decided to try the experiment of reverting to old-fashioned pile foundations. Nearly eight hundred fifty-foot piles were used, and on them were placed two layers of heavy oak timbers, forming a criss-cross grille bolted into the piles. This formed a base for a mattress foundation of concrete reinforced by steel I-beams which was cantilevered out around the edges to support the enclosing wall of the building. The outer wall was thus erected in immediate contact with the older party walls of the adjacent buildings without exerting any weight on their foundations. This method proved to be entirely successful. The remainder of the construction was, by this time, standard practice. The columns, girders, and floor-beams were of riveted steel structural forms encased in fireproof tile; floors were of flat-arched hollow tile construction; partitions of hollow tile; stairways of steel with marble treads. Mechanical equipment included five passenger elevators and one freight elevator, all of the fastest hydraulic type.

The exterior of the Schiller Building (Pl. 50) differs considerably in effect from that of the Wainwright Building. Although designed in fundamentally the same manner, the difference in the size and shape of the plot, together with the necessity of signalizing the theatre entrance by appropriate architectural features, accounts for the novelty of the form as a whole. The exterior is faced by a light brown terra cotta, with a darker reddish brown terra cotta in the decorative trim. The ground story on the street is taken up by entrances to the building, shielded by a projecting canopy of ornamental iron. Above this is a very rich balcony across the whole front of the second story, slightly curved out and treated with a light arcade in terra cotta, embellished by busts of German poets, artists, and philosophers. This balcony is patently an ornamental feature, as the strong vertical façade piers may be seen back of the arches. Since it is largely concealed from the sidewalk by the canopy, and its curved open-work does not suggest a strong architectonic support for the façade piers, its value in the composition, whether seen from below or above, is somewhat dubious. Above the second story, however, the composition is "cast in one jet," clear, soaring, beautifully integrated. The chief motive in the design is the seventeen-story tower, which is positively expressed in the lower stories by the strong relief of the vertical piers carried upward throughout its whole height "without a single dissenting line." The window spandrels are subordinated to these verticals, as in the Wainwright Building, but are here left undecorated.

Of particular interest, considering the later development of zoning-laws, is the set-back system employed in the Schiller Building to obtain the necessary light. Built on a long, narrow plot, with the six-story Borden Block on one side and an old five-story structure on the other, the problem of admitting outside light to all the offices was a difficult one. The full width of the plot is utilized in front by a block nine stories high but only thirty-five feet in depth, and at the back by the stage building and offices over it. Between front and back is a narrow connecting wing, set in from the lot line about eighteen feet on each side, forming long lateral light-courts. (This treatment does not occur in the lower six stories, occupied by the theatre, which needed no outside light.) Thus the offices in the long wing were assured adequate side light, and the offices in the nine-story front block were lighted both by windows in the front façade and others on the light-courts. Above the ninth story, the façade is set back to the line of the connecting wing, assuring an ample amount of light for the upper part of the tower.

The nine-story wings of the façade are treated with continuous oriels running from the third to the eighth story, topped by decorated panels, and these in turn serve as parapets for little loggias fronting the ninth-story windows. The ninth story is capped by a rich terra cotta frieze and projecting cornice. The treatment of these wings is clearly detached from the tower in the middle of the façade, and at first glance they do not seem to be parts of the building.

In the tower itself the spandrels between the fifteenth- and sixteenth-story windows are ornamented by terra cotta panels with heads of the heroes of Germanic folklore. The vertical piers are connected by round arches at the top, instead of the simple rectilinear scheme of the Wainwright Building. The seventeenth story serves as a rich frieze, decorated by rectangular panels of ornament enclosing little arcades. The tower is concluded by a strong block cornice with a decorated face, and since it served as an observation platform, it is surmounted by an ornate little belvedere giving access to the roof. The building is the highest of Adler & Sullivan's skyscrapers.

The interior arrangement is quite complex, involving as it does the inclusion of a theatre with 1,300 seats, a large stage, two whole floors of club rooms with dining-room, kitchen, 342 offices, and the necessary lobbies, foyers, cloak-rooms, corridors, elevators, stairways, etc. The entire ground floor, except for two stores, is given to the entrance halls and theatre. (Fig. 11) The theatre occupies a solid block in the middle of the building, fifty-five feet wide and eighty feet long exclusive of the stage, and six stories in height. It is entirely surrounded by a thick fireproof wall, and there are no connections between it and the office portion. The parquet is reached by tunnel entrances on the ground-floor level leading to the dress circle, and by broad stairs leading to a foyer on the second floor which communicates with the rear seats—an arrangement similar to that of the Auditorium. Corridors running outside of the fire walls connect with the stage on the ground floor and with the proscenium boxes on the second floor. The balcony is also reached from foyers on two floors, the third floor being attained by stairways within the theatre, and the fourth by an entrance from the gallery stairs. The gallery is reached by a separate stairway to the fifth-floor level.

The theatre, being relatively narrow, has the advantage of requiring no intermediate structural supports, and there are no
columns to obstruct the view of the stage from either parquet,
balcony, or gallery. The proscenium opening is spanned by a series
of eight large arches, arranged in steps expanding upward and
outward from the curtain, extending some twenty feet over the
floor. These arches are semicircular, rather than elliptical as in the
Auditorium. Their surfaces are covered with rich and delicate ornament, similar to that employed in the McVicker's Theatre, in a color
scheme of green and gold. The three proscenium boxes on each
side are framed by large arches with sculptured lunettes by Richard
Bock, depicting incidents from Schiller's poems. Although a smaller
theatre than the McVicker's, the Schiller is nearly its equal in the
beauty of its architectural form and decoration. Its acoustic properties maintained the standard previously set by Adler & Sullivan.[5]

The seventh story is used for offices, except over the stage where
the height of the rigging loft demands an extra story, and the eighth
to the twelfth floors (Fig. 11) are devoted entirely to offices. The
thirteenth and fourteenth stories were designed for a German downtown club of large membership, and have several large club rooms,
an assembly hall with a small stage, a restaurant and kitchen, and
several storerooms. All of these eight upper stories are carried over
the theatre by heavy steel trusses, carrying a load of three hundred
tons each. The fifteenth, sixteenth and seventeenth stories are in the
tower, and contain eighteen offices.

The Schiller Theatre became the "Dearborn" in 1898, and in the
early 1900's it was secured by the Shuberts and renamed the "Garrick." For years it was the leading Shubert house in Chicago, but
was abandoned by the drama in 1928. Except for a few minor
changes in the shop-fronts and theatre entrances and exits, to con-

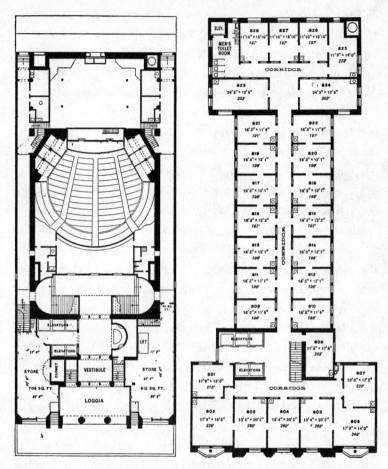

Figure 11. Schiller Building, Chicago. Plans of the first and ninth floors.

form with changing ordinances, it is still today as it was originally built.

The most striking skyscraper design of a whole generation came from Adler & Sullivan's office at the time when the Schiller Building was under erection. It was to be a "Fraternity Temple," built by the Independent Order of Odd Fellows on a site in the heart of downtown Chicago. The project called for a skyscraper of tremendous dimensions, far larger and higher than any contemplated up to that time. Just how far the project developed before its untimely death is difficult to ascertain; it may have been merely some ambitious realtor's dream, but on the other hand the facts and figures prepared by its sponsors for submission to the I.O.O.F. have a concreteness which suggests that the scheme may have been near to realization. The project was made public in September, 1891, in a brochure containing detailed descriptions of the proposed building, the financing scheme, and several plans and a rendering of the exterior by Adler & Sullivan. A site of nearly 43,000 square feet in area had been purchased, but its location, for reasons of "policy," was not stated. Montgomery Schuyler, in his review of the work of Adler & Sullivan published in 1895, stated that the project was "very seriously meant, and it came near being executed before the law intervened to limit the height of buildings." [6] This is the only hint as to the ultimate fate of the project which has come to light.

At any rate, the rendering of the exterior (Pl. 51) is an architectural document of no little importance. Its peculiar interest, of course, lies in its anticipation of the modern set-back style familiar since the passage of the New York City Zoning Law of 1916. No other large skyscraper building or design before 1908 shows so completely developed a system of set-backs. In the latter year Irving K. Pond published drawings in the *Brickbuilder* demonstrating the effect of high buildings on available light in city streets, and recommended means of control substantially the same as those later embodied in the New York zoning ordinances. Undoubtedly the system of set-backs in the design of the Fraternity Temple was devised primarily as a means of admitting outside light to the inner offices of an unprecedentedly large building block. But that the larger implications inherent in this system were recognized by Adler & Sullivan at the time seems entirely probable. For one thing, having just finished the design of the Schiller Building, they must have been acutely conscious of the difficulties in obtaining proper light for a building under the crowded conditions of building sites then available. Their own building, the Borden Block, considerably aggravated the problem of obtaining light for the Schiller Building, and they must have realized that the short-sighted demands of real estate operators in insisting on a maximum amount of floor space over a given area must inevitably lead to difficulties of this kind.

Sullivan wrote in the *Autobiography:* "The tall steel-frame structure may have its aspects of beneficence; but so long as man may say: 'I shall do as I please with my own,' it presents opposite aspects of social menace and danger . . . the tall office building loses its validity when the surroundings are uncongenial to its nature; and when such buildings are crowded together upon narrow streets or lanes they become mutually destructive. The social significance of the tall building is in finality its most important phase." [7] Certainly Montgomery Schuyler realized the implications of the Fraternity Temple design. Speaking of it, he said: "The scheme . . . is evidently that which promises the most abundant supply of air and light to its own tenants, and also that which threatens the least interference with the easements in these respects of neighboring owners. Given a detachment complete enough, indeed, and absolute protection against fire, there is no reason why a thirty-five story building should be any more an example of 'incivism' than one of ten stories. One can imagine a building of the dimensions of the 'Fraternity Temple' at the center of each square mile, or even less, of a crowded city. . . ." [8] (This latter fancy calls to mind the numerous recent schemes of LeCorbusier, Corbett, and others, for isolated tower cities.)

The design shows a building occupying an entire block, with various masses terminating in set-backs above the tenth and twenty-second stories, and a central tower thirty-six stories high capped by a pyramidal roof. The projecting balcony around the tower at the thirty-fourth floor is presumably an observation platform. The building was to have been four hundred and fifty feet high. The lower two stories form a base, penetrated by two large entrance arches, and above this the design is similar to that of the Wainwright Building, with vertical piers and an enriched frieze. The omission of the projecting cornice at the tenth story is worthy of note; if the one over the twenty-second story and the projecting balcony and pyramidal roof on the tower had also been omitted one could imagine it as a skyscraper of the late twenties.

The interior plans and construction of the building are described fully in the brochure above-mentioned, and only a few of the more interesting items need concern us here. The foundations contemplated were evidently to be caisson foundations reaching down to bed-rock; this is the first suggestion of the kind in Chicago architecture, and of interest in connection with the Stock Exchange Building erected two years later. The main lobby in the center of the building was to have eighteen elevators and four main stairways. The fraternity club rooms were to be located on the third, fourth, fifth, sixth, and tenth stories, and the remainder of the building was to contain 1,110 offices. The construction was to employ a riveted steel frame with extensive diagonal bracing against the wind-pressures on so tall a structure; fireproof tile insulation; steel stairs, mosaic floors, etc. If the Fraternity Temple had been built it would not only have been by far the largest and highest skyscraper in the world, but an inescapable demonstration of sound construction and good design; it might conceivably have stemmed the wave of classicism after the Fair and advanced the development of modern style in the high building by a generation.

The Union Trust Building in St. Louis (Fig. 12) was the third skyscraper built by Adler & Sullivan. As in the Wainwright Building, Charles K. Ramsey of St. Louis was an associate. It was designed in 1892, and construction completed on November 1, 1893. The plan is much the same as that of the Wainwright Building except that it is reversed, the open court facing south instead of north; this divides the main façade into separate blocks with a recessed court between them. The base of two stories differs considerably from the restrained simplicity of treatment of the Wainwright Building. To be sure the ground story is extremely plain, consisting of plate glass windows and rather slender piers, but the second story with its series of round windows is teeming with ornament. The heraldic lions in terra cotta are done with considerable gusto, but their value as architectural decoration is perhaps open to question. This base would seem to satisfy Sullivan's description in "The Tall Office Building" more closely than does that of the Wainwright Building: "Beginning with the first story, we give this a main entrance that attracts the eye to its location, and the remainder of the story we treat in a more or less liberal, expansive, sumptuous way. . . ." The base is topped by a cavetto cornice, richly ornamented.

The shaft of the building occupies ten stories, the projecting vertical piers being topped by arches as in the Schiller Building. The windows are grouped in pairs in each bay, separated by intermediate posts or mullions. The two top stories and cornice form an enriched capital for the building, defined from the shaft by string-courses terminating in most lively and entertaining animals described in the building prospectus as "bearcats." The rich cavetto cornice, although graceful in shape, does not seem so appropriate in its place as does the strong block cornice of the Wainwright Building. There is a fifteenth story under the roof, used for mechanical utilities, but this appears nowhere in the exterior design.

It is quite apparent that the Union Trust Building departs in many respects from the mode of design set forth by Sullivan in his article on "The Tall Office Building." It certainly cannot be termed a strictly "functionalist" skyscraper, nor on the other hand can it lay claim to the clean-cut perfection of form of the Wainwright Building. Yet in one respect it may satisfy the structuralist more than does the latter: each vertical pier contains a steel column. In 1903 three bays were added to the north side of the building; and in 1924 the base was completely remodelled.

One other skyscraper in St. Louis was projected during the years in which the Union Trust Building was built. This was to have been a Trust and Savings Bank building, just across the street from the Union Trust Building. The building was never erected, but there are two renderings of the projected exterior. The first of these was probably done in 1892, the second (Pl. 52) in 1893. The earlier design is for a twelve-story building, with four large arches forming the base, richly decorated with reliefs about the main entrance. The later design is for a sixteen-story building, the base being reduced in height and treated almost exactly in the manner of the Guaranty Building in Buffalo with columns under the piers and the display windows slanted back around the shafts to reveal the capitals. The treatment of the main groups of stories is almost identical in the two designs. The grouping of the windows in pairs under arches is perhaps the most satisfactory treatment of the wall

Figure 12. Union Trust Building, St. Louis. 1892–93.

which Adler & Sullivan achieved. The enriched attic and projecting cornice vary in detail in the two designs, but neither is especially effective.

These two designs, combined with the Wainwright, Schiller, and Union Trust Buildings, suggest that Adler & Sullivan had arrived at a more or less standard treatment of the skyscraper, since there is a fundamental similarity in all five designs. It was a treatment far better suited to the tall commercial building than any other that had been achieved up to that time: coherent, direct, suitable in its expression of the general structural and functional nature of the skyscraper, and entirely modern.

In view of this apparent crystallization, the Meyer Building in Chicago (Pl. 53) is of very great interest. It is the only skyscraper to Adler & Sullivan which has never heretofore been published, and this seems the more extraordinary since it is quite unique and seems to anticipate by a full generation one of the most general characteristics of recent architectural style. The Meyer Building was built in 1893 as a wholesale store building. It was a very inexpensive seven-story structure, practically devoid of ornament. The construction employed a steel frame and exterior wall of brick.

The striking feature of the architectural design is the continuity of the broad horizontal bands of wall between the rows of windows, with all verticals subordinate to them. The vertical piers, although on the same plane as the horizontal bands, are crossed by narrow bands of ornament at the levels of the window sills, and, except at the corners, by projecting mouldings at the level of the lintels. These details, slight as they are, suffice to emphasize the horizontals of the design. The building originally had a top cornice of slight projection and some ornament, similar to that of the Walker Warehouse, but this has since been removed and the wall concluded by an absolutely plain brick parapet. Except for the heaviness of its construction and the lack of long strip-windows of plate glass at the surface plane, the Meyer Building might easily be taken as an example of the "International Style" current in Europe and America today. This is not to suggest that it was a direct influence in the development of that style, as it seems always to have been an obscure building, and was entirely unknown in Europe where the International Style first developed. But it does demonstrate that the verticalism or the horizontalism of Sullivan's skyscrapers cannot reasonably be interpreted merely as an expression of the steel construction, since the construction is essentially the same in both types of design. As in the Wainwright Building, we are forced to conclude that the details of the design depend entirely on the form of the whole, and that this form, although a general expression of the function and structure, differs considerably in different buildings according to their expressional qualities.

The largest of Adler & Sullivan's skyscrapers was the Chicago Stock Exchange Building, built in 1893–94. (Pl. 54) The construction was the standard fireproofed steel-frame skyscraper type, and offers little of interest except in the foundations. The west wall adjoined the Chicago Herald Building, built a few years previously by Burnham & Root. Following the successful use of pile foundations in the Schiller Building, Adler determined to employ them again in the Stock Exchange Building. But it was deemed inadvisable to subject the foundations on the west to the heavy impact of a pile-driver since the Chicago Herald presses were running night and day and the delicate machinery might be damaged and incur a lawsuit for the clients. Adler discussed the problem with General William Sooy Smith, who had acted as consultant on foundations on previous occasions. The General had advised carrying foundations to rock bottom for the Fraternity Temple, and he again recommended this procedure for the Stock Exchange Building, although he would not himself undertake the responsibility of designing them. Adler decided to follow his advice. Bed-rock is about seventy-five feet below the surface in that locality, and in order to excavate to such a depth the shafts had to be water-proofed to prevent seepage of ground water into the excavations.[9] These were the first caisson foundations used for building in Chicago, and apparently the first anywhere. Reinforced concrete piers were built up in these shafts to form the foundations for the west wall of the building.

The exterior of the Stock Exchange Building is quite unlike that of the Wainwright Building and the others in its group, and at first glance seems a reversion to the earlier and more picturesque style of the buildings prior to the Wainwright. It may be argued that the design actually dates from early in 1891, or before, since mention of the projected building, naming Adler & Sullivan as the architects, appeared as early as July of that year.[10] Apart from the fact, however, that any designs of that date would almost certainly have been redrawn shortly before the beginning of construction in 1893, the executed building itself displays a stylistic character which distinguishes it from the earlier buildings. This resides chiefly in the conception of the wall as a plane rather than as the plastic surface of a mass or volume. The Walker Warehouse, the Wainwright Building, and other skyscrapers except the Meyer Building, have pronounced relief: the elements employed have projection and clarity. The Stock Exchange approaches the conception of the wall as a flat plane surface, a conception more clearly seen in the Carson Pirie Scott Store, designed several years later.

The application of the term "plane surface" to a wall which is corrugated by nine-story projecting oriels, three on one façade and six on another, needs some explanation, to be sure. But it may be submitted that these oriels bear no essential relation to the form of the whole. Whereas the oriels on the St. Nicholas Hotel, with which these may be compared, are essential to the whole composition, these oriels are certainly not decoratively conceived, nor do their verticals, which stop above and below in the air, suggest a structural articulation. They obviously have nothing to do with the steel frame and they do not give a dominantly vertical expression to the composition as a whole. Although they have a single window sill at each story, their diagonal projections prevent any continuous movement in a horizontal direction. They certainly do not dissolve the surface in that flickering granulation which is characteristic of the earlier "impressionistic" style. In short, prominent as they are at first glance, the oriels are not especially significant in the architectural scheme. Their presence is, perhaps, on the whole unfortunate; possibly they were demanded by the clients, but they may represent a choice of the architects.

Regarding the wall surface between these oriels, one sees a perfectly flat plane penetrated by simple rectangular window openings bounded by slight mouldings. There is no attempt at either structural symbolism or decorative adornment; there is not even an effect of dominant verticalism or horizontalism. The wall is simply a surface plane, the thinness of which is emphasized by the slight reveals of the windows.

The base of the exterior is three stories high—perhaps too high in proportion to the total height. The main story is the second, approached directly from the La Salle Street entrance by a wide stairway. This main entrance, with its ample arch and lace-like low-relief ornament in terra cotta, is one of the most beautiful single features in all Sullivan's work. The exchange room occupies two stories in the middle of the building, and although it nowhere penetrates to the street fronts, it is signalized in the exterior design by the two-story arches and rich terra cotta ornament. The building is thirteen stories high, and contains a total of 480 offices. The cost of the building was $1,131,555—Adler & Sullivan's largest commission after the Auditorium. The most convincing evidence of the functional efficiency of the building rests in its rental records: during the forty years of its history it has had one of the best records of all downtown buildings in Chicago, and has remained on the average 95 per cent rented during the recent depression.

The last work of the firm was the Guaranty Building in Buffalo, (Pl. 55) begun in 1894 and finished in 1895. The Guaranty Building, last of the skyscrapers, is closest in style to the first, the Wainwright Building. The programs of the two buildings were essentially similar, the same logic of design obtained, and with the exception of minor details, the buildings are twins. As remarked before, Sullivan's article on "The Tall Office Building Artistically Considered," published in *Lippincott's Magazine* in 1896, applies more directly to the Guaranty Building than to the Wainwright; the former, indeed, being more immediately in mind, doubtless served as the starting-point for the argument.

The chief differences between the two buildings are results of variations in the programs. The Guaranty Building is erected on a smaller lot but has more offices, and is accordingly higher. The exterior wall is entirely of terra cotta, instead of stone for the base and brick for the piers. The second story is not subdivided by office partitions, but is attained by wide staircases and has the large open floor areas demanded for mercantile use. Otherwise the conditions were practically the same. Both buildings occupy corner sites; both have open light-courts at the back; approximately the same floor heights; the same number of elevators; top stories devoted largely to mechanical utilities; and the two represent an equal degree of efficiency in planning, the net rental area per typical floor being 53 per cent of the lot area.

The exterior of the Guaranty Building combines a fundamental

simplicity of form with very great richness in detail. The color of
the walls is a warm terra cotta red which distinguishes the building
sharply from its neighbors and demonstrates that at a time when
most architects were content to work in the "chaste white" of the
Renaissance tradition (actually ranging from the glaring bathroom
white of glazed terra cotta to the grays of various building stones)
Sullivan was conceiving of modern architecture as a thing of rich
color. The two lower stories form a base clearly defined from the
shaft by a strong horizontal moulding, and treated with broad surfaces and ample openings in a simple rectilinear scheme. The
height of the building is emphasized by the unbroken continuity of
the vertical piers, and by their close spacing between every window,
two windows to each interior office. The top story forms a richly
ornamented frieze, penetrated by round windows, each of which is
the center of development of an intricate decorative pattern. This
treatment is effective in itself but with the piers terminating in an
arcade, instead of a flat line, the frieze is insufficiently bounded and
lacks the positiveness of the broad and definite belt around the
tenth story of the Wainwright Building. The cornice, too, is thinner,
and the immense masses of decorative foliage spreading upward
from the corner piers to overflow the face of the cornice are not
architectural in conception.

From close at hand the most striking feature is the rich play of
surface ornament. (Pl. 56) Sullivan expresses the fact that the
terra cotta sheathing which gives fire-protection and keeps out the
elements is not self-supporting masonry, but merely a casing. The
system of piers and spandrels is patently thin, and their flat surfaces are delicately enriched. It is axiomatic that ornament should
be confined to non-structural parts of an architectural composition,
such features as bases and supporting piers to be left undecorated.
Although Sullivan transgresses this rule, he does so in a manner

which does not vitiate the structural integrity of the design. The reticulation of the surface ornament varies considerably with the part ornamented, and although from near at hand the ornament takes its place as such and is unsurpassed of its kind, from a distance the effect is merely that of a rich texture on plane surfaces which are broad, simple, and essentially architectonic; the wall is not disturbed by the detail with which it is enriched, and the effect is one of stability and repose.

All of the exterior ornament, with the exception of the capitals of the columns, was detailed by Elmslie, while the interior ornament was detailed by Sullivan himself. The forward projection of the plate glass windows of the ground floor at a point about two-thirds the height of the columns seems to be an unsatisfactory compromise between the practical and the aesthetic, attempting to reveal the detail of the capitals and at the same time to enlarge the display-window space. The main entrances are sumptuously treated but the arched lunettes serving to accent them do not suit the rectilinear openings of the second story.

The interior lobbies and stairways (Pl. 57) are extremely rich. Floors are of mosaic, walls are panelled in marble with a mosaic frieze at the top, and the elevator grilles and stair-rails are of ornamental iron-work. The Guaranty Building is the richest, both without and within, of all Adler & Sullivan's skyscrapers, and affords the best study of Sullivan as a decorator. The building was renamed the "Prudential Building" in 1899, and stands today with no material alterations or remodellings.

The Guaranty Building was the last work of the partnership of Adler & Sullivan. In July, 1895, Adler retired from the profession of architecture to go into business. At that time Adler was fifty-one years old, Sullivan nearly thirty-nine. The firm had practiced more than fourteen years and had won a position of acknowledged leadership in the Middle West. But in spite of the large number of buildings designed by the firm between 1881 and 1895—over a hundred in all—architecture in the middle nineties was not a lucrative calling. The panic of 1893 and the ensuing depression lasting to the closing years of the decade had hit the building business severely. Architects simply went without commissions, or, if they undertook to design a building, often had to accept stock in the enterprise in place of cash payment, and the par paper frequently became valueless through receiverships. Adler & Sullivan were hit with the rest. The only building finished in the year 1894 was the Stock Exchange, and most of the work on that had been completed in 1893. Virtually the only work during 1894 and 1895 was the Guaranty Building, and this, of course, did not go far toward the rent of the large offices in the Auditorium Tower or the maintenance of the staff of over fifty draftsmen, engineers, and designers which had been so busy in the early nineties. As work ran out, the office force had to be cut, and finally the partners themselves felt the financial pressure. Adler, with three children, two of them boys only approaching wage-earning age, necessarily had greater expenses than Sullivan who was unmarried. Consequently, when Richard T. Crane offered him a ten-year contract as consulting architect and general sales manager of the Crane Elevator Company, at an annual salary greater than the amount he had ever made in any one year in the profession of architecture, Adler was almost forced to accept although with great regret at leaving his chosen calling. He published an open letter dated July 11, 1895, in the *Inland Architect*, announcing his retirement from the profession.[11] Sullivan was left alone to carry on the work in the offices of the Auditorium Tower.

Richard Crane and Dankmar Adler were good friends, but both were men of virile character, inflexible will, and a strong liking for independence. Adler soon found himself anxious to get back to his life's work, and possibly Crane felt he had drawn a Tartar. At any rate, after only six months the contract was terminated by mutual agreement, and Adler returned to the practice of architecture in January, 1896. Adler wished to re-form the firm of Adler & Sullivan, but Sullivan refused—unquestionably an error in business judgment, but he had felt Adler's abandonment of the firm at a crisis rather keenly. Adler decided to practice alone, working on small commissions and maintaining a small office on the Wabash Avenue side of the Auditorium Building. During the four remaining years of his life the two men saw but little of each other.

The work of the last years of Adler's life was divided between designing and writing, the latter chiefly on technical and legal questions connected with architecture. A brief account of these years is contained in the Appendix. He died of apoplexy, after an illness of ten days, on April 16, 1900. He was fifty-six years old. The funeral was held in the Anshe Ma'ariv Synagogue, and he was buried in Mount Ma'ariv Cemetery. One of the red granite columns from the entrance of the Central Music Hall stands over his grave.

[1] Francisco Mujica: *History of the Skyscraper*, p. 22.

[2] Sullivan: "The Tall Office Building Artistically Considered," *Lippincott's Magazine*, vol. 57, p. 403, March, 1896.

[3] *Autobiography*, p. 298.

[4] Sullivan: "The Tall Office Building Artistically Considered," *Lippincott's Magazine*, vol. 57, p. 403, March, 1896.

[5] A few years ago when the theatre was being used for cinema purposes it was equipped with sound mechanism for talking movies. The firm which installed the equipment found that the acoustic properties were so good that less than half the amplifying power normally employed in theatres of that size was necessary.

[6] Montgomery Schuyler: "A Critique of the Work of Adler & Sullivan,"

*Architectural Record*, Great American Architects Series, no. 2, December, 1895.

[7] *Autobiography*, p. 313.

[8] Montgomery Schuyler: *op. cit.*

[9] It is not clear whether the modern type of pneumatic caisson, with sufficient air-pressure in the working chamber to keep out water, and a decompression chamber above, was employed. There would seem to be no other possible method. Woltersdorf, in his biographical sketch of Adler, and Sullivan in "The Development of Construction" state merely that "caisson foundations" were employed.

[10] *Industrial Chicago*, vol. I, p. 231.

[11] *Inland Architect and News Record*, vol. 25, no. 6, p. 61, July, 1895.

# VI. SULLIVAN ALONE

THE story of Louis Sullivan's career from the dissolution of the partnership with Adler to the time of his death is in many ways a tragic chapter. In the fifteen years from 1880 to 1895 Sullivan had designed more than a hundred buildings; during the nearly thirty years that remained of his life he built only twenty buildings. In other words, his practice fell away on the average to a tenth of what it had been in number of buildings, and to far less than a tenth in size of commissions. These are facts which speak for themselves. Naturally Sullivan knew poverty and bitterness. He was forced in time to give up his offices in the Auditorium Tower, to sell his property, to give up his clubs, to dispose of his library, to borrow money with little hope of returning it. It is perhaps fortunate that we know little of the painful details of this last period of his life; Sullivan himself mentions nothing of them in the *Autobiography*.

But because of this very obscurity, legends have sprung up since the time of his death implying that his professional decline was due to some kind of personal disintegration. To be sure, Sullivan was at times during these many years unhappy, bitter, solitary, and seemingly listless. But this may well be explained as effect rather than cause of his professional "decline." That it was a "decline" remains to be proved: the record of his buildings and his writings is ample evidence that in creative force and power of thought he fell little, if at all, below the standard already set. To any who knew Sullivan, to any who realized the intensity of his faith, the ardor of his hope in a new architecture, the conviction is inescapable that such bitterness and cynicism as marked his later years was due to a sense of failure in his mission: the failure to bring about, try as he would, any considerable and widely apparent progress toward a new architecture. Therein was his failure, and he felt it keenly.

For the most part, however, he remained his old self. William L. Steele, one of the recruits of those days, described the office life of the post-Adler era: "We knew from afar his firm springy tread, and at the first brisk swing of the outer door we instantly subsided into graven images of unremitting toil. . . . Louis' methods with his draftsmen were severe. We did not love him, but we had a great respect for him, and a great admiration for his vigorous personality. His standards were unremittingly high. He allowed sloppy draftsmanship on no terms whatever. He did not care how much time was consumed in the drafting room as long as the work was done up to his exacting taste. Louis Sullivan composed all his own specifications while I was in his office, excepting one little one that he let me do. His method was to stride up and down dictating eloquently and copiously. His specifications were models of clarity and precision. His thought seemed aimed at nothing but the best interest of the job to be done. . . . He was a natural leader of men, but was either too independent, or too indifferent, to lend himself to any of the arts of the politician. He was profoundly interested in his theory of democracy, especially in its relation to art as the self-expression of free men. On the other hand, in his way of life, his mode of dress, his manner of speech, he was an aristocrat of whom any old Bourbon might have been proud. Wilful, passionate, ambitious, domineering; a hard taskmaster as well as a fine raconteur and bon vivant, he held his handsome head high." [1] Certainly this does not sound like a man who had lost either his professional or his personal standards.

A much more practical explanation of Sullivan's later difficulties is that he simply was not a good businessman. This again depends on the point of view. Undeniably he could be haughty and short with clients who displeased him, and he would never compromise his own ideals of what was fitting in order to make a sale. He lost commissions in this way. But if he was not an accommodating salesman of his wares, he was a good businessman in another way: he delivered the goods as promised. He never resorted to cheap or shoddy materials, nor on the other hand was he extravagant of his client's money. In the very difficult task of estimating costs in advance he rarely underestimated only to demand additional funds for the completion of the building later on.

A characteristic picture of his mode of procedure is contained in an anecdote told by the president of the People's Savings and Loan Association Bank at Sidney, Ohio, which was designed by Sullivan in 1917. Sullivan was called to Sidney, and the directors outlined for him in informal conference their requirements for a new building. The site was then an empty corner lot. Sullivan retired to the opposite corner, sat on a curbstone for the better part of two whole days, smoking innumerable cigarettes. At the end of this time he announced to the directors that the design was made—in his head, proceeded to draw a rapid sketch before them, and announced an estimate of the cost. One of the directors was somewhat disturbed by the unfamiliarity of the style, and suggested that he had rather fancied some classic columns and pilasters for the façade. Sullivan very brusquely rolled up his sketch and started to depart, saying that the directors could get a thousand architects to design a classic bank but only one to design them this kind of bank, and that as far as he was concerned, it was either the one thing or the other. After some conference, the directors accepted the sketch design and the bank was forthwith built with not a single essential change in the design and at a cost $1,000 below Sullivan's estimate, despite the fact that it was built during the war years.

The loss of Adler from the firm is most often cited as the cause of Sullivan's failure to obtain commissions after 1895. Undoubtedly there is much truth in this, but it must be remembered that during the ensuing five years, at least, the nation-wide depression made building very sluggish. During those five years Sullivan's commissions as an independent practitioner were, if not more numerous, larger and much more important than Adler's, for during these five years Sullivan did three major skyscrapers, Adler none.

Probably the chief cause of Sullivan's paucity of commissions in later years was neither a personal breakdown nor a lack of business acumen, but simply that he was ill-attuned to the spirit of the generation he lived in. That he realized this is clearly evident in many passages in the last chapters of the *Autobiography*. With acute historical perception, he selects Daniel H. Burnham both as an antithesis to his own personality and as a symbol of the generation they both lived in. His picture of Burnham is skilfully drawn in sentences here and there in the *Autobiography*. As Sullivan saw him, Burnham had a kind of dual personality, a combination of practical hard-headedness and romantic sentimentality; and Burnham was successful precisely because the temper of the American people at large was just such a combination of hard practicality and vague idealism. Sullivan speaks of Burnham's insatiable desire for bigness, evident even as a young man. "During this period there was well under way the formation of mergers, combinations and trusts in the industrial world. The only architect in Chicago to catch the significance of the movement was Daniel Burnham, for in its tendency toward bigness, organization, delegation, and intense commercialism, he sensed the reciprocal workings of his own mind." But Sullivan also found Burnham "a sentimentalist, a dreamer, a man of fixed determination and strong will—a man who readily opened his heart if one were sympathetic." Burnham's desire for bigness was a dream, "a fixed irrevocable purpose in life, for the sake of which he would bend or sacrifice all else." Yet he combined with that dream the capacity for compromising, in the practical sphere, with necessities. Burnham's notion of democracy was quite opposite to Sullivan's; he said to Sullivan: "It is not good policy to go much above the general level of intelligence."

It was Daniel H. Burnham who was the father of the World's Columbian Exposition in 1893, and it was the World's Columbian Exposition, more than any other single factor, which led to Sullivan's decline in popularity. Burnham was appointed Chief of Construction of the Fair in the fall of 1890, and John Root was made Consulting Architect. But even before Root's premature death in January, 1891, it became apparent that one man could not do such a vast amount of work in so short a time. Burnham was authorized to appoint a Board of Architects, and he selected five from the East and five from the West. At a meeting of this board in February, 1891, Richard Morris Hunt presided and Sullivan acted as Secretary. "Burnham arose to make his address of welcome. He was not facile on his feet, but it soon became noticeable that he was progressively and grossly apologizing to the Eastern men for the presence of their benighted brethren of the West. Dick Hunt interrupted: 'Hell, we haven't come out here on a missionary expedition. Let's get to work.' " It was this sense of cultural inferiority in Burnham which permitted the Eastern architects to control the architectural program of the Fair.

It is unnecessary to describe this program in detail. Suffice it to say that the Roman Classic style, executed in plaster and staff on temporary wood and steel frameworks, with the exteriors all of a pure and chaste white, was agreed upon for all the major buildings. The disposition of the buildings was determined along major axial lines, formally symmetrical, and affording vistas along lagoons, the whole tied together by a uniform cornice line at a height of sixty feet. The task was herculean, and Burnham was throughout the guiding spirit. Sullivan says: "Burnham performed in a masterful way, displaying remarkable executive capacity. He was openminded, just, magnanimous. He did his great share." But if the White City was a dream of beauty, it was a dangerous and spurious kind of beauty, spurious because it appropriated the forms of a culture not its own, dangerous because it seemed to do this so successfully. It represented the acme of all that Sullivan had fought against during his whole life. His criticisms of the Fair are vitriolic, but their justness renders them worth quoting at length.

"These crowds were astonished. They beheld what was for them an amazing revelation of the architectural art, of which previously they in comparison had known nothing. To them it was a veritable Apocalypse, a message inspired from on high. Upon it their imagination shaped new ideals. They went away, spreading again over the land, returning to their homes, each one of them carrying in his soul the shadow of the white cloud, each of them permeated by the most subtle and slow-acting of poisons; an imperceptible miasm within the white shadow of a higher culture. A vast multitude, exposed, unprepared, they had not had time nor occasion to become immune to forms of sophistication not their own, to a higher and more dexterously insidious plausibility. Thus they departed joyously, carriers of contagion, unaware that what they had beheld and believed to be the truth was to prove, in historic fact, an appalling calamity. For what they saw was not at all what they believed they saw, but an imposition of the spurious upon their eyesight, a naked exhibitionism of charlatanry in the higher feudal and domineering culture, enjoined with expert salesmanship of the materials of decay. . . . The virus of the World's Fair, after a period of incubation in the architectural profession and in the population at large, especially the influential, began to show unmistakable signs of the nature of the contagion. There came a violent outbreak of the Classic and the Renaissance in the East, which slowly spread westward, contaminating all that it touched, both at its source and outward. The selling campaign of the bogus antique was remarkably well managed through skilful publicity and propaganda, by those who were first to see its commercial possibilities. . . . Thus did the virus of a culture, snobbish and alien to the land, perform its work of disintegration; and thus ever works the pallid academic mind, denying the real, exalting the fictitious and the false, incapable of adjusting itself to the flow of living things, to the reality and the pathos of man's follies, to the valiant hope that ever causes him to aspire, and again to aspire; that never lifts a hand in aid because it cannot; that turns its back upon man because that is its tradition; a culture lost in ghostly *mésalliance* with abstractions, when what the world needs is courage, common sense and human sympathy, and a moral standard that is plain, valid and livable.

"The damage wrought by the World's Fair will last for half a century from its date, if not longer. It has penetrated deep into the constitution of the American mind, effecting there lesions significant of dementia.

"It was here that one man's unbalanced mind spread a gauzelike pall of fatality. That one man's unconscious stupor in bigness, and in the droll fantasy of hero-worship, made him do his best and his worst, according to his lights, which were dim except the one projector by the harsh light of which he saw all things illuminated

and grown bombastically big in chauvinistic outlines. Here was to
be the test of American culture, and here it failed. Dreamers may
dream; but of what avail the dream if it be but a dream of mis-
interpretation? If the dream, in such a case, rise not in vision far
above the general level of intelligence, and prophesy through the
medium of clear thinking, true interpretation—why dream at all?"

The effects of the Fair on American architecture were twofold:
it gave a great impetus to the use of the historic styles, especially
the Roman and its Renaissance derivatives; and it greatly enhanced
the prestige of the academically trained architect. Regarding the
first, it may be noted that although the major buildings of the Fair
were in the Roman Classic style, almost all other historic styles
were represented in the "state" and "foreign" buildings and the
bazaars along the Midway. Many of these, to be sure, were "more
scenery than solid," and to describe them as of any particular style
necessitates a rather elastic conception of the history of architecture; but in intention, at least, they were historical. For instance,
among the "state" buildings were the following: the Massachusetts Building, a replica of the John Hancock House in Boston; the
Pennsylvania Building, with the tower of Independence Hall,
Philadelphia; the Virginia Building, a replica of Mt. Vernon; the
Connecticut, Kentucky, Maryland, Ohio and Nebraska Buildings, all
in versions of the American Colonial, Georgian, or Neoclassic; the
California Building, a partial reproduction of the old San Diego
mission; the Maine Building, Romanesque; the Indiana Building,
French Gothic; the Iowa Building, Early French Renaissance; the
Arkansas Building, French Rococo (!); the New York Building, a
scholarly version of the Medici Villa in Rome by McKim, Mead
& White; and the Minnesota Building, another Italian Renaissance
villa. The foreign government buildings included the Elizabethan
style in England's "Victoria House"; the Islamic style in the East

India Building, by Cobb; the Spanish Gothic in the Spanish Building; Japanese and Swedish Buildings in appropriate national
styles; and the German Building, a large and elaborate medieval
*Rathaus* on the shore of Lake Michigan.

The justly famed "Midway" was originally conceived as a part
of the ethnographic exhibit, consequently its architectural setting
had a strong flavor of the aboriginal, with an Eskimo village, a
Dahomey village, a Lapland village, a Javanese village, a Samoan
village, Diamond Dick's Indian village, a Turkish village, an Al-
gerian village, and the Ruins of Yucatan; but mingled with these
were accomplished imitations of the buildings of the more civilized
societies, Old Vienna, the German village, two Irish villages (one
containing bits of Blarney Castle, the other Donegal Castle surrounded by "Druidical stones" and Celtic crosses), and perhaps
the greatest attraction of them all, A Street in Cairo, containing a
Mohammedan mosque and minaret, a large Temple of Luxor, and
genuine original Egyptian harem muscle-dancing, all complete.
Amidst the riot of mining-camps, ostrich farms, and scenic railways, were other choice bits of architecture: a Moorish Palace, a
Persian Palace, the Chinese Theatre, a Japanese bazaar, the Italian
Gothic structure of the Venice-Murano Glass Company, and a
Malayan Palace entitled "The Bungalow of the Sultan of Johore."

The Fair was, in reality, the triumph of the romantic eclecticism
that had been blossoming throughout the generation following the
Civil War. But it was also the beginning of the more exact and
scholarly eclecticism that characterized the architecture of the succeeding generation. Most of the chief architects of the Fair had
studied in architectural schools—the first ones to be founded in
this country or at the Ecole des Beaux-Arts in Paris—and they had
acquired a much more thorough book-learning concerning the
styles of the past than had been generally current in the preceding

twenty years. Thenceforth with the aid of photographic documents it was possible to design a building with a much more genuine aura of the past. Architects became scrupulously exact in detail; a Tudor Gothic structure, for instance, might be decked with all the suggestions of medieval antiquity—rough-faced masonry walls and small windows, picturesque dormers and chimney-pots, the roof-ridge sagging from centuries of the overburdening weight of heavy slate roof-tiles carefully stained at the eaves to simulate a growth of moss, the windows with crazy diamond-leaded panes, even the door-steps artificially hollowed out to reveal the wear of generation on generation of plodding feet. Ralph Adams Cram and Bertram Grosvenor Goodhue appeared on the scene to become the high priests of a revived medievalism. McKim, Mead & White upheld the banner of an impeccable classicism. Every architect worked in a style, and the less successful had to offer a choice of several. In Chicago, the firm of Daniel H. Burnham & Co. succumbed more and more to the wave of Classic and Renaissance emanating from the East, and for twenty years it decorated its huge commercial structures with a classic colonnade below and a Bramantesque arcade above, *con variazione*. The Fair had aimed a death blow at the new style which had been evident in the work of the Chicago School before 1893; Richardson and John Root were dead, Sullivan as far as the public was concerned was moribund, and Wright had yet to make his mark.

Small wonder that Sullivan wrote in the *Autobiography:* "Meanwhile the architectural generation immediately succeeding the Classic and Renaissance merchants, are seeking to secure a special immunity from the inroads of common sense, through a process of vaccination with the lymph of every known European style, period and accident, and to this all-round process, when it breaks out, is to be added the benediction of good taste. Thus we have now the abounding freedom of Eclecticism, the winning smile of taste, but no architecture. For Architecture, be it known, is dead. Indeed let us gather, in procession, in the night, in the rain, and make soulful, fluent, epicene orations to the living dead we neuters eulogize.

"Surely the profession has made marvellous improvements in trade methods, over the old-fashioned way. There is now a dazzling display of merchandise, all imported, excepting to be sure our own cherished Colonial, which maintains the Anglo-Saxon tradition in its purity. We have Tudor for colleges and residences; Roman for banks, and railway stations and libraries—or Greek if you like—some customers prefer the Ionic to the Doric. We have French, English and Italian Gothic, Classic and Renaissance for churches. In fact we are prepared to satisfy, in any manner of taste. Residences we offer in Italian or Louis Quinze. We make a small charge for alterations and adaptations. Our service we guarantee as exceptional and exclusive. Our importations are direct. We have our own agents abroad. . . . Our business is founded and maintained on an ideal of service, and a part of that service we believe to consist in an elevation of the public taste, a setting forth of the true standards in design, in pure form, a system of education by example, the gradual formation of a background of culture for the masses."

But while the World's Columbian Exposition led to a renewed fever of borrowing from Europe, Europe itself was more appreciative of Sullivan than of his imitative contemporaries. In 1893 when M. André Bouilhet, a Commissioner of the *Union Centrale des Arts Décoratifs* of Paris, visited the World's Fair, he was more impressed by the Transportation Building and the Chicago Auditorium than by any other buildings, and in his report to the society he devoted more attention to Sullivan than to any other American architect. Speaking of the Fair, he said: "It is a great city of palaces the architecture of which awakens no novel sensations in Europeans for we find here again more or less accomplished imitations of the monuments of Greece and Rome. With its domes, with its colonnades, its porticoes, its terraces, its gardens filled with statues, one might think he was looking at the realization of the dream of a young architect in quest of a magnificent *projet* which might open to him the portals of the Villa Medici. Only one of these palaces, which struck me the first time that I entered Jackson Park, is truly original; it is the work of a young American architect, formerly a student of our own *Ecole des Beaux Arts*, Mr. Sullivan. I refer to the Transportation Building. It is one of the most successful and original buildings, well conceived and of fine proportions; and it has the special merit of recalling no European building." [2]

M. Bouilhet requested of Sullivan some material for the *Musée des Arts Décoratifs* in Paris, and secured a number of his original drawings, many photographs of his buildings, and some casts of details of his ornament. Sullivan gave him a model of the Golden Door of the Transportation Building and casts of the doors of the Wainwright Tomb and Getty Tomb. [3] This material was assembled in a special Sullivan section of the museum, and after its exhibition created so much interest that the directors of an art gallery in Moscow asked to have duplicates made of the things on display. Subsequently so many other requests of a similar nature came in that the museum granted special permission to a firm in Paris to make replicas for various institutions throughout Europe. In 1894 the *Union Centrale des Arts Décoratifs* awarded Sullivan three medals, in gold, silver, and bronze, for the Transportation Building.

The eminent French writer, Paul Bourget, was more interested in the mammoth commercial structures of downtown Chicago than

in the accomplished imitations of the White City. That he appreciated the spirit that animated all of Sullivan's designs is evident in
the following passage from *Outre-Mer Impressions of America:*
"At one moment you have nothing around you but 'buildings.'
They scale the very heavens with their eighteen and twenty stories.
The architect who built them, or rather, made them by machinery,
gave up all thought of colonnades, mouldings, classical decorations. He ruthlessly accepted the speculator's inspired conditions
—to multiply as much as possible the value of the bit of earth at
the base by multiplying the superimposed 'offices.' One might
think that such a problem would interest no one but an engineer.
Nothing of the kind! *The simple power of necessity is to a certain
degree a principle of beauty;* and these structures so plainly mani-
fest this necessity that you feel a strange emotion in contemplating
them. It is the first draught of a new sort of art—an art of democracy made by the masses and for the masses, an art of science,
where the invariability of natural laws gives to the most unbridled
daring the calmness of geometrical figures." [4] It should be remarked that M. Bourget had seen the skyscrapers of New York
before those of Chicago, and had not been moved to any such
enthusiasms.

An anecdote from Mr. Max Dunning illustrates a characteristi-
cally French appreciation of Sullivan. Mr. Dunning was in conversation, in 1900, with a M. Pascal in one of the ateliers of the Ecole
in Paris. The talk turned on the Transportation Building, for which
M. Pascal expressed a great admiration, and then on Sullivan's
work in general, with which M. Pascal seemed to have kept in close
touch. One of his remarks was: "I consider that Louis Sullivan in
his work has exemplified better the real essence of *Beaux-Arts*
teaching than any other American." Another Frenchman, Jean
Schopfer, writing of the architecture of New York City in 1900,

spoke of Sullivan's Bayard Building as "The best skyscraper yet erected." [5] In the same year a Danish reviewer, writing on the "Art of Optimism," cited Louis Sullivan's work as just cause for his thesis. Some years later, when Anders Zorn visited Chicago, he said: "What is the matter with you Chicago people? There in the Auditorium Tower sits your country's greatest living architect, one of the world's leaders in his profession, doing nothing. This could not happen in Europe." (*Sic!*)

In this country, where Sullivan's achievements might naturally have received the most notice, only five published articles before 1900 display any real appreciation of his importance in American architecture; these were written by Montgomery Schuyler, Barr Ferree, Robert Craik McLean, Charles H. Caffin, and Russell Sturgis. But it should be unnecessary to argue further that Sullivan was a prophet without honor in his own country. The very paucity of his commissions indicates how little he was appreciated. It was this fact, primarily, rather than any limitation of Sullivan's, which led to the decline during the last part of his life. A decline, not in creative power—the buildings he did design amply attest this fact —but a decline in the capacity of his professional contemporaries, and of the country at large, to recognize his talents or to realize his significance.

The first buildings erected by Sullivan after Adler left the firm were three skyscrapers, begun in 1897, 1898, and 1899. In 1896 there had been projects for two large skyscrapers, one in St. Louis and one in Cincinnati, but after the designs were made the enterprises collapsed. The first structure actually built after the dissolution of the partnership was the Bayard Building (Pl. 58) in New York. This was designed with Lyndon P. Smith, a New York architect, as associate, and was erected in 1897–98. It was later known as the Condict Building, and it is still standing on the north side of

Bleecker Street, opposite Crosby Street, just off Broadway. It is a twelve-story office building, steel-framed, and sheathed in terra cotta. The architectural scheme is fundamentally the same as that of the great skyscrapers prior to 1895, but it is most nearly akin to the unexecuted designs for the St. Louis Trust and Savings Bank. (Pl. 52) The treatment of the ground story, with display windows slanting back around columns at about two-thirds of their height, is the same as in the second of these designs. The alternation of heavy steel-bearing piers with lighter terra cotta mullions in the shaft of the building, and the decorated terra cotta spandrel panels and large arches connecting the main piers in the attic are almost identical with the corresponding features in the first of the Trust and Savings Bank designs. The chief difference is in the embellishment of the top story and attic by a kind of tracery in the heads of the large arches and the introduction of large figures of angels with outspread wings, rising from the primary piers to the cornice. Although Montgomery Schuyler remarks in defense of the fenestration and enrichment at the top of the building that the two top stories are internally one story, the upper floor being a gallery surrounding an open room two stories in height which is lighted from above, this fact hardly seems to justify the exterior treatment. The general effect is rich and exuberant, but it does not accord with the remainder of the design.

In spite of this infelicity, the Bayard Building was a prophetic apparition in New York; its freedom from historical preconceptions, its directness and fundamental simplicity made it far superior to its contemporaries and suggested the proper solution of the vexing problem of skyscraper design. Consequently it was the first of Sullivan's skyscrapers to be hailed by the Eastern critics, and we find it attracting more attention, due merely to its proximity, than had such landmarks as the Wainwright Building and the Schiller Building six and seven years before. Russell Sturgis, whose buildings of the late sixties had also been prophetic, wrote in the *Architectural Record:* "There is here no pretense that the building is a massive structure of cut stone, and no pretense that it allows of treatment in the modern classical way with orders and with classical proportion. The whole front is a careful thinking-out of the problem, How to base a design upon the necessary construction in slender metal uprights and ties. Were it not for the most unfortunate treatment of each great opening between the uprights with an arch and a seeming system of tracery in the head, this front might be pointed to as completely realistic in design. Even as it is, if the reader will eliminate by a mental process these five great arches with their subordinate arches and the oculi which fill their heads, he will have the architectural treatment of the future metal building of our cities in the form which it must pass through if it is to reach any serious architectural success." [6]

Montgomery Schuyler employed the Bayard Building as the climax of his article "The Skyscraper Up to Date." "It is an attempt, and a very serious attempt, to found the architecture of the tall building upon the facts of the case. The actual structure is left, or rather, is helped, to tell its own story. This is the thing itself. Nobody who sees the building can help seeing that. Neither the analogy of the column, nor any other tradition or convention, is allowed to interfere with the task of clothing the steel frame in as expressive forms as may be. There is no attempt to simulate the breadth and massiveness proper to masonry in a frame of metal that is merely wrapped in masonry for its own protection." [7]

Concerning the reduction of the base of the building from two stories (as in the Wainwright and Guaranty Buildings) to one, Schuyler goes on to say: "Even the second story 'counts in' with the superstructure, to which it logically belongs. . . . It is not a question whether two or three stories would not be more effectively proportional to the superstructure than one. It is a question of fact. The result, whatever else one may think of it, is a sense of reality very different from what we get from the skyscrapers designed on conventional lines. It puts them to the same sort of shame to which the great roof trusses of the Manufacturers Building in Chicago (at the World's Fair) put the imitative architecture with which they were associated. Not that the gauntness and attenuation of the resulting architecture are in this case altogether agreeable to an eye accustomed to the factitious massiveness of the conventional treatment. But at the worst, this front recalls Rufus Choate's famous toast to the Chief Justice: 'We look upon him as the East Indian upon his wooden idol. We know that he is ugly, but we feel that he is great.' . . . Meanwhile the aesthetic, as distinguished from the scientific attractiveness of the Bayard Building, without doubt resides in the decoration which has been lavished upon it, and which is of a quality that no other designer could have commanded. . . . The Bayard Building is the nearest approach yet made, in New York at least, to solving the problem of the skyscraper. It furnishes a most promising starting point for designers who may insist upon attacking that problem instead of evading it, and resting in compromises and conventions." [8]

The Gage Building (Pl. 59) on Michigan Avenue, Chicago, was begun in 1898 and completed in 1899. In this commission Sullivan was an associate of the firm of Holabird & Roche. Stanley McCormick commissioned Holabird & Roche to design a building in three units to be used largely for the millinery business. The three units were of different heights, the southernmost being only six stories high, the middle one seven, and the northernmost eight; the south unit, moreover, was narrower than the other two. Sullivan was requested by Mr. McCormick to design only the façade of the north unit, occupied on completion by Gage Brothers & Company. Sullivan's façade was executed in ornamental iron at the base and brown terra cotta above, whereas the other two units had façades of red brick. The architectural scheme in all three units is similar, with slender vertical piers sheathing the steel columns and dividing the façades into bays. The thinness of the wall, since it actually served only as a screen, is apparent in the lightness of proportion of these piers and the reduction of the wall to narrow spandrels between the strips of continuous windows in each story and even more in the flat treatment of the base, a mere external casing of the skeleton. There is patently no attempt to simulate masonry construction.

The chief difference between the façades of the different units is in the window treatment. All three units employ very large windows, of nearly the same size, but in the two southern units Holabird & Roche filled the entire window with transparent plate glass. Sullivan dropped a four-foot curtain of translucent glass from the top of the window, reducing the transparent windows to continuous horizontal strips about four feet high. This has been criticized as an example of Sullivan's "impracticality." A member of the firm of Holabird & Roche wrote in his reminiscences many years later: "The building was for a millinery business, and when artificial light was as poor as it was in those days, it was important that there be as much daylight as possible. Now we would have run the windows up just as far as they could go, for the light at the top carries further. But against our judgment Sullivan insisted on putting four feet of ornamentation at the top of the windows . . . and the store was ruined for a good many years, until artificial light approximating daylight had been developed." This criticism sounds plausible, but it will not bear examination. The arrangement of windows in the two south units is undoubtedly the one calculated to give the most light to the back parts of the rooms, since light entering at the top of a window penetrates farthest into the interior. But at the same time it affords too strong a light for the parts of the rooms adjacent to the windows. Direct daylight, and especially direct sunlight which strikes these façades throughout the morning, is often too strong for exact ocular work such as reading or needle-work; that this is true in this instance is revealed by the fact that almost every window-shade is drawn down half-way to diminish the amount of light. This is true even of Sullivan's façade, which was alleged to cut off so much light as to "ruin the building." Sullivan's window treatment effects a compromise between admitting a proper amount of light and too brilliant a glare. Although he was in this instance criticized for denying functional needs for the sake of "decoration," it becomes apparent that in reality he made a much more discerning study of the functional needs than did his critics—and had his "decoration" to boot. For an all-glass window treatment, one has only to inspect the Carson Pirie Scott Store, begun the year that the Gage Building was finished; here the function was different, the light was needed—and supplied.

Architecturally, the resolution of the horizontals and verticals in Sullivan's façade is far more positive and successful than in the façades of the other two units. The ornamental detail is perhaps of more questionable merit. The broad band of ornamental iron framing the show-windows and the small terra cotta decorations in the spandrels are, to be sure, admirably inventive if possibly over-exuberant. We know that Sullivan regarded such touches as "grace-notes"—free, lyric enrichments without which the basic theme might have been too austere. And just as certain virtuosi over-embellish their piano playing, Sullivan was sometimes too little restrained in his decorative fancy. The huge foliations spreading from the tops of the two piers seem too large for the building and too conspicuous, although as transition features from piers to cornice they are admirable examples of Sullivan's conception of ornament as an organic exfoliation, seeming to "grow out" of the structural parts in both a literal and imaginative sense. They represent an attempt to increase the plasticity of a structurally rather flat composition. In 1902 four stories were added to the Gage Building by Holabird & Roche, Sullivan's design being carefully preserved, and the attic, with its ornament and cornice, lifted bodily to the top.

The most important building designed by Sullivan independently was the large department store built for the Schlesinger & Mayer Company in Chicago, and since 1904 occupied by Carson Pirie Scott & Company. (Pl. 60) This takes its place as of equal significance with the Wainwright Building, since it was the first department store designed by Sullivan, and as revolutionary and influential a solution in its field as was the Wainwright Building in the field of office structures, although the two are almost contradictory in appearance.

The old building of the firm of Schlesinger & Mayer, built shortly after the Chicago Fire, occupied the southeast corner of State and Madison Streets, known to Chicagoans as "the World's Busiest Corner," and although not very large, was signalized by a curved angle pavilion somewhat like that of the old Palmer House. The adjacent buildings to the south on State Street were of miscellaneous sizes and styles. As early as 1891 the firm of Schlesinger & Mayer evidently contemplated the enlargement of their store southward two hundred feet along State Street, changing the various façades into one uniform front eight stories high, and engaged Adler & Sullivan as the architects for this work. Apparently this project rested in abeyance for the next eight years, and in the meantime Adler & Sullivan had separated. The actual construction was taken up in 1899, and Sullivan rather than Adler was selected as the architect. The first unit, built in 1899, was a small section on Madison Street nine stories high, but only three bays (about sixty feet) wide. There was another lapse of three years before the major part of the structure, extending west on Madison Street to the corner, and south on State Street about 150 feet, was undertaken. The old buildings occupying this extensive site were demolished in 1902 and the new structure built in 1903 and 1904. It was three stories higher than the first unit, but otherwise the same in design. Before the building was fully completed, the firm of Schlesinger & Mayer sold out to Carson Pirie Scott & Company, and the latter firm occupied the new building in the summer of 1904. The monogram "S & M" may still be seen, however, in the ornamental iron work of the exterior and interior. In 1906 Carson Pirie Scott & Company added a third unit, consisting of five bays (105 feet) extending to the south on State Street. D. H. Burnham & Co. were the architects for this portion, but the design, except in the attic story, is the same as in the previously completed structure.

Taken as a whole, the Carson Pirie Scott Store represents one of the most intelligent solutions of the problem of the large department store that has ever been made, and for its time it was epoch-making. That it is still, after thirty years, not only adequate but highly satisfactory in spite of changing conditions, is a tribute to the genius and foresight exhibited in its planning.

The construction was of the skyscraper type, with steel frame resting on caisson foundations, and a terra cotta exterior. Since the fundamental interior arrangement was that of unbroken floor spaces for the display and sale of merchandise, it was important to have windows which would admit the maximum amount of daylight into these interior spaces. The problem was thus essentially different from that of the Gage Building, or any of the commercial office structures. The natural boundary of these windows would be the steel frame itself; the width determined by the distance between columns, the height by the distance from floor to floor. These large window-openings, of uniform size, established the basis of the exterior design. Since their major dimensions were horizontal, they naturally suggested a horizontal scheme in the whole design; the horizontal surfaces of terra cotta are thus slightly wider than the vertical piers and they are continuous throughout the whole length of the building, whereas the vertical piers are broken by two narrow bands of ornament at each floor level.

This dominant horizontality, so contrary to the dominant verticality of the Wainwright Building, although both are constructed on steel frames, should be conclusive proof that the horizontality of the one or the verticality of the other cannot consistently be interpreted as reflecting Sullivan's intention to reveal the steel frame. As pointed out before, the form in each case is an aesthetic choice, based to be sure on practical considerations, but far removed from literal structuralism. On the other hand, it may be remarked that as an aesthetic choice the horizontality of the Carson Pirie Scott Building was by no means a universal mode of design applied by Sullivan to any and all buildings, as is sufficiently obvious, and that therefore the great interest which this building has for modern European critics as a forerunner of the "International Style" is accidental. The American horizontalism which directly influenced Europe in the early decades of the twentieth century was that of Frank Lloyd Wright, Sullivan's most famous disciple. Sullivan's own direct influence on modern European architecture has been much more a matter of theory and philosophy than of specific stylisms.

Sullivan's feeling for the need of some kind of accent at the top of a façade is evident here as in his other buildings. There is no real cornice, but the twelfth-story window system is recessed, and a heavy shadow cast by the overhanging roof slab serves to delimit the façade at the top. This serves the expressional purpose of the earlier projecting cornices far more logically in terms of actual construction. Sullivan also employs narrow bands of terra cotta relief to ornament the small round columns and the tops of the corner piers. An irregularity not often noticed is the reduction in height of the top three stories, a treatment requested by the owners as an economy, but one also which gives interesting variety to the façade.

The three-quarter-circle curve of the main corner is an effective motive in the design, its curvilinear form and circular mullions contrasting nicely with the rectilinear severity of the two façades. It is defined by a strengthening of the bounding piers, and by its reëntrant angles (it is actually slightly more than three-quarters of a circle) especially evident at the cornice. This curvilinear motive was designed at the request of Schlesinger & Mayer as a reminiscence of the curved pavilion on the same corner of their old building. It is an appropriate and distinctive feature in its new form. It also serves a practical purpose: with the numerous doors around the curve it facilitates entrance and egress in several directions, thus distributing traffic at a busy corner.

To later eyes the most debatable feature of the design has been the two-story base sheathed in a rich casing of ornamental iron. (Pls. 61, 62) This sheathing is only a veneer about a half-inch thick, and quite apart from its decorative value it represents an amazing technical achievement. The detail, designed by Elmslie who had remained with Sullivan as chief designer, is extremely fine and intricate, and some of it is free-standing. Kristian Schneider, an artist-craftsman who worked with Sullivan more than twenty years, made the plaster models of the ornament from Elmslie's pencil drawings. He was very talented in this work, and modelled practically all of the ornament of Sullivan's buildings for execution in iron, terra cotta, or plaster from the time of the Auditorium to the late banks. Schneider's models were cast very precisely by the firm of Winslow Brothers by means of new and improved technical processes. The result was that unprecedented virtuosities became possible in this technique, and the mere technical achievement remains just cause for amazement.

As to the design, Mr. Elmslie has explained the conception of the ornament as a rich frame to a rich picture. The window-displays were intended to attract the chief attention but it was considered appropriate to frame these as beautifully as possible with a rich and delicate kind of ornament, rather feminine in character. The detail is worthy of careful study. Certainly in no other buildings than Sullivan's can one find such arresting originality, fertility of invention, sensitiveness, movement, and love of true creation pervading the whole. Undeniably in certain features, notably the weighty canopy over the Madison Street entrance, the virtuosity of rendition conceals any melody and loses all relation to the underlying structural form. Conventional modern taste would doubtless prefer to frame the display-windows in smooth and lustrous surfaces of white metals and marbles, but as the years go by architecture may well develop toward a richness now undreamed of. At present, however, the reaction against all kinds of ornament is so widespread that we judge quality in this aspect of architecture with difficulty.

During the years in which the Carson Pirie Scott Store was under construction Sullivan designed several industrial structures, and an office building for Crane Company in Chicago. (Pl. 63) The latter was built in 1903–04, and is a very simple brick structure, five stories high, a cubic block in shape, and absolutely devoid of ornament. The windows are connected by continuous sills and lintels, giving the intermediate horizontal bands of wall a slight emphasis over the vertical lines of the piers. Although the wall is quite plain, every fifth course of brick is laid with headers, a variation giving a certain interest to the surface texture. Most noteworthy is the complete omission of a cornice, the wall being terminated by a simple parapet and stone coping. This is architecture reduced to its simplest terms, the form being most suggestive of some of the best German industrial work of the next decade.

In 1905 Sullivan designed a small store building in Chicago for Mr. Eli B. Felsenthal. (Pl. 64) It is made of tapestry brick, so that there is a rather specious color and richness of texture in the wall surface. Such decoration as there is derives its character from the material, the bricks being laid to form rectangular panels at the top of the wall. Two inset terra cotta panels are used on one wall, and two relief panels on the other. Despite its humble purpose and obvious inexpensiveness, the building has considerable dignity and force, the large areas of unbroken wall-surface emphasizing the solidity of the mass. With this building Sullivan's skyscraper period is over. It is the first of the low suburban buildings which the creator of the skyscraper style was called on to do during the rest of his life.

Sullivan designed only two residences during this whole period. Both were fairly elaborate buildings in which cost was a secondary consideration, and they are of particular interest for the comparisons which they afford with Frank Lloyd Wright's residences of the same years. The first was a residence built for Mr. Henry Babson in Riverside, Illinois, in 1907. (Pls. 65, 66) The house is set well back from the road and surrounded by several acres of fine lawns and trees, with stable, garage, and service buildings located at some distance to the northwest of the house. Facing broadside to the road, shielded by trees, and built on very low foundations, the house presents an appearance of comfortable amplitude, dignified privacy, and admirable adaptation to its site. The use of projecting porches and porte-cochère adds to the sense of unity with the surroundings. The wall up to the level of the second-story window sills is of maroon tapestry brick, enlivened by a few inset terra cotta panels of intricate design and of a sea-green color touched with light blue. The second story is of dark-stained cypress wood, with horizontal battens and a broad projecting roof. The under side of this roof projection is plastered and tinted a dull rose, echoing the color of the brick wall below, but at a far lower intensity. The windows have leaded glass, especially designed by Elmslie, and suggestive of Wright's work. The chief decorative feature of the main front is a large balcony projecting from the second story, executed entirely in wood. At first sight a somewhat overwhelming *tour-de-force*, this balcony becomes with familiarity a remarkably interesting and appropriate feature. It appears less weighty in actuality than in photographs, and the small arcade with delicate incised carving is in itself a most graceful feature. Functionally it has its obvious uses and architecturally it gives character to a façade that might otherwise be tame and excessively longitudinal.

An interesting comparison has been made between this residence and Frank Lloyd Wright's Coonley residence, in Riverside, built the following year, in a well-illustrated article in the *Architectural Record*.[9] Both houses are completely non-historical in style and emphasize long-drawn-out horizontals in the general composition. Of the two, the Coonley house undoubtedly represents the more radical departure from tradition in plan and general arrangement, and the more brilliant and imaginative use of plane surfaces and cubic volumes in the architectural composition. An unusual effect is achieved by concentrating all the living quarters of the house in the second floor, leaving the ground floor for service rooms and corridors and treating it with an almost solid wall. Since the house is very low on the ground, and the stories are of the minimum height, the effect is almost that of a one-story house. The plan is more complex than that of the Babson residence, with numerous projecting wings reaching over driveways and embracing the gardens and pool, so that the house is intimately united with its surroundings. The plastered walls give an effect of mobility and lightness. The Babson residence is clearer in its disposition, the plan can be "read" more easily from the exterior, and the higher wall of brick gives an effect of greater solidity and durability. Sullivan's house is conceived more in terms of substantial mass; Wright's in terms of light, hollow volumes. Both are masterpieces of their own kind. Since Sullivan's historical achievement was particularly in the field of large buildings, and Wright's in the field of house design, it is worth pointing out that even here Sullivan has very characteristic virtues.

The interiors of the Babson residence are more traditional in effect, but are of interest for the woodwork and for Sullivanesque details such as the rugs and lighting-fixtures. A large part of the designing was actually done by Elmslie, and he was retained for later additions to the house and the construction of a quadrangle of service buildings just prior to the War. These are in the style of the main house, and form an appropriate addition to the estate.

The second of the two residences was built for Mrs. Josephine Crane Bradley at Madison, Wisconsin, in 1909. In plan it is T-shaped, with the main façade fronting south, and a long wing extending northward from the middle of the back. The south façade (Pl. 67) is a long, low mass, similar to the Babson residence, except that the horizontal lines are broken at intervals by strong vertical piers of brick, extending from foundation to cornice and projecting some eighteen inches from the wall surface. In the middle is a polygonal projecting bay, similar to that on the garden front of the Babson residence except that it is only one story in height. The two ends of this main block offer the most extraordinary features of the house: large overhanging porches on the second story, supported by steel cantilever beams, encased in wood, with projecting ends elaborately sawed. The gable at the west end overhangs an open porch enclosed by a brick parapet (Pl. 68); the gable at the east end, exactly the same in form, overhangs a side entrance on to the lawn. The parallelism with Wright's projecting gables of this period is evident, but there is a superior vigor and force in the weight and salience of these features as compared with Wright's. The wing extending toward the back is quite wide, and the roof consists of two gables, presenting twin gable-ends side by side over the rear façade. The main entrance is from a porte-cochère at the back of this wing, from which one enters a long hall. (Pl. 69) Built for a large family of children, the house has numerous bedrooms, two sleeping porches, and large playrooms, and since the Bradley family left it, has served admirably for a fraternity house. It seems just to attribute the design of this house to at least an equal coöperation between Sullivan and Elmslie.

Sullivan's most important commission after the Carson Pirie Scott Store was the National Farmers' Bank at Owatonna, Minnesota. This was the opening wedge for what was to become the most extensive field of practice of Sullivan's later years, and almost his only means of support. Eight of his last eleven buildings were built for small banks, scattered throughout the farming communities of the Middle West.

At the World's Columbian Exposition in 1893, according to many accounts, the building which most drew the great public—the uncultivated masses—was the Transportation Building. The man on the street admired, and was impressed by, the Roman grandeur of the great buildings surrounding the Court of Honor, but he really liked the Transportation Building. Just why this should be is difficult to explain. The nationalist would readily assume that it was due to the fundamental soundness of taste in the mass of the American people. Perhaps one should not even call it "taste," for to them "taste" already meant admiring the things that the "best people" admired. The general liking for the Transportation Building was something more than this; it was, perhaps, an instinctive response. For it had, although in a language unfamiliar to them, the simple qualities which they admired. It did not require them to accept "forms of sophistication not their own"; it was exotic but not "foreign"; in short, they liked it for the excellent reason that it was good Fair architecture. One likes to think that something of this common-sense approach, this native flair, stayed alive in the small farming towns of Ohio, Minnesota, Wisconsin, Indiana, and Iowa while the cosmopolitan centers lost their cultural independence. This may be a too sanguine estimate of rural American culture, but the fact remains that ten out of eleven of Sullivan's last buildings were built in small communities rather remote from metropolitan spheres of influence, whose populations never exceeded a few thousand.

These buildings stand out like jewels on the shoddy main streets of the prairie towns. Tallmadge says of Sullivan's banks: "Their color, brilliance and gaiety entirely put in the shade the thin, awkward and wan examples of the country builder, and to the same degree the pallid and pudgy Roman frontispieces of the city architect. . . . The ornament, by its intricacy and vitality, compels the interest of the commoner who would, as we, pass by a mile of eggs and darts without sensing their existence. . . . These banks are a book of wonders to a people who all of their lives have been contemptuous of or oblivious to architecture." [10]

The bank at Owatonna was the first, and is often considered the best, of the series. In 1907 the bank officers decided to carry out long-contemplated plans for a new building. The vice-president of the bank, Mr. Carl K. Bennett, described in an article their search for an architect: "The layout of the floor space was in mind for many years, but the architectural expression of the business of banking was probably a thing more felt than understood. Anyhow, the desire for such expression persisted, and a pretty thorough study was made of existing bank buildings. The classic style of architecture so much used for bank buildings was at first considered, but was finally rejected as being not necessarily expressive of a bank, and also because it is defective when it comes to any practical use. Because architects who were consulted preferred to follow precedent or to take their inspiration 'from the books,' it was determined to make a search for an architect who would not only take into consideration the practical needs of the business but who would heed the desire of the bank officers for an adequate expression in the form of the building of the use to which it would be put. This search was made largely through the means of the art and architectural magazines, including the 'Craftsman,' with the hope of finding some architect whose aim it was to express the thought or use underlying a building, adequately, without fear of precedent, like a virtuoso shaping his materials into new forms of use and beauty." [11] It so happened that one of Sullivan's articles, entitled "What is Architecture? A Study in the American People of Today" had been published in *The Craftsman* in the preceding year,[12] and this article attracted the attention of the officers of the bank as revealing the architect they sought. Through it Sullivan obtained the commission.

The National Farmers' Bank was begun in 1907, and completed in 1908. (Pl. 70) Since only part of the lot was necessary for the bank itself, the remaining land at the east was utilized for a two-story wing containing two stores, several offices, and a small warehouse. This wing is independent of the banking room, but treated in the same material and style.

As in all of Sullivan's later buildings, only a partial impression of the beauty of both exterior and interior can be obtained from photographs, since the effect of the original depends so largely on color. The exterior of the bank has a base of reddish brown sandstone ashlar, laid in courses of different heights, and penetrated by simple rectangular door and window openings. Above this the wall is faced by rough shale brick in soft and variegated colors, the general effect being a rich dark red. The walls are opened by two great arched windows thirty-six feet in span, with wide flat archivolts consisting of ten concentric header courses of brick. The glass is set in vertical steel mullions. The walls are treated as large rectangular panels framed by an outer band of enamelled terra cotta relief in bronze-green accented with brown, and an inner five-inch band of brilliant glass mosaic dominantly blue in color but with touches of green, white, and gold. The wall is capped by a heavy cornice of unique design (Pl. 71), consisting simply of corbelled courses of brick bounded above and below by bands of brown terra cotta. The total effect is very rich, with the colors blending softly from a distance, but strongly individual at close range.

The interior is a large square room, rich in decorative detail and glowing in color, although the total effect of light spaciousness absorbs the detail so that it is never obtrusive or over-brilliant. The room is amply lighted by the great arched windows on, two sides and a skylight overhead, and there is a curious quality to the light—a greenish tinge, like sunlight passed through sea-water. The windows are of double thickness: plate glass outside, and opalescent leaded glass inside, with an hermetically sealed air-space between for protection against extremes of cold and heat. The inner windows are marbled green and buff in color, with center patterns of buff and violet. On the opposite walls, under arches of the same size as the window arches, are two large mural paintings by Oskar Gross representing dairy and harvest scenes. The wide archivolts and outer soffits of all four arches are beautifully colored; on the archivolts a stencilled pattern in jade green, brick red, dull green and buff colors; on the soffits, terra cotta relief sheathed in gold leaf. (Pl. 73) The banking offices project into the room on three sides as one-story enclosures. The walls are of red Roman brick, topped by a cornice of enamelled green terra cotta. The counters and deal plates are of Belgian black marble, and the cashiers' grilles are of bronze. (Pl. 74) Noteworthy details are the green terra cotta enframement of the clock, the decorative panel over the entrance door, and the lighting fixtures, the shades of which are miniatures of the whole building. The furniture, including the check desks, was all especially designed.

The plan is admirably adapted to the purpose of a farmers' bank. (Fig. 15) In addition to the strictly banking rooms, there is a farmers' exchange room intended for the private business or social transactions of the bank's clients; a women's parlor; a private consultation room for conference with the bank's officers; and the president's office. All of these are furnished in quarter-sawed white oak, with walls and ceilings panelled in broad, smooth surfaces, built-in benches cushioned in dull red leather, and specially designed tables and writing desks, carpets, chairs, etc. In the president's office there is a small mural painting by John Norton, dated 1923. This is undoubtedly the best painting to be found anywhere in association with Sullivan's architecture. Most of the interior details were designed by Elmslie, and the idea of the single great arches of the façade was his, being substituted for three smaller arches in Sullivan's early sketches. Thus Elmslie, who was never formally a partner of Sullivan, was at this time a truer collaborator in design than Adler had ever been.

Sullivan's next commission was for the People's Savings Bank in Cedar Rapids, Iowa, built in 1911. (Pl. 75) Coming after the highly successful achievement at Owatonna, one would expect a repetition, with minor variations, of the general scheme of the Owatonna bank. But Sullivan now had time to work out each commission freshly. A different problem called for a different solution, and the two buildings are entirely unlike. As Montgomery Schuyler said: "Every one of his buildings is the solution of a particular problem, and the result is a highly specialized organism, which is as suitable for its own purpose as it is inapplicable to any other. It is as inimitable in the mass as in the detail." [13] The program of the Cedar Rapids bank called for a larger amount of space to be devoted to accessory rooms than in the Owatonna bank, and the basis of the plan became a public room surrounded by accessory offices, rather than a room with the offices projecting into it. The bank consists, essentially, of a central hall, the main banking room, two stories high and about twenty-five by fifty feet in dimension. This is surrounded by subordinate rooms one story high —vestibule, officers' quarters, clerks' cubicles, the vault, etc.

The exterior is simply the envelope of the interior, expressing

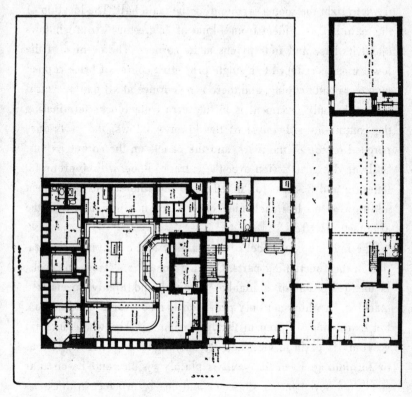

Figure 15. Plan of National Farmers' Bank, Owatonna, Minn.

it in the simplest and most direct terms. There is almost no ornamental detail, and the mass is severely rectilinear in shape. The
wall is faced by tapestry brick, opened by small windows low
down to light the rooms surrounding the main hall. The location of
the main hall is evident from a kind of "clerestory" with windows
about its base and four pylons at its corners. The cornice of the
lower mass is reduced to a single projecting course of brick capped
by a terra cotta coping, and there is no cornice at all on the central
mass. The only ornament is in the terra cotta blocks terminating
the continuous sill-course of the lower windows, the grotesques
perched on top of the piers, and the panels on the corner pylons.
Sullivan designed a sign over the entrance door, with appropriate
lettering and a sense for its effect in the whole. The subsequent
addition of no less than nine other signs has not improved the
architectural effect.

The interior is a model of availability and clarity of organization in the functioning parts. Quoting Schuyler: "This, one feels,
is the habitation of a highly organized and highly specialized
machine, in which not only provision is made for every function,
but expression is given to that provision." [14] The whole internal
economy is plain to view and friendly in feeling, not mysterious
or forbidding. Even the vault is plainly visible, and its circular
steel door seven feet in diameter and nearly two feet in thickness
is an impressive element in the architectural effect. The interior
materials are rich, but there is far less decorative detail than in
the Owatonna bank. The counters are of white marble; all partitions and other woodwork of oak. This is treated with broad unbroken surfaces. Five columns on each side of the main hall support the "clerestory"; they are of steel sheathed in wood, and
adorned only by carving around the necks and on the faces of the
abaci. Above these columns in a kind of "triforium" division are

long mural paintings by Philbrick which effectively complete the architectural scheme.

At the same time that Sullivan was working on the People's Savings Bank, he was busy on plans for a church in Cedar Rapids. Although this was not erected until three years later, when Sullivan had nothing to do with its construction, the major part of the design is due to him. The history of the project is rather distressing. The Official Board of St. Paul's Methodist Episcopal Church of Cedar Rapids decided to erect a new church building in 1909. Their program was unusual, since they desired a structure with far more than the customary amount of space for the use of the Sunday school, and for other social and recreational activities. A number of architects were invited to submit plans in competition, and of the twelve sets of plans submitted, Sullivan's was chosen. He was accordingly engaged as architect in October, 1910. "His distinct invention in this case was the combination of a rectangular school and social building with a semicircular auditorium along one side, having its stairhouse entrances outside the semicircle, and providing a great wall, separating these buildings, with ample openings. This simple arrangement met every fundamental requirement for what was later to be filled in." [15] But although Sullivan's conception was accepted as the basis for the design, his first set of detailed plans was rejected as too expensive, and then a second set likewise. In March, 1912, Sullivan resigned as architect because of financial disagreements. The church board kept his plans, and in November turned them over to an obscure and undistinguished architect who had done several churches in Chicago. By virtue of making a few minor changes and substituting "store-bought" ornament for Sullivan's especially designed ornament, the cost was brought down sufficiently for the project to be executed. Fortunately Elmslie was able to go over the revised plans thoroughly, without compensation, and eliminate most of the more glaring anomalies. The church was built on these plans between April, 1913, and May, 1914. This procedure, although doubtless "legal" enough, was protested in a brief editorial in the *Western Architect* entitled "A Sullivan Design That Is Not Sullivan's," [16] and certainly the whole affair was unfortunate. Of course, the church itself is the chief loser, as anyone may see in observing the cheap "art-glass" of the main skylight, or the banal stencilled ornament in the Sunday school classrooms. But the church as built is fundamentally Sullivan's conception.

The plan consists of a rectangular block at the back used for the Sunday school, offices, and social rooms, and a semicircular auditorium sixty-five feet in diameter extending in front of this. (Fig. 16) The exterior (Pl. 76) is quite unlike conventional ecclesiastical architecture. The main front is a semicircular wall three stories high, sheltered by a broad cornice. The auditorium is entered by two stair towers detached from the sweeping curve of the wall, projecting at the southeast and southwest. Above is a simple curved roof of low pitch, with a bell-tower in the center. The junction of the church auditorium and the school building is indicated on the outside by a low wall crossing the roof and by pylons at the sides. The only noteworthy change from Sullivan's scheme for the exterior is the substitution of square piers for free-standing columns around the curved auditorium at the third story.

The interior of the auditorium is interesting in plan. Just within the curved wall is a broad corridor running around the back of the pews. Eight aisles converge from this toward the pulpit, and the pews are arranged between these in concentric circles, every seat facing the pulpit which is at the focus of all the radiating lines. There is a downward slant of four feet in the floor, affording a

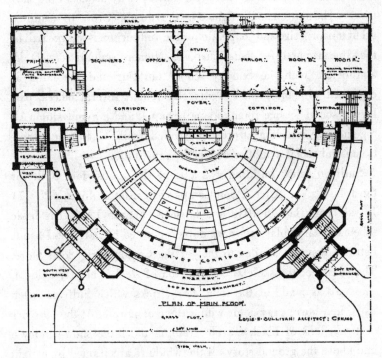

Figure 16. Plan of St. Paul's Church, Cedar Rapids, Iowa.

clear view of the pulpit. The acoustic properties are excellent. The main floor has seven hundred seats, and four hundred more are contained in a gallery which is built over the outside corridor and the last two rows of pews. Access to the gallery is by means of the stair towers. The auditorium is lighted by the two upper rows of windows, all of uniform size and shape. Below the auditorium is a large hall of the same size used for social purposes. Numerous doors connect the auditorium with the Sunday school building and the latter is equipped with more than twenty classrooms, several offices, parlors, a social service room, a small chapel, and a gymnasium. Altogether the building affords unexcelled facilities for the educational and social activities of a church institution.

Sullivan's next building was a large dry-goods store built for the John D. Van Allen & Son Company in Clinton, Iowa. (Pl. 77) It was begun late in 1913 and finished early in 1915. The basic scheme of large plate glass windows separated by horizontal bands between floors is similar to that of the Carson Pirie Scott Store. The nature of the skeletal construction of steel is clearly evident. The wall is made of the long, thin bricks which Sullivan often used, in a burnt gray color with a tinge of purple. At the base are vertical slabs of black marble framing the large show-windows, and above the ground story all the windows are framed by a light gray terra cotta. There is a very slight cornice. The extraordinary feature of the design is apparent at the first glance. On the main façade of the building are three slender mullions running through three stories, from ornate corbels at the second-floor level to huge outbursts of terra cotta foliage in the attic. Corbels and finials (if so they may be called) are a vivid green in color. Just above the finials, and forming a background for them, are inset tile panels in Dutch blue and white. These curious features must have been purely decorative in intention. They are non-structural, occurring in the middle of the bays between the steel-enclosing brick piers. At the same time there seems to be no valid decorative excuse for them. They do not serve to express or to emphasize the fundamental form of the building, which is a series of horizontal bands; they do not seem to be a part of the form, but merely applied on it; the exuberant naturalistic foliations comport poorly with a structure otherwise so geometrically rectilinear; even the color does not seem in place. In short, one cannot understand why Sullivan put them there. Occasional details such as this appear in other of his buildings, and we feel in them a tendency toward purely lyrical outbursts, like some passages in his writing, but no others seem so entirely illogical, or, it must be admitted, so unsuccessful in effect.

The next six buildings, chronologically, were banks, built between 1913 and 1919. The first of these is the Henry C. Adams Building (Pl. 78), in Algona, a small town in northwestern Iowa. Intended by Mr. Adams for a bank building, and designed by Sullivan as such, the contemplated bank failed to receive a charter and the building was first used as a real estate building known as the Land & Loan Office. Although one of the smallest and most unassuming of Sullivan's buildings, it is one of the best—a simple rectangular block, with no cornice, and sparing but effective ornament. It is so obviously a direct statement of the problem, and that problem was so simple, that it needs little comment. Few buildings of that period, however, either in this country or in Europe, match it in quality.

The Merchants' National Bank in Grinnell, Iowa, was built in 1914. (Pl. 79) Although a smaller building than either the Owatonna or the Cedar Rapids banks, it is fully as monumental in effect. The exterior walls appear almost solid, although the interior is amply lighted. The material used is a wire-cut shale brick of mixed shades, ranging in color from a blue-black to a golden brown, the general effect being a deep tapestry red. The cornice is of brown terra cotta, richly modelled and inlaid with gold. Although it does not project beyond the face of the building, small finials rise against the skyline, causing a slight indistinctness in the silhouette which does not accord with the otherwise clean-cut geometry of the mass. The great window on the east side, measuring about fifteen feet in height by forty feet in length, is an impressive feature. Enclosed in a rectangular opening, and recessed from the wall surface, it is fronted by nine slender colonets. As their attenuated proportions suggest, these colonets are of iron, but they are sheathed in gold leaf and the combination of gold and dull red is in stunning harmony. The window itself is of double thickness, as at Owatonna, with plate glass outside and leaded colored glass inside. The two small windows at the corner light the directors' room, and the window to the left of the door lights the women's lounge. The clock projecting from the corner was a relic of the old bank building.

The most striking feature of the exterior is the entrance door with its huge sunburst of ornament above. All of this detail is executed in gray terra cotta, except the heraldic lions and certain portions of the ornament which are gilded. The sunburst above the door centers about a kind of "rose-window" in stained glass, and is a remarkable fantasy in superimposed circles, squares, and diamonds, with both naturalistic and geometric details. As a study in decorative design *per se* it is of great interest; as a part of an actual building it is far too large, too complex, and too heavy for the position it occupies. Like similar features on other late buildings, it must be ascribed to Sullivan's innate tendency to burst out at times into overwrought lyricism.

The interior is much less richly ornamented than the Owatonna bank, but is by no means bare. (Pl. 80) The walls have a high brick dado topped by a finishing strip of dark-stained oak. Above this they are of light plaster. The brick wall at the back, over the vault and the safe deposit room, has a rich band of fire-gilt terra cotta ornament. Gold terra cotta trim also occurs on the tellers' cage at the back, and on the capitals of the square piers carrying large flower-bowls. The large window in the east wall is of leaded glass, with a ground of marbled yellow and lavender, with central insets in peacock blue and bright green colors. The skylight colors are cream and turquoise blue. Certain details are worthy of note: the clock over the entrance set in a glass mosaic field; the suspended lighting fixtures of oak and frosted glass; and the circular window of the façade, in brilliant colors. Although the bank is not large, an unusual sense of spaciousness is given by the complete openness of the interior above the low partition walls.

The Home Building Association Bank at Newark, Ohio (Pl. 81) was built at the same time as the Grinnell bank. The lot was of very small dimensions but the officers of the company desired accommodations for quite a large business. Consequently it was necessary to erect a two-story structure, and it was in reality a three-story building since the basement was designed for business use. The exterior is faced by greenish gray terra cotta slabs with ornamented borders. The long rectangular panel over the side windows is of glass mosaic in light green, and the entrance front has another very rich panel of green glass mosaic with the legend "The Old Home" emblazoned thereon in gold lettering. The general effect of the exterior is not good, and one has the feeling that the whole enterprise was cheap. Indeed, with the present obliteration of the building by red and gold signs, it looks as nearly ordinary as one of Sullivan's buildings could.

The interior of the Newark bank (Pl. 82) is extremely rich in decoration. The counters and wall dado are faced by intricately veined black marble; the wall is a polychromatic frieze; and even the ceiling beams are richly ornamented. The glaring white porcelain lights, it is hardly necessary to remark, were not a part of the original installation. The colors of the frieze at the top of the wall are brick red (the large star motives), dull green, dull blue, and gold-buff. The best feature of the interior is the treatment of the plate glass shield partitioning the tellers' cage from the public space. This consists merely of broad panels of polished plate glass on both front and top, from which depend inverted bronze troughs as light-reflectors, and bronze tellers' wickets inserted over the deal-plates. The arrangement is functionally admirable, and the effect of the polished glass and metal surfaces is like the gleaming precision of fine machinery.

The Purdue State Bank in West Lafayette, Indiana, was also finished in 1914. It was the smallest and least expensive of all Sullivan's banks. The chief interest of the building is the manner in which it is adjusted to a small triangular and sloping site within the acute angle formed by the junction of two streets, utilizing the entire available area very skilfully in the plan of the interior. The exterior most closely resembles the Henry C. Adams Building at Algona.

Finest of all the bank buildings designed by Sullivan, and one of the outstanding works of his whole career, is the People's Savings and Loan Association Bank at Sidney, Ohio. (Pl. 83) Sullivan himself considered this building the best of the series. One's first impression of the building is not so much of its form as of its beautiful harmony of soft, rich and luminous colors. The walls and base serve as a deep ground color against which the lighter and more brilliant glass mosaic and terra cotta ornament are relieved, like the melodic passages of solo instruments against the sustained full harmonies of an orchestral accompaniment. The red of the bricks is not a flat opaque color, but the rich and vibrant red of tapestry brick of varied tones. The base consists of two-foot slabs of verde antique marble, strongly veined and almost black. On the entrance façade the jambs and architrave of the door, the heraldic lions, the belt-course and impost moulding of the arch, the arch itself and the corbels on which it rests, are all in richly modelled terra cotta of a dull turtle green color. The tympanum of the arch, executed by Louis J. Millett, has a ground of light blue glass mosaic, with the single word "Thrift" in gold letters, and an inner archivolt in two shades of green, buff, and purple, the purple dominating. This is the "solo melody" of the façade, and even from a distance its frank, clear color is readily apparent. The foliage designs in the corbels, the strong projection of the arch, and its enriched soffit, are all full of vigor and spirit. On the long west façade, the tremendous windows lighting the banking room are boldly framed by strongly projecting sill, dividing mullions, and lintel, all in terra cotta. The color changes from mottled green below into brown above, gradually becoming lighter and merging into warm golden buff in the cornice. The long rectangular panel over the windows has a ground of light green glass mosaic, and the name of the bank in gold letters.

Many features of the exterior design call for attention. There are, for instance, the four square brick lamp-posts bordering the streets, designed by Sullivan to give the setting of the building something of its own quality. One can imagine these replaced by the ubiquitous and ugly Aladdin posts of cast-iron which adorn most of our Main Streets. Then there is the fine lettering in gilded bronze across the upper part of the façade, beautifully placed and in keeping with the whole. The robust foliage designs in terra cotta forming the corbels below the belt-course and the escutcheons above are worthy of careful study. The enframement of the great side windows is, however, too powerful and the way it is "pinned" to the wall by the brooch-like projections is of a disturbing plastic symbolism. Here character ends and caricature begins.

The interior (Pl. 84) is simpler and finer than that of any other of Sullivan's banks. As at Grinnell, the room is left open and unobstructed above a fringe of offices surrounding the central space, an arrangement giving the maximum effect of light and spaciousness. The range of windows in the west wall has opaque leaded glass in subdued colors—a light sea-green ground, with central ornaments in tomato and pale amber colors. The skylight is an iridescent mother-of-pearl color. The public space is screened from the tellers' cages, offices, etc., by a low brick wall topped by verde antique marble which forms the counter. At intervals projecting slabs carried on legs form check desks. Above the counter square brick piers carry a beam of natural oak, with incised patterns and a two-inch strip of inlaid terra cotta ornament. The rectangular openings above the counter thus formed are either left open or filled by large panes of plate glass, in which the bronze tellers' wickets are inserted. At the south (back) end of the public space there is no solid wall, but in its place a single sheet of plate glass, through which may be seen the huge door of the vault, exactly centered on the main axis. This door, a beautiful and powerful mass of polished steel, is the focus of one's first view of the interior and not only symbolizes the function of the building but is an important part in the decorative scheme. Sullivan has been accused of seeming "unaware of the machine as a direct element in architecture, abstract or concrete," [17] but here is an instance of a perfect concrete meeting of architecture and the machine. An example of Sullivan's meticulous care in details is his forethought in finding out from the bank's officers whether the vault door would normally during the course of banking hours be left open or closed; finding that it would be open, he placed the door just enough off axis so that when swung open on its great hinges it would fall on the center line. With the exception of a few corridor and office fixtures, all lighting is indirect. Counters and desks are lighted by overhead bronze reflecting troughs set with frosted glass, and the room as a whole is lighted by electric lights placed in troughs on top of the oak beam and in the large vases topping the four corner piers. The women's parlor (Pl. 85), with gray-pink marble floor, gray brick wall and natural-finished oak trim, is an extremely simple but distinguished apartment.

The mechanical equipment of the bank was very advanced, especially in the system of air-conditioning. Detailed information on this is contained in an article by Tallmadge in the *American Architect* of 1918.[18]

The Farmers' and Merchants' Union Bank in Columbus, Wisconsin, was built in 1919 and is the last of the series. The exterior (Pl. 86) is made of tapestry brick, ranging widely in color through browns and golden yellows. The general form, as at Grinnell and Sidney, is severely rectilinear, with broad expanses of plain wall surface against which the decorative enrichment of the portal and range of side windows stands out the more vividly. The small façade has only two openings below: the entrance door and a large window opening on the officers' platform within. Resting across these is a huge decorative lintel, or panel, with the name of the bank lettered on a polished slab of verde antique marble framed by lavish terra cotta ornament in a mottled green color. The arched opening above has a lunette with colored glass, and a recessed archivolt in four faces, a treatment less effective than that at Sidney. The heraldic lions perched on Sullivanesque fasces also seem somewhat out of place. The side wall, slightly battered in its lower half, has a massive solidity akin to that of the Egyptian style, but with the lyric ornament of the row of arched windows, nothing of its ponderous character.

The interior (Pl. 87) is a long narrow room, affording space for tellers' cages only on one side, but the arrangement of these is essentially the same as in the bank at Sidney.

Sullivan's last work, designed in his sixty-fifth year, was a small music store built for William P. Krause on Lincoln Avenue, Chicago. The plan and interior of this building were designed by William C. Presto; only the façade was by Sullivan. Since the building was used for a residence as well as a shop the façade has two entrances at the sides and a display-window occupying the middle. Deeply recessed and richly framed, the window is conceived as a picture that dominates the lower part of the façade. Above, the façade is faced by terra cotta panels in a dull green color, simply treated except for a central motive rising from an enriched corbel and projecting above the cornice. It is not one of his best designs, but again we have only to compare it with the conventional façades of the adjacent stores which have since been built up around it, to realize as forcefully as ever that even in his least significant works Sullivan was still a master.

The whole story of Sullivan's personal life from 1895 to his death in 1924 will probably never be known. As mentioned before there are no details concerning it in the *Autobiography*, and only a few items may be gleaned from the reminiscences of those who knew him. We know, for instance, only the mere facts of his marriage: that he was married to Margaret Hattabough on July 1, 1899, and that they were separated on January 29, 1917. Those who knew him say that he always spoke respectfully of his wife, and warmly admired certain of her qualities, but that they lived in different spheres, emotionally and intellectually. They lived separately many years before the divorce took place. There were no children from the union. Sullivan thought and wrote a great deal from 1900 on. *Kindergarten Chats*, weekly articles published in an architectural journal throughout the whole year in 1901–02, were a book in proportion. While writing them Sullivan worked usually at a desk in the Cliff Dwellers club, writing late at night—sometimes until two or three—only to appear at the office the next morning apparently fresh and eager for work.

He read a great deal. The books in his library reveal some rather esoteric interests. There were several books on Japan and Japanese art, and he possessed a small but choice collection of Oriental rugs, Chinese and Japanese vases, bronzes, and jade carvings. He had about a dozen books on gems and precious stones, from the designs of which it has been suggested that he derived motives for his ornament, although this is not true. *Gray's Botany* influenced his ornament more than any other single source. He had a dog-eared copy, showing extensive use in studying the morphology of plants and their curious and marvellous differentiations within species. He referred the book to students frequently. His sketch-book was full of drawings from this source: complex organic developments from single germinal ideas. There were a few books on the history of music, others on musical analysis, harmony, etc., and fourteen volumes of oratorios. Several books on psychology and psychic phenomena reveal a profound interest in this field. There were in addition well-worn copies of Walt Whitman's *Leaves of Grass* and Nietzsche's *Thus Spake Zarathustra*, especially suggestive to the student of his writings.

The lack of commissions reduced him to desperate straits by 1909. It was at that time that he had to give up the office in the Auditorium Tower and to auction off his library and many of his household effects. He was also forced to dispense with the assistance of Elmslie in the office, thus being left completely alone. The last buildings that Elmslie helped with were the Bradley residence in Madison and the bank at Owatonna. There were many years of enforced inactivity, and the idleness and loneliness made inroads on his health. Frank Lloyd Wright renewed his friendship with Sullivan in 1914, and the two saw each other frequently in the subsequent years. Wright stood by loyally, and many interesting passages in his *Autobiography* tell of these meetings, especially toward the end. In 1918 Sullivan attempted to obtain war work with the Bureau of Construction of the Ordnance Department, but here again his services were not wanted.

In June of 1918 Claude Bragdon urged him to rewrite and publish in book form the *Kindergarten Chats*, and Sullivan worked throughout the summer and autumn at this task. Sometimes he took his work out to Washington Park, but more often he wrote at the Cliff Dwellers. The revision was finished in December, but no publisher was found. During 1922 and 1923 Sullivan wrote *The Autobiography of an Idea*. This work renewed his vitality and interest in life, and he was probably happier during these last years than he had been for a long time. The improvement in his health at this time was marked. To accompany the *Autobiography* he designed a series of nineteen plates of ornament, and these and the *Autobiography* were published in book form by the Press of the American Institute of Architects in 1924.

But in February and March of 1924 Sullivan was in ill health. Neuritis developed in his right arm, and his heart was seriously dilated from an over-use of stimulants. In April he failed rapidly. Just a few days before he died Mr. Max Dunning was able to visit him in his small rooms in the Warner Hotel and place in his hands the completed copy of his book and the plates of his "System of Architectural Ornament." Mr. Dunning writes: "Mr. Sullivan considered, I believe, that these two efforts constituted his life's greatest accomplishment, and I believe that I am stating the truth when I say that his last days were among the most pleasant he had experienced for many years, as he felt that his life's work had been splendidly consummated." On the evening of April 13 he went to sleep, a sleep from which he never wakened. He died early in the morning of April 14, 1924, from heart trouble. Funeral services were held in a small chapel, and Sullivan was buried next his father and mother in Graceland Cemetery. A small monument was later erected by his friends; it stands very near the Ryerson Tomb, and not far from the Getty Tomb. Truly of him can it be said: *"Si monumentum requiris, circumspice."*

[1] From an Address to the Chicago Chapter of the A. I. A. on May 8, 1928.

[2] André Bouilhet: "L'Exposition de Chicago," *Révue des Arts Décoratifs*, vol. 14, p. 68, 1893–94.

[3] List of gifts and accessions in the official report of the vice-president of the Museum Commission, March 16, 1894, *Révue des Arts Décoratifs*, vol. 14, p. 324, 1893–94.

[4] Paul Bourget: *Outre-Mer Impressions of America*, 1895, p. 14.

[5] Jean Schopfer: "American Architecture from a Foreign Point of View: New York City," *Architectural Review*, vol. 7, (vol. 2 new series), no. 3, p. 25, March, 1900.

[6] Russell Sturgis: "Good Things in Modern Architecture," *Architectural Record*, vol. 8, no. 1, p. 101, July–September, 1898.

[7] Montgomery Schuyler: "The Skyscraper Up to Date," *Architectural Record*, vol. 8, no. 3, p. 231, January–March, 1899.

[8] Montgomery Schuyler: *op. cit.*

[9] "A Departure from Classic Tradition," *Architectural Record*, vol. 30, no. 4, pp. 327–338, October, 1911.

[10] Thomas E. Tallmadge: "The Farmers' and Merchants' Bank of Columbus, Wisconsin," *Western Architect*, vol. 29, no. 7, p. 63, July, 1920.

[11] Carl K. Bennett: "A Bank Built for Farmers," *The Craftsman*, vol. 15, no. 2, p. 176, November, 1908.

[12] *The Craftsman*, vol. 10; nos. 2–4; May, June, July, 1906.

[13] Montgomery Schuyler: "The People's Savings Bank of Cedar Rapids, Iowa," *Architectural Record*, vol. 31, no. 1, p. 45, Jan. 1912.

[14] Schuyler: *op. cit.*

[15] Descriptive and historical pamphlet issued by the Church Board at the dedication, May 31, 1914.

[16] *Western Architect*, vol. 20, no. 8, p. 85, August, 1914.

[17] Frank Lloyd Wright: *Autobiography*, p. 104.

[18] Thomas E. Tallmadge: "The People's Savings & Loan Association Building of Sidney, Ohio," *American Architect*, vol. 114, no. 2235, October 23, 1918.

# VII. SULLIVAN'S ARCHITECTURAL THEORY

SULLIVAN's importance as a prophet of modern architecture lay equally in his theory and in his practice. Some other architects of his generation anticipated in isolated buildings the form of a modern architecture, but there was no consistent achievement. Such a case was John Root's Monadnock Building of 1891; undeniably a primitive of the modern style, the Monadnock Building was nevertheless a unique example which its architect never duplicated. Similarly many critics during the nineteenth century had had premonitions of a new philosophy of architecture. It might be argued that no essential point of Sullivan's theory was entirely new; every one of his ideas had already been expressed. But no one before him had tied them together into a consistent system of thinking. Sullivan was probably the first man of his times to set forth both by precept and by example the clear outlines of a new philosophy and a new art of building. As Lewis Mumford has said: "Sullivan was the first American architect to think consciously of his relations with civilization. Richardson and Root both had good intuitions, and they had made effective demonstrations; but Sullivan knew what he was about, and what is more important, he knew what he ought to be about." [1]

In attempting to arrive at an understanding of Sullivan's theory of architecture we are confronted by two facts: that his theory was far too complex to be summarized in the catch-phrase "form follows function," and that even with a more complete exposition of his ideas no full realization of their import can be achieved without a sense of the passionate conviction that lay behind them. His was not a mere theory of architecture, nor even a philosophy of architecture; it was a religion of architecture. His writings are winged with poetry and shot through with emotional intensity. For this reason no mere analysis of Sullivan's credo is sufficient; its significance resides so largely in his manner of expression and choice of words that many passages in this account are quoted directly from his own writings.

Sullivan wrote extensively, but unfortunately the greater part of his published articles and addresses appeared in comparatively obscure periodicals which have long since ceased publication, and bound volumes may be found on the shelves of only one or two libraries. Moreover two or three of his best addresses and his longest book were never published. Consequently it has been difficult for any but the closest students of his life to make use of the great wealth of material which he left. Eighteen published articles and addresses and two published books are listed in the Sullivan bibliography at the end of this work, and in addition six unpublished manuscripts are named.[2] It is impossible within reasonable limits to discuss in detail each of these articles, but it may be helpful to indicate briefly the general nature of those which are best known and those which may be considered most important.

The earliest essay by Sullivan which has been preserved to us is a paper read before the Western Association of Architects in 1885, entitled "Characteristics and Tendencies of American Architecture." This was written when he was twenty-nine years old, yet it represents the point of view, in nearly complete form, from which he never essentially departed in forty years of further writing. It was published in full, with commendations, in the *Builders' Weekly Reporter* of London, but apparently aroused no great interest in this country. Although it is the earliest of Sullivan's essays preserved to us, there is no reason to suppose that his characteristic point of view had not been evolved before 1885. According to the *Autobiography* Sullivan had conceived the notion of formulating a "Clopet demonstration" for architecture while he was still a student in the Ecole, about 1875.[3] Certainly the account of his ambitions during the first year in the firm of Adler & Sullivan, 1881, is most explicitly "functionalist" in character: "He could now, undisturbed, start on the course of practical experimentation he long had in mind, which was to make an architecture that fitted its functions—a realistic architecture based on well defined utilitarian needs—that all practical demands of utility should be paramount as a basis of planning and design; that no architectural dictum, or tradition, or superstition, or habit, should stand in his way." [4] While it is possible that in this passage the man of over sixty-five was reading back into the mind of the youth of twenty-five ideas which he had not clearly formulated at that time, and while we know definitely that the actual phrase "form follows function" did not appear in any known writings of Sullivan prior to 1896, nevertheless it is reasonable to suppose that in a mind so original and active a well-defined point of view may have been formed during the early years.

At any rate Sullivan's famous "Inspiration" essay, read before the Third Annual Convention of the Western Association of Architects in Chicago in 1886, is generally conceded to have marked his intellectual majority. Over three hundred architects were present, from a territory extending as far west as Denver, east to Rochester, north to Minneapolis, and south to Atlanta. Sullivan, according to an eye-witness, "ascended the platform with an air of mingled diffidence and self-esteem, dark-complexioned, with scant black hair and chin whiskers" and held the audience in a state of close attention during a reading which occupied some forty minutes. It was a prose-poem, rhapsodic and lyric in utterance (Sullivan later considered it somewhat "sophomoric and over-exalted"), and it is doubtful whether more than a handful of his listeners understood what this remarkable effusion on a supposedly architectural subject meant. But they received it courteously, and a few young men remembered it for years, for in the foreword was contained a complete summary of Sullivan's theory of architecture as organic growth, and in the body of the work poetic passages of memorable beauty. The essay fell into three parts: "Growth—a Spring Song"; "Decadence—Autumn Reverie"; and "The Infinite —a ɔong of the Depths"; the transition from part to part effected by two interludes.

The following two articles, one on the relationship of details to mass in architecture and the other on "Ornament in Architecture," coming in 1887 and 1892, are further developments of the idea of art as organic growth, the former containing some of his most eloquent passages. In "Objective and Subjective," an address read before the Twenty-eighth Convention of the A.I.A. in New York in 1894, Sullivan discusses the source and rise of artistic knowledge and, as a necessary corollary, launches into his first detailed attack on academic education, in particular the education imparted by the architectural schools of his day. This was a theme to which he devoted some of his most acid criticism in later years —in fact, it was perhaps his major destructive attack, just as the idea of a functional and organic architecture was his major constructive effort.

In 1896, just after the completion of the Guaranty Building in Buffalo, Sullivan published his article "The Tall Office Building Artistically Considered." Originally appearing in *Lippincott's*, this was at various later dates reprinted in the *Inland Architect and*

*News Record, The Craftsman,* and the *Western Architect,* and is probably the best-known of his writings after *Kindergarten Chats* and the *Autobiography.* As A. W. Barker has pointed out,[5] it must be admitted that Sullivan's tendency to metaphor and the fluency of his thought often left his writings overloaded and somewhat obscure, but here his prose style is at its best. The simple and direct English of the essay is excelled only by the logic and clarity of its reasoning. It is the clearest and most concise statement of Sullivan's whole architectural theory that may be found. Those parts of it pertaining specifically to the skyscraper have been quoted at length in the discussion on the Wainwright Building.

Two shorter and less important articles appeared in 1899, and in the same year the finest of his poems, a long work entitled "The Master," finished and dated on the day of his marriage, July 1st. This was never published.

From 1900 to 1902 Sullivan wrote a great deal. The partnership with Adler had broken up five years before and during these years there were few commissions in the office. A note of bitterness crept into his writing; his attacks on the existing order were more virulent, while he restated his credo with more eloquence. His style became less urbane, more epigrammatic. He was, in spite of himself, being forced to become not an architect but a teacher. In this situation he addressed himself more and more to the youth of the land as the hope of the future. "The Young Man in Architecture," an address to the Architectural League of America; "Reality in the Architectural Art"; and "Education," also read before the Architectural League, all appeared in these years. But the most famous work of this era was *Kindergarten Chats.*

*Kindergarten Chats* was Sullivan's first sustained literary effort. The "Chats," mostly a page or two in length, appeared in weekly issues of *The Interstate Architect and Builder,* running through a whole year from February 16, 1901, to February 8, 1902. For purposes of a vital and dramatic presentation of his thoughts, Sullivan chose the form of a series of dialogues between an imaginary teacher and pupil, the latter assumed to be a "young, well-educated, self-confident and unsuspecting hopeful" in whose mind the master might plant the seeds and cultivate the growth of a true conception of the architectural art. The title reflects Sullivan's conviction that the simple and intimate methods of kindergarten training are the only educational process that we have developed which is worthy of serious approval. "It is my main contention against prevailing educational methods, that their general, traditional tendency is to shut off Nature's stimuli and substitute book stimuli, or else the spectres of medieval theological doctrine. From this arraignment I specifically except the kindergarten, manual training school, gymnasium and athletic field, which are the best in educational method that we have." Sullivan sought an "architectural kindergarten" in which simple and obvious truths might be presented without complication or obfuscation by pseudo-aristocratic learning. Concerning the method of the "Chats," Sullivan addressed his pupil as follows: "First I would dissolve for you this wretched illusion called American architecture, and then cause to awaken in your mind the reality of a beautiful, a sane, a logical, a human, living art of your day; an art of and for democracy, an art of and for American people of your own time."

It is a remarkable series. Ranging from scathing sarcasm and unbridled criticism of the commercial, the insincere, and the pretentious in the architecture of that day, through long passages of close reasoning concerning the true nature and function of architecture, to moods of inspired feeling and pure poetry, it is the most complete record of Sullivan's range of thought and imagination. His fearless attacks on contemporary architecture—even of specific buildings without regard to the prestige of the architects concerned—often seem unduly bitter, and the work is occasionally marred by trivialities or lapses in taste, but on the whole its constructive truth outweighs these minor defects. Twenty years later Claude Bragdon wrote: "The Chats proved to be a vigorous, bitter, bludgeoning assault upon the then existing architectural order, . . . but they pointed out a way to freedom to any sincere young architectural talent stifling in the tainted air of our industrialism or bogged in the academic morass. Large, loose, discursive, a blend of the sublime and the ridiculous . . . Kindergarten Chats remains in my memory as one of the most provocative, amazing, astounding, inspiring things that I have ever read." [6] During the latter half of 1918 Sullivan revised *Kindergarten Chats* with a view toward their re-publication, and this version, edited by Claude Bragdon, was finally published in book form by the Scarab Fraternity Press late in 1934.

From 1905 to 1910 Sullivan's writings centered on his conception of a true democracy. "Natural Thinking: A Study in Democracy" was a long address given before the Chicago Architectural Club in 1905. It contains his definitions of feudalism and democracy as two opposed world-forces, an interpretation of history as the rise of feudalism with its two chief institutions of the aristocracy and the priesthood, and the gradual growth out of this of the democratic idea. Education as the outgrowth of "natural thinking" is analyzed and held up as the prime essential of a democratic society, and demonstrated as fundamentally democratic in nature. This address was never published, but several passages from the manuscript are quoted below.

"The Possibility of a New Architectural Style," published in 1905, was a very brief and lucid summary of the point of view developed in previous writings, demonstrating in particular that various current suggestions concerning the "appropriateness" of the Gothic style for modern American use were as beside the point as arguments for any other style-revival. This definite stand has particular interest in view of the fact that it appeared just prior to the completion of Cass Gilbert's West Street Building in New York, the first of a long series of Neo-Gothic skyscrapers which took as their point of departure the vertical emphasis of the high building which Sullivan had first clearly shown in the Wainwright Building, and proceeded to "express" this with a vocabulary of Gothic ornament. Nothing could demonstrate more clearly the manner in which Sullivan's distinguished contemporaries seized at the superficials of his work and failed utterly to grasp its fundamental thesis. "What is Architecture?—A Study in the American People of Today," published in 1906, was a brief summary of principles previously enunciated.

During the years 1906–08 Sullivan worked on a book which was to be the most complete statement of his whole social and artistic philosophy. It was to be entitled *Democracy: A Man Search*, and on the title page is a note in Sullivan's neat handwriting: "The revision of this book was completed by me at the Chicago Club, Chicago, at 1:42 A. M. April 18th, 1908." The manuscript was the longest he ever wrote. Although unpublished, it was in some ways the most remarkable of his books. Broader in scope than the "Chats," and displaying a far wider knowledge of previous philosophic writings and of the panorama of human history, it was at the same time more restrained in phrase but equally intense in poetic feeling. Like his other works, *Democracy* is somewhat baffling to the casual reader accustomed to reading poetry as poetry, philosophy as philosophy, criticism as criticism, sociological theory as sociological theory, and so on, each sphere of thought or feeling separated and presented as such. Sullivan merges all of these into one copious outpouring, as integral as life itself. Consequently its literary, or philosophic, or scholarly merits are difficult to isolate and estimate. As poetry we find it too philosophical, or as philosophy too poetic. One critic, in reviewing it, found "an immense amount of truly sensuous language snowed under by abstract language," or more appropriately from his standpoint, "full of grains of gold swept along in swift mud"; another found it of compelling power in the construction of original and forcible thoughts, but confused by redundant and over-fluent moonshine. The fact is that *Democracy* requires a breadth of approach which shall, in Sullivan's own language, "illuminate the heart, expand the range of the creative power of the mind, and certify the spiritual integrity of man" before it can be properly appreciated. Few persons of the author's acquaintance have read the manuscript, and none of these has felt fully competent to pass judgment upon it in its entirety. Certainly he feels less qualified to do so than many others, yet it seems valid to hazard an opinion that this might some day be taken as one of the great literary achievements of modern times.

From 1908 until the last years of his life Sullivan wrote almost nothing. These were undoubtedly his darkest years. He was kept partially busy by the trickle of commissions for small banks and a few other structures between 1907 and 1919, and one or two unimportant articles came from his pen. William L. Steele, in his memorial address on Sullivan to the Chicago Chapter of the A.I.A. on May 8, 1928, said: "To us who knew and believed in Louis Sullivan and who followed his colorful and romantic career, it has not been easy to interpret him in any but tragic terms. Here was this gifted man, this genius, immensely capable, ready to do what was needed to be done in a complete and powerful way—and yet, we saw him ignored when he was not ridiculed. . . . It is amazing how, when the time came, so few noted his absence from his accustomed place. It was as though he had been away in a far country when, just before the end, he came back from nobody knew where and wrote his valedictory. It was a shadow of the powerfully built, broad-chested athlete of former days, but a quietly triumphant old man, who nightly sat at a table in the Cliff Dwellers Club writing what was to be his literary masterpiece."

This latter-day acclaim, never very vociferous, but affording Sullivan some gratification in his last years, began with *The Autobiography of an Idea*. In January, 1922, when Sullivan was sixty-five years old, Charles A. Whitaker, managing editor of the Press of the American Institute of Architects, wrote Sullivan to ask for a series of articles for the Journal of the A.I.A. which might later be reprinted in book form. From this request grew the conception of an autobiography, and Sullivan plunged into its writing with enthusiasm. The work began in February, was continued through 1922 and brought to completion in August, 1923. It appeared serially in issues of the *Journal* from June, 1922, to August, 1923. During the late summer and fall Sullivan revised certain passages, and the completed series was published in book form in March, 1924. As related before, Sullivan received the bound copy on his death-bed.

*The Autobiography of an Idea* needs no description here, since it has been reprinted by W. W. Norton in the "White Oak Library" series within the past year, and has been available to anyone interested in Sullivan. However, for this very reason, present-day conceptions of Sullivan are perhaps based too largely on the book. The majority of those who have heard of Sullivan at all know him only by the *Autobiography*, and perhaps three or four of his buildings. It is well to keep in mind that the *Autobiography* was written when Sullivan was over sixty-five years old; that it came after a period of nearly fifteen years of comparative inactivity which had wrought their inevitable effects; that it treats largely of his long-gone youth, only partly of his professional career during the Adler & Sullivan days, and practically not at all of the years after 1893. For these reasons, it is only partially satisfactory as a biography, and as an exposition of his "Idea" of architecture it cannot be compared with the much more lucid articles of the nineties and early 1900's. This is not to suggest that the *Autobiography* is not an interesting, and even a great, book; but in my opinion it is by no means his literary masterpiece, nor yet an adequate source for a complete understanding of his philosophy. For this reason, in summarizing Sullivan's beliefs, an effort will be made to draw very largely on those sources which are earlier in date and less accessible to the general reader.

During the same months that Sullivan was writing his auto-biography he was working on a series of large drawings to illustrate a system of architectural ornament, originally requested by the Burnham Library of the Art Institute of Chicago. The Press of the American Institute of Architects asked for the publication rights, and the work was carried on as a companion volume to the *Autobiography*. Nineteen large drawings were done between January, 1922, and May, 1923. Sullivan wrote a brief introduction and explanatory comments on several of the drawings. The plates for the book were finished in time for Sullivan to see them before his death, but it was not finally completed until May, 1924. Published in folio under the title "A System of Architectural Ornament According with a Philosophy of Man's Powers," the book affords a glimpse of Sullivan's amazing powers of draftsmanship. That such marvels of lightness and delicacy could have been executed by a man of over sixty-five is no less astonishing than the fertility of invention, the richness, and the flexible strength of the drawings themselves. Yet even these may not be compared with some of the earlier drawings—the preliminary drawings for the ornament of the Auditorium, for instance—to see Sullivan as a draftsman at his best.

During the last years of his life, the editors of several architectural periodicals became aware of the genius in their midst and asked for articles from his pen. "The Tall Office Building Artistically Considered" was republished in the *Western Architect* in January, 1922. A brief but caustic article on the "Chicago Tribune Competition" was published by the *Architectural Record* in February, 1923. In this Sullivan unerringly and forcefully pointed out the merits of Eliel Saarinen's design which was awarded second prize, hailing it as "the most beautiful conception of a lofty office building that has been evolved," then proceeded to analyze the defects of the first prize design—an estimate of the two in which most subsequent criticism has concurred. In April, 1923, Sullivan's appreciation of Frank Lloyd Wright's work was published in an essay "Concerning the Imperial Hotel, Tokyo." This was followed a year later by "Reflections on the Tokyo Disaster," after the Imperial Hotel had successfully withstood the great earthquake and fire of September, 1923. In both these articles, written while *The Autobiography of an Idea* was under way, Sullivan displays a new optimism, a sense that his life's work had not been in vain.

Coming to a general statement of Sullivan's theory of architecture, it must be reiterated that we are dealing with something comparable to a religion. Sullivan's conception of architectural design is far more vital than mechanical or utilitarian functionalism on the one hand, or than "abstract composition" on the other. It takes on the dimensions of a whole life, and as such it must be approached. To understand Sullivan's ideas concerning architecture it is necessary to know something of his conception of God, his ideas of man and of human powers, and his beliefs about the social order. All of these are indissolubly fused with his ideas of architecture.

*The Infinite.* It has been observed that Sullivan was irreligious because he attacked the institution of the Church. It should be unnecessary to remark that this is a superficial observation. Sullivan was profoundly religious. Although he never used the word "God," preferring the phrase "Infinite Creative Spirit" or more often simply "The Infinite," the concept of an ultimate source of all Nature and life was ever-present and active in him. This Infinite was to him the immanent spirit in all the myriad phenomena of Nature, and as such it becomes evident to man. Although Sullivan was not given to speculation about its exact nature, it seems evident that he did not conceive of the Infinite as either personal or causal—that is, he did not necessarily distinguish between it as the creator and the phenomena of Nature and the universe as the created. But although the Infinite is resident in and integral with all Nature, and can be perceived or realized by man through Nature, its apprehension is ultimately a personal process. This belief is probably most closely allied to modern pantheism, in the sense that it suggests that the universe, taken as a whole, is God; that there is no other God than the combined forces and laws manifested in the existing universe. Sullivan did not conceive of the Infinite as either conscious or intelligent, and he was not the least interested in the notion of life after death. But it is hard to overestimate the vital importance to him of Nature. He loved and worshipped Nature from childhood on, and countless passages reveal its inspiration to him in every day of his life. From the rank weed in a roadside ditch to the grandeur of a summer storm or the vast stretches of lake and prairie, Sullivan saw fascinating beauty and thrilling perfection. The Infinite, through Nature, was the very source and life-blood of artistic inspiration, as of life itself.

"I must insist, very earnestly, upon the great practical value in our daily lives of this conviction that the Infinite is partly intelligible, and wholly useful to us. All the more I must impress it upon you, because precisely the contrary is taught, and because it is generally and tacitly assumed by the unthinking and the cynical that the Infinite is apart from us. Under such conditions of belief the Infinite has become in our minds an academic, an abstract symbol, instead of a living presence—and our unison with it official, delegated, perfunctory and occasional. The simple conception of the Infinite, that I am herein setting forth, has been so distorted for us by the theologians, the ecclesiastics of all denominations, creeds and sects, so cobwebbed, and obscured and blended with the conception of a Deity, that the Infinite has become, literally, in practice a thing remote from us.

"The traditional notions, however sincere, were based upon the conception of the Infinite as a Monarch, and our relations to him distant—with the sense of fear and our own sinful unworthiness predominant.

". . . I purposely herein have separated the Infinite from the religious conceptions that have descended to us, because these have as their axis of revolution the thought of a hereafter. I wish to deal with the present. I deem it vastly more important. What becomes of a man's soul in a theoretical hereafter is of insignificant value to the people at large in comparison with the social or anti-social use he puts it to here.

"Natural thinking must, as a prerequisite, rest upon an elevated, a humane, an enlightened and natural appreciation of the Infinite

—on adequate realization of our close identity with It, with Nature, and with our Fellow Men." [7]

*Man.* Man, to Sullivan, is the perfectly designed receiving-set for the impulses emanating from Nature. The five senses, when keenly attuned, are marvellous channels for the transmission of her stimuli to the organs of perception, and the result is objective experience. However, these senses may become dulled through perverse education or other causes, the channels become blocked, and in this case man is without the essential primary nutriment for right thinking or right feeling. Sullivan insists on the necessity of keeping the senses keenly attuned; he cites the difference between merely *hearing*, as a passive process, and *listening* as a vital and attentive process of hearing, and recommends that people should be taught to "listen" with all five of the senses, as children normally do.

Objective experience is but the first step in the apprehension of Nature. It is the primary material. But just as food is assimilated by the bodily organs into the blood stream, objective experience must be translated into subjective experience before it can become of vital use. This is accomplished by three faculties, or powers: the intellect, the emotions, and intuition. The intellectual powers are those commonly known as observation, memory, reflection, and reasoning; acting upon objective experience, they translate it into subjective experience which has meaning and the possibility of use. Similarly, the emotions endow objective experience with qualities of value and intensity, rendering it through a process of selection and reinforcement of potential value in expression. Intuition, which can be defined only as "that acute and instant scent in matters objective leading to matters subjective," endows objective experience with a unitary significance. Like the physical powers

(the senses) these mental powers may become slackened or ob-
structed, and the translation of objective experience into subjective
experience may not occur with its proper force and clarity. Sullivan's only prescription for this is sound education, sound physical
health, and the constant use of the powers which Nature has given,
for through use they become stronger and more perfect. With a
normal vital education in natural living and natural thinking the
potentialities of the human mind are almost unlimited.

"Never doubt the possibilities of your own mind, for they are
there, waiting for you to discover them, to know them, to use them.
You cannot hope to know your own powers until you test them
with the force of will and the backing of character to overcome
obstacles. It is almost folly to talk of the limitations of the mind.
I tell you that the limitations of your mind are much further off
than you suppose. The so-called average mind has vastly greater
powers, immeasurably greater possibilities of development than
is generally supposed." [8]

"It is quite the fad to discourse upon genius as a form of in-
sanity, and to assert its essential identity with degeneracy and
crime. The argument is specious; there is something in it. It is a
fragment of truth. But its discovery is so enthusiastically cherished
by the alienist that he does not sense the center of gravity around
which his satellite of truth must necessarily revolve, namely, the
organic *sanity* of genius as an expression of race-intellect forced
up sporadically through the human mass by the same persistent
urge of Nature that is striving today, as it has ever striven, to make
the sanity of the genius *normal and universal*; and that it is toward
this physical and spiritual equilibrium that Nature is striving to
shape Mankind. When intuition and imagination are absentees, the
alienist is not likely to suspect their supreme value as agencies in
the human intellect. He is pleased to speak in compliment of the

creative-power of genius, yet . . . he discusses genius as almost all men artificially educated treat almost all things natural; that is to say, as an accident, a perversion.

"It is my profound conviction that every infant born in what is generally called normal health, is gifted by Nature with a normal receptivity, which if cherished and allowed to be nourished . . . will unfailingly develop those normal, natural and sane qualities of mind to which, today, under a completely inverted conception of the Infinite, of Nature and of Man, we give the name Genius—as we would give name to a thing strange, and apart from the people.

"In our study of social science, altogether too much importance has been attached to heredity and too little to environment. In my view there is no normal heredity but that which Nature intended, namely, health, vigor and beauty. In a humane and democratic philosophy there is not room for such a thing as an unfit human being—except in a very limited and strictly pathological sense— and indeed this would disappear." [9]

Thus far we have traced what might be called Sullivan's episte-mology—his theory of the source and rise of mental content, the way in which knowledge and insight are achieved. The use of this content, the reverse process—the "objectification of the subjective" —is creative activity.

Creative activity presupposes the achievement of the kind of insights and values heretofore mentioned as a first requisite. With-out vital experience, both objective and subjective, man cannot create vital things. As a man is, so also is that which he creates. There can be no art without some prior experience of Nature and of Life, and the measure of an art is the depth and breadth of the experi-ence which calls it forth.

"I would give you of our art some adequate notion of its possible beauty, its endless capacity for expression, its fluency, its lyric quality, its inexhaustible dramatic power—when it comes into kinship with Nature's rhythms. And how can you know this unless you have felt it? And how can you understand it if you have not known it? And how can you *express* it unless you have *lived* it and understood it? You cannot express unless you have a system of expression; and you cannot have a system of expression unless you have a prior system of thinking and feeling; you cannot have a system of thinking and feeling unless you have had a basic system of living. When all is said and done, the great masterpiece, or the little masterpiece, is but the condensed expression of such philosophy of life as is held by the artist who creates it." [10]

Creative activity occurs by means of three processes or agencies: Imagination, Thought, and Expression. Imagination is that intuitive union of the senses, the intellect, and the emotions in an instantaneous integration which determines at once the whole character of the creative act. It is an "illumined instant," a revelation that has lain dormant but potential, in short, what we call inspiration. In Sullivan's words, it is "the very beginning of action because it is a sympathy that lives both in our senses and our intellect—the flash between the past and the future, the middle link in that living chain or sequence leading from nature unto art, and that lies deep down in the emotions and the will." Thought, on the other hand, is the cumulative factor, which weighs and tests and lends validity to the act of the imagination. It is "the faculty which doubts and inquires, that recognizes time and space and the material limitations, that slowly systematizes, that formulates, that eventually arrives at a science of logical statement that shall shape and define the scheme and structure that is to underlie, penetrate and support the form of an art work." Expression is the physical embodiment of the emotional experience which gives beauty and communicative power to the creation. "Exuberant in life and movement, free, supple, active, dramatic, changeable, it is the part of Expression to clothe the structure of art with a form of beauty; for it is the perfection of the physical, the physical itself, and the uttermost attainment of emotionality." Thus the spiritual, intellectual and emotional must be bound together in a complete harmony; the whole process must be a unitary impulse, "for otherwise and without this unitary impulse our expression, though delicate as a flower, our thinking as abstract as the winds that blow, our imagination as luminous as the dawn, are useless and unavailing to create:—they may set forth, they cannot create."

Creative activity, then, somewhat as in the process above described, grows organically and naturally out of experience. It cannot spring by a purely intellectual process out of sets of objective criteria such as rules of proportion or rules of composition. The word "composition" was anathema to Sullivan, because to him architecture is not composition, but growth and organization. Similarly "proportion" as a set of rules for the achievement of an harmonious relationship of parts is false and artificial: "proportion is a result, not a cause. It may be imprisoned for a while in architectural ratios, but it does not reside in them." Sullivan insisted on architecture as *organic* in nature, meaning it must have the quality of life because it is an embodiment of life.

"All life is organic. It manifests itself through organs, through structures, through functions. That which is alive acts, organizes, grows, develops, unfolds, expands, differentiates, organ after organ, structure after structure, form after form, function after function. That which does not do these things is in decay! This is a *law*, not a word! And decay proceeds as inevitably as growth:— functions decline, structures disintegrate, differentiations blur, the fabric dissolves, life disappears, death appears, time engulfs— the eternal night falls. Out of oblivion into oblivion—so goes the drama of created things—and of such is the history of an organism." [11]

If true creation cannot be learned in already created formulae, but must be the result of the growth of the power to experience and embody, a necessary corollary is that architectural design, in itself, cannot be taught directly. It can be taught only indirectly through bringing out in the student the creative power which a full and vivid experience insures. In other words, one does not *learn how* to create beauty; one *becomes the kind of person* who can and does create it. While this doctrine may seem at first glance discouraging, since it upsets our whole notion of education as something literal and formal and susceptible of strictly rational management, it is in reality the most optimistic of all doctrines, for it asserts that true creative power is potential in all mankind; genius is normal, not abnormal, if we would only release ourselves from artificial and false training. The conception of architectural education as mere lesson-learning is responsible for most of our present-day architectural ills.

"I know that the secret of our weakness lies primarily in the utterly purposeless education we have received. I know that the architectural schools teach a certain art or method of study in which one is made familiar with the objective aspects and forms of architecture. I know that this is, as far as it goes, conscientiously and thoroughly done. But I also know that it is doubtful, in my mind, if one student in a thousand emerges from his school possessed of a fine conception of what architecture really is in form, in spirit and in truth: and I say that this is not primarily the student's fault. I know that before entering his architectural school he has passed through other schools and that they began the mischief: that they told him grammar was a book, algebra was a book, geometry another book, geography, chemistry, physics still others;

they never told him, never permitted him to guess for himself how these things were actually intense symbols, complex ratios, representing man's relation to Nature and his fellowman; they never told him that his mathematics, his geography, his chemistry and physics, came into being in response to a *desire* in the human breast to come nearer to nature;—that the full moon looked round to the human eye ages before the circle was dreamed of.

"Our student knows to be sure, as a result of his teaching, that the Greeks built certain-shaped buildings, that the Goths built certain-shaped buildings, and that other peoples built other buildings of still other shapes. He knows, moreover, a thousand and one specific facts concerning the shapes and measurements and ratios of the whole and the parts of said buildings, and can neatly and deftly draw and color them to scale. He moreover has read in the philosophies, or heard at lectures, that the architecture of a given time gives one an excellent idea of that time.

"This, roughly speaking, is the sum total of his education, and he takes his architectural instruction literally, just as he has taken every other form of instruction literally from the time he was a child:—because he has been told to do so, because he has been told that architecture is a fixed, a real, a specific, a definite thing, that it's all done, that it's all known, arranged, tabulated and put away neatly in handy packages called books. He is allowed to believe, though perhaps not distinctly so taught, that, to all intents and purposes, when his turn comes, if he wishes to make some architecture for Americans or for this generation at large, he can dip it out of his books with the same facility that dubs a grocer dipping beans out of a bin. He is taught by the logic of events that architecture in practice is a commercial article, like a patent medicine, unknown in its mixture and sold to the public exclusively on the brand.

"He has been seriously taught at the school, and has been encouraged in this belief by the endorsement of people of culture, that he can learn all about architecture if he but possess the attributes of scholarship and industry. That architecture is the name of a system of accredited, historical facts as useful, as available, and as susceptible to inspection as the books of a mercantile house." [12]

"Better no architectural school than schools of the kind we have. Better the vulgarest of homely vernaculars than learned folly of speech. Indeed, a *true vernacular* in our art is what you are to seek: a sane, an organic art of expression, which shall arise from you, and from the heart of hearts of your land and people." [13]

What, then, should a proper architectural education be like? It must, in Sullivan's thought, be an education whereby subjective values are built up naturally and spontaneously out of immediate objective experience. It should foster the desire to absorb and to emit; the desire to receive and to create. This should begin as one of the earliest parts of the curriculum of a general education. Such an inter-play of in-taking and out-giving is certainly not to be found in books as such, but rather in direct contact with Nature—contact so close that the result is not merely sensuous experience, but a communion with, an entering into the soul of Nature. Education at present is submission to the authority of forms of thought accumulated in the past, with no thought of testing them in the light of the present. Architectural schools, in Sullivan's view, are teaching artificial and objective canons rather than the subjective significance of architecture.

But if the old objective canons are to be abandoned, what is to be substituted for them? Evidently architectural design, according to this new conception, must be an exceedingly flexible matter. Any rule which is set up must be as fundamental and all-embracing as the fundamental unity of life itself; it must be a rule which allows place for both objective and subjective values; it must permit the utmost individual creative freedom. Sullivan's life-long search in architecture was for a "rule so broad as to admit of no exceptions." This rule, as he evolved it from his experience with Nature, is the simple one that *form follows function*. To Sullivan, this was simply natural law. It was a direct adaptation of a great biological principle to the sphere of architecture. Unfortunately, this rule sounds simpler than it really is. Taken at its face value, it was accepted by some of Sullivan's contemporaries, and has been more widely accepted since, as the text of modern "functionalist" theory, and has frequently been perverted into something which Sullivan never intended. A similar fate befell Cézanne's phrase, that "all nature can be reduced to terms of the sphere, the cone, and the cylinder"; as employed by the Cubists, it by no means comprehended Cézanne's theory of painting. Thus the truths of one generation become the clichés of the next, as Sullivan himself realized:

". . . formulas are dangerous things. They are apt to prove the undoing of a genuine art, however helpful they may be in the beginning to the individual. The formula of an art remains and becomes more and more rigid with time, while the spirit of that art escapes and vanishes forever. It cannot live in text-books, in formulas, or in definitions." [14]

To Sullivan, "function" meant, first and most obviously, the use to which a building is put. As straight utilitarianism, this was nothing new, having been proclaimed as a mode of architectural design by previous nineteenth-century writers; in combination with Sullivan's virulent attacks on eclecticism, it was, however, of new force. It meant, simply, that architectural form will express the purpose of the building which it clothes; the function of a library is different from that of a railroad station, and that of a church different from that of a residence. This is elementary. Their disposition of masses, of openings, their treatment of decorative detail—everything about them should proclaim that they are what they are. A library will not attempt to look like a Gothic cathedral, nor a railroad station like a Roman bath, nor a bank like a classic temple. Secondly, it meant that architectural form will express the structural nature of a building. If it has a steel frame, this should be expressed, not made to look like solid masonry construction. If the structure of a building demands a blank wall, the wall should be left blank, not interrupted by false windows or other features of structural origin for the sake of symmetry or rhythm or other qualities of purely formal design. In short, architecture should be first of all honest and truthful.

This all sounds very simple. But there are complex overtones. Just what is the "use" to which a building is put? If it is a house, certainly it will minister to more than creature comforts; it will have to satisfy something more than physiological man; it will be more than "a machine to live in." It must contribute insofar as possible to man as an intellectual, an emotional, a spiritual being. In short, the word "function" meant to Sullivan the *whole life* that would go on in a building. Similarly, structure has imaginative and emotional qualities. For example, an office building is two hundred feet tall in terms of finite measurements. There is inherent in this physical fact the emotional overtone of loftiness; this loftiness must be given expression, and when it is the structural nature of the building is enhanced, clarified, given human meaning. It will be noted that Sullivan never talks about the *revelation* of function and structure, but the *expression* of function and structure. This means the "expression or symbolization of a thought, feeling, or quality"; certainly nothing merely utilitarian or mechanical is here. Furthermore, with regard to the expression of parts of a building, Sullivan says specifically, "you should add, that, if the work is to be organic the function of the part must have the same *quality* as the function of the whole, and the parts, of themselves and by themselves must have the quality of the mass— must partake of its identity."

Sullivan's functionalism, then, means something far more than mechanism and utilitarianism. It means that a building must be organic, unitary, that it must have life; it means that a building must express intellectual and emotional and spiritual realities. The fact that he insists that expression grow out of actual experience keeps him tied to earth; but in his insistence on expressiveness as well as on adequacy he goes beyond pure functionalism as it exists in its most bald form today; that is a form which he would have considered as unsensitively materialistic as the eclecticism which he so passionately condemned.

"We may talk for years on the inter-relationship of function and form, and get only an average and a fairly good start. But it will be a right start, I believe. We may, perhaps, see where the end lies, but it will be, like a star in the sky, unreachable and of unknown distance; or it will be like life itself, elusive to the last, even in death. Or it will be like a phantom beacon on a phantom stormy sea; or as a voice calling afar in the woods; or, like the shadow of a cloud upon a cloud, it will remain diaphanous and imponderable, floating in the still air of the spirit." [15]

"I value spiritual results only. I say spiritual results precede all other results, and indicate them. I can see no efficient way of handling this subject on any other than a spiritual or psychic basis.

"It is for this reason that I say all mechanical theories of art are vanity, and that the best of rules are but as flowers planted over the graves of prodigious impulses which splendidly lived their lives, and passed away with the individual men who possessed these impulses. This is why I say that it is within the souls of individual men that art reaches its culminations. This is why I say that each man is a law unto himself; and that he is a great or a little law in so far as he is a great or a little soul.

"I regard spiritual facts as the only permanent and reliable facts—the only solid ground. And I believe that until we shall walk securely upon this ground we can have but little force or directness of purpose, but little insight, but little fervor, but little faith in material results." [16]

In a narrow functionalism there would be no place for ornament on a building. Sullivan himself asserted that it would be greatly for our aesthetic good if we should refrain entirely from the use of ornament for a period of years, but this only as a purgative measure, in order that the remains of ornamental detail of previous ages persisting in our architecture might be completely eliminated, and the way prepared for the "production of buildings well-formed and comely in the nude." But he felt that a truly appropriate system of ornament is desirable, and that an architecture completely lacking in ornament cannot realize its highest possibilities. Ornament is the most subtle and gracious aspect of expression; after the basic form of the building has been made in itself expressive, the creative impulse should be carried on into the ornament. It will be organic, growing out of the mass rather than applied to it, expressing the nature of its material, and partaking of the fundamental rhythms of the building itself. But it will appear, not as something merely receiving the spirit of the structure, but as a thing expressing that spirit by virtue of differential growth. Furthermore, it follows that a certain kind of ornament should appear on a certain kind of structure ("just as a certain kind of leaf must appear on a certain kind of tree"), and that the ornamental systems of buildings of various sorts should not be interchangeable between these buildings. Buildings should possess as marked an individuality as that which exists among men. Ornament is no more a closed system of forms than are the structural parts and the ever-changing uses to which buildings are put. It should grow in endless variety from man's imagination, inspired by Nature.

"The decoration of a structure is in truth, when done with understanding, the more mobile, delicate and sumptuous expression of the creative impulse or identity basically expressed in the structure; it is the further utterance, the more sustained and delicate rhythmical expression thereof. For the *new architecture* a new decoration must evolve to be the worthy corollary of its harmonies, a decoration limitless in organic fluency and plasticity, and in inherent capacity for the expression of thought, feeling and sentiment. And when this power of plastic modulation, of rhythmical fluency, shall characterize your expression, throughout the entire being of a structure, you will have arrived at the heights of that art of expression I wish you to attain." [17]

*Society.* But even though man as an individual achieves the experience which is given forth through the crucible of personality as creative activity, and every product of creative activity is stamped with its own and its author's individuality, yet the sanction and the worth of this achievement is not individual but social. Higher even than the individual is the social order, and this, to Sullivan, meant true Democracy. Like Whitman before him, Sullivan was an ardent believer in the democratic ideal. By Democracy he meant, not the extant American government and social system, nor even an ideal political system, but a perfect social order in which the political system is of relatively minor import because man shall have become more perfect in brotherhood, in love, and in character. This he believed to be possible of achievement, like genius in creative expression, through right education. In fact, the only valid education he termed democratic education. Opposing the forces leading toward true Democracy are all anti-social manifestations, which he lumped together under the term Feudalism. It is important to realize the comprehensiveness of these two terms in Sullivan's thinking. Like his conception of functionalism, they embrace far more than is ordinarily included in the definition of the words themselves. They are symbols of positive and negative, constructive and destructive forces in the social order. All social manifestations, such as architecture, education, business, religion, are estimated by Sullivan as either Democratic or Feudal.

The two principles on which a Democratic society rests are individual freedom and individual responsibility.

"We live under a form of government called Democracy. It is of the essence of Democracy that the individual man is free in his body and free in his soul. It is a corollary therefrom, that he must govern or restrain himself, both as to bodily acts and mental acts; —that in short he must set up a responsible government within his own individual person. It is the highest form of emancipation—of liberty physical, mental and spiritual, by virtue whereof man calls the gods to judgment, while he heeds the divinity of his own soul. It is the ideal of Democracy that the individual man should stand self-centered, self-governing—an individual sovereign, an individual god." [18]

"Personal responsibility and personal accountability must, absolutely, be cardinal doctrines in every branch of our education, if democracy is to survive. Educational methods in general must take cognizance of this principle, and hence prepare the youthful individual for his coming responsibilities—first, by making him aware of the nature of those responsibilities, and second, by training his character as well as his mind to accept and meet them." [19]

Architecture is to be judged by social principles. "Architecture is not merely an art, more or less well or more or less badly done, it is a social manifestation. If we would know why certain things are as they are, in our architecture, we must look to the people; for our buildings as a whole are an image of our people as a whole, although specifically they are the individual images of those to whom, as a class, the public has delegated and entrusted its power to build. Therefore by this light, the critical study of architecture becomes, not the study of an art—for that is but a minor phase of a great phenomenon—but, in reality, a study of the social conditions producing it, the study of a new type of civilization. By this light the study of architecture becomes, naturally and logically, a branch of social science." [20] Similarly, the study of the history of architecture becomes, not a history of "styles," but a history of civilization. "To begin with, disabuse your mind of this word 'styles.' It is a misnomer, or at the least reckoning, it is a term devoid of genuine significance. If for the word 'style' we substitute the word 'civilization' we make at once a pronounced stride in advance toward an intelligent understanding of the values of the historical monuments of architecture. Bear also in mind, that while the continued and customary use of the word 'styles' tends to confirm a popular notion that there were in the past *many* architectures, there is now, as ever there has been and as ever there will be, but *one architecture,* of which the so-called styles were and are variants expressive of differences and changes in civilization." [21] Style is really the crystallization of the thought of certain peoples, done more or less consciously, but unerringly. It is valid only for the time and people which created it.

The function of the architect is primarily a social one: "The true function of the architect is to initiate such buildings as shall correspond to the real needs of the people: . . . to vitalize building materials, to animate them with a subjective significance and value, to make them a visible part of the social fabric, to infuse into them the true life of the people, to impart to them the best that is in the people." Yet instead of this, the majority of our architects, lost in a morass of artificial learning, false social standards, and a fear of reality turn backward to the imitation of past "styles."

"American architecture is composed, in the hundred, of ninety parts aberration, eight parts indifference, one part poverty and one part Little Lord Fauntleroy. You can have the prescription filled at any architectural department-store, or select architectural millinery establishment." [22]

"Yet there is a certain grim, ghastly humor in it all; for instance:—A banker sitting in a Roman temple; railway tracks running into a Roman bath; a Wall Street broker living in a French chateau; a rich vulgarian living in a Trianon; a modern person living in a Norman castle; a hive of offices built up of miscellaneous crippled fragments of ancient architecture, firmly fastened to a modern steel frame; university buildings with battlements and towers, but no cross-bow-men. Libraries that might be mistaken for banks, hospitals that might be taken for libraries, department stores that might be taken for hotels; a Doric column proposed as a memorial to the hardy American Pioneer; the suggestion to transform the city of Washington into a modern Rome, and to make of the Potomac an American Tiber. The suggestion in general that if anything in particular is to be done it shall be done in the most unnatural way:—in other words, like some other thing, some prior thing, that bears no traceable relationship to it. We see: factories with Corinthian columns; domes upon 'pure Greek' buildings; Greek temples set upon the tops of office buildings; façades of Roman temples inserted in the middle of apartment buildings; Northern dwellings in the South; Southern dwellings in the North;

buildings at variance with climate, or purpose—'architecture' lugged to buildings and pasted thereon wherever place may be found. And all these things meaningless, the real building always obscured, never revealed:—all purposeless, all in essential bad faith, all masquerade, scene-painting, theatrical, presumptuous— all discordant, even riotous, inept even where quiet and 'scholarly' —all inept—all an imposition upon honest intelligence." [23]

"I urge that you cast away as worthless the shop-worn and empirical notion that an architect is an artist—and accept my assurance that he is and imperatively shall be an interpreter of the national life of his time. If you realize this, you will realize at once and forever that you, by birth and through the beneficence of the form of government under which you live—that you are called upon, not to betray, but to express the life of your own day and generation. That society will have just cause to hold you to account for your use of the liberty it has given to you, and the confidence it has reposed in you. You will realize, in due time, as your lives develop and expand and you become richer in experience, that a fraudulent and surreptitious use of historical documents, however suavely presented, however cleverly plagiarized, however neatly re-packed, however shrewdly intrigued, will constitute and will be held to be a betrayal of trust. It is futile to quibble, or to protest, or to plead ignorance or innocence, or to asseverate and urge the force of circumstances. Society is, in the main, honest—for why should it not be?—and it will not ask and will not expect you to be liars. It will give you every reasonable and legitimate backing, if you can prove to it, by your acts, that artistic pretension is not a synonym for moral irresponsibility. If you take the pains truly to understand your country, your people, your day, your generation; the time, the place in which you live:—if you seek to understand, absorb and sympathize with the life around you, you will be under-

stood and sympathetically received in return. The greatest poet
will be he who shall grasp and deify the commonplaces of our life:
—those simple, normal feelings which the people of his day will
be helpless, otherwise, to express:—and here you have the key with
which, individually, you may unlock in time the portal of your
art." [24]

[1] Lewis Mumford: *The Brown Decades,* p. 143.

[2] In 1933 Mr. George G. Elmslie turned over all the original manuscripts
and typed copies of Sullivan's writings in his possession to the Burnham
Library of the Art Institute of Chicago. This constitutes a nearly complete
collection of his writings, and it is augmented by the original drawings for
the plates of "A System of Architectural Ornament" and many other interesting items of Sullivaniana.

[3] *Autobiography,* p. 221.

[4] *Autobiography,* p. 257.

[5] A. W. Barker: "Louis H. Sullivan, Thinker and Architect," *Architectural Annual,* 2nd edition, p. 49, 1901.

[6] Foreword to *The Autobiography of an Idea.*

[7] "Natural Thinking: A Study in Democracy." 1905.

[8] *Kindergarten Chats.* 1901–02.

[9] "Natural Thinking: A Study in Democracy." 1905.

[10] *Kindergarten Chats.* 1901–02.

[11] *Kindergarten Chats.* 1901–02.

[12] "Emotional Architecture as Compared with Classical." 1894.

[13] *Kindergarten Chats.* 1901–02.

[14] *Kindergarten Chats.* 1901–02.

[15] *Kindergarten Chats.* 1901–02.

[16] "What is the Just Subordination, in Architectural Design, of Details
to Mass?" 1887.

[17] *Kindergarten Chats.* 1901–02.

[18] "The Young Man in Architecture." 1900.

[19] *Kindergarten Chats.* 1901–02.

[20] *Kindergarten Chats.* 1901–02.

[21] *Kindergarten Chats.* 1901–02.

[22] "The Young Man in Architecture." 1900.

[23] "Natural Thinking: A Study in Democracy." 1905.

[24] Address to the Chicago Architectural Club, May 30, 1899.

# VIII. A CRITICAL ESTIMATE

THE general conception of the importance and significance of an architect depends largely, after all, on what has been written about him by eminent scholars and critics. Granting that a serious lack of detailed information has impeded the formation of a just appraisal, the fact remains that Sullivan's life and work have received scant recognition at the hands of our scholars and historians. As remarked in the Foreword, some of his work was enthusiastically hailed by the more discerning critics of the nineties, but in general he was then and has since been regarded as something of a freak—a genius perhaps, doubtless a well-meaning enthusiast with some talent, but out of touch with stern practical realities and inevitably destined to a life of failure. His career has been regarded as an interesting by-path, off the main highway of our architectural development.

Most of these views need not concern us since they were patently so short-sighted. A more interesting interpretation, however, appeared in an article written in 1925 by a great historian of American architecture, Mr. Fiske Kimball.[1] In my opinion this interpretation was wrong, but it was important as one of the first serious attempts to place Sullivan in relation to his times, and because it suggests a method of approach to an estimate of Sullivan's significance. Quoting from the article: "The coherence of the realistic treatment of the subject matter of modern life by Sullivan and his fellows was with the work of the realistic schools of the nineteenth century in painting and sculpture, in literature and music. Under the domination of science, the painting of Monet and the impressionists, the sculpture of Carpeaux and Rodin, the music-drama of Wagner, the novels and plays of Flaubert, Zola, Tolstoi, and Ibsen, all sought characteristic beauty through truth to nature, rather than abstract beauty through relations of form. Against this domination of art by science, there had been a reaction even before 1890. Cézanne let anatomy and photographic foreshortening in painting give way to formal organization; sculpture became 'archaic' and geometrical; there was a renaissance of verse, of 'absolute' music. The counterpart in architecture has been a renewed interest in unity and simplicity of form, as against a functional or dynamic emphasis. As in previous great periods of abstract composition of mass and space, the fifteenth and eighteenth centuries, there has been a reversion to the classic elements, regarded as a universal language of elementary geometric simplicity. Beginning in New York in the eighties with Joseph Morrill Wells, Stanford White, and McKim, triumphing at the Chicago Fair, the movement, American in its genesis, is now pressing on to foreign conquests. . . . Instead of the forerunner of the new century, Sullivan, we now see, was the last great leader of the old. He was the Monet; Wells the Cézanne. Like Monet, living on into another age, he was within his lifetime already an old master."

There are three points in this argument which demand discussion: first, that Sullivan's theory of architecture is essentially scientific in nature and that he belongs with the nineteenth-century school of realistic artists; second, that the dominant tendency of twentieth-century art has been a search for abstract beauty through geometric relationships of 'pure form'; and third, that the Classic and Renaissance revivals of McKim, Mead & White and the architecture of the World's Columbian Exposition may be taken as the most characteristic evidence in the field of architecture of this essential twentieth-century tendency.

The character of nineteenth-century art cannot be discussed at length here, but it is safe to say that it was by no means exclusively dominated by science. The nineteenth century, conscious of the limitations of the "age of reason," sought reality in new directions. Science and romanticism, although apparent opposites, were merely two phases of this search, like the two faces of a single coin. Science was a search for reality in the world of "facts," eliminating from consideration the humanistic values which earlier centuries had cherished to such an extent. In asserting that every fact and every relationship of facts perceivable by the human senses, augmented by the telescope, microscope, and sundry other implements, are fundamental truths, it sets up a series of absolutes which are now being disproved by scientists themselves, and which, even if they were not, are as quixotic as the sheerly logical absolutes of the seventeenth century, for they could make no effective working contact with that which lies beyond science. Thus the conflict between science and religion.

Romanticism, on the other hand, was an attempt to apprehend reality by means of emotional experience rather than by rational calculation. Its strength lay in the recognition of the validity of emotional experience as an avenue to reality; its weakness lay in its tendency to deny the validity of rational or scientific knowledge, and in its intense and narrow pursuit, to bog down in the emotional experience without achieving the reality. There was in it an intent to be intense, which of course failed of success, and romantic art tended, not to express a new sense of reality, but to "just plumb express." Emotional inspiration is not spun out of the individual consciousness by sheer will-power, it must come as the natural coloring of the normal experiences of life.

The romantic was usually too intense; the scientist too literal. The result was a general lack of a common outlook on life, a point of view, which might have served as the source of a genuine style in art. This accounts for the disparateness, not to say chaos, of nineteenth-century artistic manifestations. There were the "Realist" and the "Romantic" schools in sculpture and painting, and there were individual artists who were a little of both. In architecture, there was the succession of "styles" on the one hand— Classic, Gothic, French Empire, Renaissance, Byzantine, Romanesque, or what have you; and the development of iron construction, fireproofing, high buildings, plumbing, and technical progress in general on the other.

In architectural criticism, the same dichotomy of values was evident. The romantic criticism tended to evaluate architecture for its "emotional" qualities. In principle this might have been very fruitful; in practice it usually failed as romanticism itself failed, and for the same reasons. Instead of seeking the real emotional qualities inherent in buildings themselves, it paraded a mélange of ethical, literary, naturalistic and sentimental values associated with buildings either by accident or fancy. Ruskin, dean of the romantic critics, was chief offender in this respect. The criticism arising out of the realistic, or scientific, point of view is more interesting since it bears a closer superficial relationship to Sullivan's theory of functionalism. Viollet-le-Duc, greatest of the realistic critics, appealed constantly to "truth" in architecture. He saw that the stupid imitation of various past styles represented a complete failure to understand the lessons of the history of architecture, and he ridiculed the rules of the academies. In their place he sought to establish the rule of structure: that "all architecture proceeds from structure, and the first condition at which it should aim is to make the outward form accord with that structure." [2] Moreover, he constantly stressed the importance of satisfying new needs by new types of buildings, and of employing all the new materials and devices which science and the machine placed at the disposal of architecture. But Viollet-le-Duc's conception of architecture was too much thought, too little felt. His own practice, though sound and sensible and scientific to a degree, lacked the urge of a vital inspiration. His experiments in structure, conditioned doubtless by his enthusiasm for the Middle Ages and by the limited size of available members in structural iron, were in reality adaptations of the forms of late medieval vaulting to execution in iron. His decorative forms, although he strove for originality, have the family appearance of nineteenth-century Gothic.

The realistic criticism in general followed the biologic theory of the adaptation of form to function and environment, emphasizing conditions of use and structure as a means of achieving architectural beauty. It was closely allied to the mechanism and utilitarianism of contemporary philosophy. But it fell short in two essential respects. First, it was largely a matter of words rather than accomplishment; although the engineers showed the way in practice, few who professed themselves to be architects were willing to follow it to an entirely realistic conclusion. And second, even if they had, the result would not have been architecture, for the realistic attitude was too narrow. Architectural design is not a mechanical registration of the mere facts of structure and function, however honest this method may be. Although Sullivan advocated an honest acceptance and recognition of the facts of function and structure as the right *start* toward creative architectural expression, he then added, "We must now heed the imperative voice of emotion." It should be quite evident, both from his buildings and his writings, that Sullivan's conception of architecture is more than scientific, and that in searching something more than literal truth to nature he goes far beyond the nineteenth-century "realistic" artists.

Are we to assume that the dominant tendency of twentieth-century art has been a search for abstract beauty through geometric relationships of "pure form"? In my opinion such an interpretation is quite erroneous. In searching for a more universal interpretation of nature than his predecessors the Impressionists had given, through simplifying natural forms to their fundamentals of mass and color, Cézanne was working from actual visual experience toward an organic order, not from purely rational concepts of form toward a geometric order. This was the same kind of abstraction that Sullivan employed in reducing a building program to its simplest and most universal terms as an approach to creative expression. And this, it seems, was the really significant abstractionist tendency of the twentieth century, despite the fact that Cézanne was followed by the Cubists, and Sullivan by the "Classicists."

And as to the Classic and Renaissance revivals of McKim, Mead & White and the architecture of the World's Columbian Exposition representing this characteristic twentieth-century interest, it should be unnecessary to point out that such architecture was neither organic nor geometric nor abstract; it was specific and representational, and represented the worst phase of nineteenth-century academicism rather than the best expression of the twentieth century. It would be more proper to say that McKim, Mead & White were the Lord Leightons, the Alma-Tademas, the Bouguereaus; Sullivan the Cézanne.

Such an estimate, made in 1925, was undoubtedly influenced by the still-persisting dominance of the historic styles and the academic attitude toward architecture. There was little evidence, in this country at least, to show that Sullivan had been anything more than a voice crying in the wilderness. But the rapid advance of modernism in architecture during the past ten years makes it far easier now to see Sullivan in his true rôle of prophet, and there is every indication that he will achieve growing recognition as modern architecture continues to develop and as its significance is realized.

How may we view his achievement today, both as to theory and practice? As far as the influence which they exerted goes, it seems fairly certain that Sullivan's thinking was of far greater import than his buildings. It is difficult to dissociate the two, since the buildings were always, in a measure, practical demonstrations of his theories. But his system of thinking when expressed in stone and mortar was conditioned by a great many factors which tended to obscure its real significance. In the first place, thinking deals in generalizations, whereas building deals, literally and figuratively, in specifications. No matter how much Sullivan sought to reduce a building program to its simplest and most universal terms and to achieve a "true normal type," he was always confronted by the myriad facts of costs, materials, site, patronage, etc.—factors which tended to make the specific solution in each case obscure the general principle of design. To be sure, he welcomed these practical conditions and sought through them the architectural expression which he desired, but the results were not always transparently clear to those who saw his buildings. The Wainwright Building was the nearest approach to a "true normal type" and undoubtedly the most influential building which he designed. Yet as has been pointed out before its influence on other architects was a matter of superficials rather than fundamentals, results rather than methods, copying rather than thinking. Thus what Sullivan did in the Wainwright Building—which was merely to show the way—resulted in little or no further progress, but rather a crystallization into a formula of design.

Moreover, there is little doubt that the bare logic of Sullivan's architectural thinking would have been more clearly apparent to his contemporaries if his buildings had not been adorned by such lyrical enrichments in the way of ornament. These were fascinating and baffling, oftentimes totally inexplicable, and they attracted such attention that Sullivan was considered more as an ornamentalist than as an architect. That ornament was essential to Sullivan's architecture is undeniable, but it was nevertheless confusing. And like his general system of design, it was copied quite widely by lesser architects who could employ it imitatively but not creatively.

His genuine influence on the practice of architecture in this country, however, was far more extensive than is generally supposed. Acting first through his disciples of the "Chicago School," it later spread so widely as almost to establish a new vernacular style in the cities and small towns of the Middle West. Travelling through the suburbs of Chicago and in towns and cities from Buffalo to western Iowa, one frequently sees a "Sullivanesque" or else a "prairie style" building, done perhaps by a local architect of no distinction but bearing unmistakable evidence of influence from the source.

As a great architect, Sullivan had followers. There were not many; he was too uncompromising in his strictures of timidity or stupidity to be a popular idol and too urgent in his architectural proselytizing to be a comfortable companion to the mildly progressive. But there were a few hardy spirits who admired him immensely as a prophet and as a man, and these came to be known as the "Chicago School." Sullivan wanted no one to be an imitator, not even of himself, and his success as a teacher may be indicated by the way in which his followers for the most part acquired his manner of thinking rather than his specific stylisms. Some of them, armed with this start, progressed into individual styles only remotely resembling Sullivan's. From the middle nineties up to the time of the War, and even after, there was a small but vital current of fine work produced by these men, forceful and individual in character and always fundamentally sound. Perhaps the best of them were Frank Lloyd Wright, George Elmslie, George B. Maher, and Walter Burley Griffin. Others who received Sullivan's impress to a greater or less degree were: William Gray Purcell, who worked in partnership with Elmslie several years; Hugh Garden; Dwight Perkins; Robert C. Spencer; George Dean; Richard E. Schmidt, for many years in partnership with Hugh Garden; William Drummond; and Claude Bragdon. Until the work of the Chicago School is better known than it is at present, however, it will be impossible to estimate correctly the real force and character of Sullivan's direct practical influence in this country.

The influence of Sullivan's thinking was more belated, but more powerful. It did not at once reverse the current of academic theory inherited from previous generations, but it added to it new streams of vitality and freshness, and ultimately turned its direction into a new channel. The process has taken more than a generation, and is perhaps not yet complete, yet it is sufficiently advanced so that the significance of Sullivan's thinking can be far more readily understood today than it was ten years ago.

The major destructive attack in Sullivan's writings was on eclecticism in architecture, and the major constructive effort, we have seen, was the idea of a functional and organic architecture. How valid was his attack on eclecticism? Many of us have not made up our minds on this issue, and unless we do—or until we do—it will be quite impossible either to judge Sullivan or to understand modern architecture. The historic styles are still imitated in the architecture of today—indeed probably the greater part of current building is eclectic in nature—but our placid acceptance of this attitude toward architecture is beginning to be shaken by doubts. What are we to believe?

The word "eclecticism" comes from the Greek *eklegein,* meaning to select, to choose. It commonly implies the selection of certain elements from differing sources as a means of achieving a balanced and inclusive point of view. For instance, in philosophy, it is "the practice of choosing doctrines from various or diverse systems of thought in the formation of a body of acceptable doctrine" (Webster). In architecture, it commonly means the use of historic styles in modern architecture. Properly, the term should be employed with respect to a single building composed of elements from various historic styles, but in practice it is applied to the mass of modern buildings as a whole, representing a variety of historic styles. These two usages have been defined by Mr. Henry-Russell Hitchcock as "eclecticism of style" and "eclecticism of taste," respectively.

We may examine the former first. It might be represented by a church whose architect sought a new kind of eclectic architectural beauty that would satisfy admirers of the Classic, the Byzantine, the Gothic, and the Renaissance styles by combining Byzantine domes on pendentives over the nave and choir, a Renaissance dome raised on a drum over the crossing, a classic temple façade decorated along the raking cornice with Gothic pinnacles and crockets —and possibly a caryatid porch using the Beau Dieu of Amiens and Notre Dame de Paris as supports. It is easy to smile at such a fancy, and we are sure that it wouldn't be beautiful, but why?

The answer may be given, perhaps, in terms that would satisfy both the formalist and the functionalist, as follows: a work of art is a unity which is more than the sum of its parts, a unity dependent on the inter-relationship of its parts in a coherent artistic (organic) order. The whole is more than the sum of its parts because it has abstract (functional) significance. Interchange two or three parts, or take them away, and the unity is lost. Take one part away from the whole and it is not partially beautiful in proportion of its size to the size of the whole—it is not beautiful at all. It has ceased to have the aesthetic significance with which its relationship to the whole had endowed it. Thus a Doric column used by itself, as a memorial, for instance, is an aesthetic absurdity. Going one step further, the attempt to recombine elements of diverse architectural styles that have ceased to exist as stylistically or architecturally significant—to recombine these into a new style that will represent the diverse beauties of the original styles is obviously childish. It is like attempting to create a new literature out of a dozen different languages the words of which have ceased overnight to have any meaning. It is bound to result in something that has neither the merits of the individual beauties of the past on the one hand, nor of a genuine new beauty on the other; it will be neither flesh, fowl, nor good red herring. Eclecticism of style may be dismissed as of no significance—and this would be generally agreed upon today, for our eclecticism is predominately an eclecticism of taste, in which "pure" rather than hybrid styles are employed.

This more general form of eclecticism may be defined as "different styles used contemporaneously, but each building all in one style." Used in this sense, the degree of style-imitation varies considerably in modern buildings. There may be an almost exact imitation of a specific historic building, such as the Nashville Parthenon; there may be an imitation of only part of a specific historic building, such as the caryatid porch on the old Buffalo art museum; there may be an imitation of a general style but of no specific building, such as the Washington cathedral; or there may be an imitation of historic detail on a building which could not possibly be taken entirely as of a past style, such as the Chicago Tribune Tower. All of these differ in degree, not in essence; they all represent an attempt to borrow forms of beauty from the past.

Another aspect of modern eclecticism is that the historic styles are always modified in an attempt to accommodate them to modern functional needs and to take advantage of the latest modern' improvements in construction. In other words, the designers are changing the architecture without changing its expression. It must be granted at once that there is no single modern building that does not involve some kind of change in function and technique from its stylistic original. The Nashville Parthenon is not a temple to Athena; it is made of composition stone instead of Pentelic marble; machines were used in its construction instead of hand labor; in short, there are an infinite number of differences between it and the Parthenon at Athens. But one would not deny that it is Greek in style in spite of these differences. The dormitories at Yale have steel frames, concrete floors, squash-courts and electric lights, and in that sense they are not medieval buildings; but the aesthetic intention is that they should *look* medieval.

Thus limited, we conceive eclecticism to mean the imitation of historic styles, in varying degrees of strictness and completeness, for the achievement of architectural beauty; and the concurrent employment of modern engineering for the achievement of modern functional demands. Used in this sense, how valid is eclecticism as a mode of architectural design?

There are several arguments commonly proposed by the advocate of eclecticism. Let us take his side for a moment. In the first place, he would argue, insofar as architecture is an art (and we assume it is), beauty is a necessary part of it. Beauty has no necessary relationship to matters of function and structure in building; these are merely the practical conditions, and the practical and the aesthetic may be clearly separated and distinguished. For instance, the Doric column in a Greek temple is a beautiful support, but from the structural standpoint it is inefficient because it is unnecessarily heavy and because the vertical flutes which give it such an appearance of grace and strength are structural liabilities rather than structural assets. Beauty evidently has no relationship to structural fact here. The flying-buttress on a Gothic cathedral is eminently a structural feature, yet that it could serve the ends of beauty quite apart from structural necessity is attested by the fact that in many cathedrals the topmost row of flying buttresses counters no vault thrusts whatever, and indeed is anti-structural, for the buttresses would push the tops of the walls inward unless a concealed structural device under the roof were employed to prevent this. Instances from the architecture of the Renaissance could be multiplied a thousand-fold, and all would tend to show that architectural beauty has no necessary relationship to function and structure.

What is beauty, then, and how is it achieved? Beauty, the eclecticist would answer, is something that pleases the eye, and it is not something which is invented overnight but is inherited from the past. The enduring kind of beauty, like morality, is a social product that has taken thousands of years in development. It represents the accumulated experience of the race. We have the priceless lessons of the past on which to build: restraint, simplicity, unity, balance, careful refinement of proportion and detail. These lessons are embodied in the great architecture of the past. To abandon them would be to abandon our cultural heritage and to risk almost certain chaos. It is folly to talk of "modern civilization" as though it began a generation, or even a century, ago; our roots are in the past, we owe a great debt to Greece, to Rome, as also to the Middle Ages and the Renaissance. And to employ the architectural styles of these epochs is no more than a just and appropriate recognition of that debt. Culture is a continuous stream, and cultural expressions, like architectural styles, are valid for us today because they represent our roots in the past.

These arguments in favor of eclecticism are plausible; taken together they may be quite convincing. But they are nevertheless hopelessly wrong. Let us attempt to answer them one by one, if need be sentence by sentence.

In the first place, in asserting that beauty is an essential element of architecture, we too often run into the error that it is the *primary* element, necessarily implying that requirements of function and structure be subordinated to it wherever there may be conflict. Architecture is a utilitarian art, not a fine art, and utility is far more important than beauty. It might well be worth inquiring of every building, first: "Was it worth building?" and only secondarily "Was it beautifully done?" But the question of the priority of beauty or utility is in any case an academic one. For in all the great architecture of the past the practical and the aesthetic have not been separated. Function, structure, and beauty have been wholly integrated. Beauty has been derived *out* of function and structure, not *in spite* of them. The separation of the practical and the aesthetic into two separate categories is false and artificial and at the root of most of our architectural follies. We may use the example of the Doric column, which embodies perfectly the relationship between structure and beauty: its weight and its vertical flutes are no mere aesthetic accident, they are essential because they symbolize or express the structural purpose and nature of the column as a support. The column must not only be strong; it must *look* strong. It is not a matter of "pleasing lines" or "nice proportions"; the reason why we find the column pleasing is not because of any inexplicable magic of proportion, but because it is an apt structural *expression*. A similar explanation might be given of the top-of-wall buttresses in a Gothic cathedral. Although mechanically unnecessary, they carry to completion the expression of the general structural system of the cathedral. They demonstrate perfectly the close relationship between structure and beauty.

What about the second argument? Is architectural beauty something of permanent value, representing the accumulated experience of the race? Assuredly it is, but what conclusions are we to draw from this fact? Quoting an argument in defense of eclecticism: "If, then, it is true that we are co-heirs with our brothers who have not yet emigrated of the glory and the grandeur that were Greece and Rome; if the same blood that joined thrust to thrust in the dizzy groins of Amiens, that hung the vault of St. Peter's so little below the firmament, that flecked the streets of London with the white fingers of Wren's churches—if the same blood flows in our veins, why should we give up this royal heritage? It is ours as much as it is theirs across the seas." Does this then mean that we should *imitate* that heritage? Indeed we have the Parthenon and Amiens Cathedral, just as we have Dante and Chaucer; it would be folly to destroy them, but why build a modern Parthenon any more than write a modern novel in medieval Italian or Chaucerian English? Was the beauty of the Parthenon or of Amiens achieved by imitating something that had been done centuries before in another country and for another civilization? Architectural beauty may be permanent, but it is not permanently the same. The succession of the historic styles, representing an ever-changing beauty, is ample demonstration. How can we argue that because our whole culture and civilization has its roots in the past we are therefore to perpetuate the ancient forms of cultural expressions? True enough, culture is a continuous stream, but this very analogy suggests that it is not fixed, but changes. As a matter of fact, only limited portions of past culture are valid for us today. We owe much to Hebraic culture, but those aspects of it which are the expression of a primitive pastoral society are no longer valid for us today: who believes in eye-for-an-eye justice? We owe much to Greek culture, but Platonic philosophy is contrary to our whole notion of reality. We owe much to the Middle Ages, but its scholastic theology is of little concern to us. In short, only such inheritances from the past as are valid for us today form a part of our culture, and is this not properly *modern* culture, rather than ancient cultures? And if, in actual practice, the eclectic architect is to defend his use of the historic styles as a recognition of our debt to the past, how is he to explain the fairly frequent use of Islamic, Oriental, Maya-Aztec, and even Neolithic styles today, when the debt of modern culture to these sources is almost nil? Also, in what way does a skyscraper, a railroad station, a cinema theatre represent a debt to the past—and therefore why should we make them Gothic, or Classic, or Louis XIV?

We have studied much the "priceless lessons of the past," but the one all-embracing and vital lesson that we have failed to learn is that architecture in all the great periods of the past has been a creative art, not an imitative art. In previous periods, architects and master-builders have always built, simply, modern architecture. They did not consciously elect to build in the "Gothic style" in thirteenth-century France; they built in the best manner of their day. Genuine beauty, and genuine style, are the result of a creative approach to architecture: the determination of building needs, the solution of technical problems, and the evolution of an architectural form appropriate to and expressive of those needs and those technical solutions. And since the needs and problems of one age are different from those of another age, the architectural form will change correspondingly. Of course this change will progress slowly, just as language and civilization develop slowly, and it is more important to respect the tradition of the past than to attempt to invent a new beauty without reference to that tradition. "Strive not," said Sullivan, "after what is called originality. If you do you will be starting in exactly the wrong way. I wish distinctly to impress upon you that what I am advocating and what I am striving to point out to you is a normal development. . . ." [3]

But "respect for tradition" does not imply a slavish subservience to the past. "I do not see and cannot comprehend how anyone who truly reveres the great works of the past can for a moment dream of imitating them. . . . Nor does it avail in the least to say that such imitation professes the reproduction, in our day, of forms of ancient origin which the world has long held noble. That is merely a superficial begging of the question; an out and out sophistication. For in the first place, you can revivify nothing that is dead; and the men who made these works have long gone to their fathers. Those men alone could have made other works in the same *spirit*. In the second place, if your mind is lofty enough to come into a genuine companionship and communion with theirs, you will wish, through such communion, to do what they did, namely, to *produce;—to interpet the life of your own people*." [4]

The most deplorable result of the eclectic approach is that it kills or stultifies creative thinking and imagination. Is "creative genius" so rare? It is my conviction that a genuine attitude toward architecture, calling for a creative approach to every new problem, will in itself generate creative power, or reveal it where it exists. The imagination does not act where there is no stimulus and no necessity for it to act. But where it is clearly demanded its quiescent potentialities may become apparent. Herein lies the possibility of a future architecture that will be creative, not imitative; genuine, not spurious. It may seem that we have devoted overmuch attention to slaying the dragon of eclecticism. But that it is no imaginary dragon, let him read who runs through the streets. It should be clearly evident that Sullivan's thinking in this connection is almost as much needed today as it was a generation ago.

Is Sullivan's constructive theory of an organic and functional architecture still valid today? We have only to look at the "new architecture" as it has developed in Europe and America during the past few years. Clean-cut, angular, of an elementary simplicity, swift in line, it seems to answer the description of a new kind of architecture. The form-relationships bear no resemblance to the mode of "abstract composition" of the past; there is neither mass, specious monumentality, rigid symmetry, nor formal division of wall-surfaces, there is no classic decorative detail, nor Gothic; in fact, there is almost no decorative detail whatsoever. In short, the organization of these new forms seems to rely on some entirely different principle than that of following rules of composition and grammars of detail. What that principle is we have to find out only by consulting the buildings themselves or the architects who designed them. And the testimony is well-nigh universal. LeCorbusier, Gropius, Lurcat, Miës van der Rohe, Oud, and many others have stated and reiterated their faith, and it is always the word "functionalism." Some have only partially understood it, and have regarded functionalism as a matter of pure mechanical and utilitarian revelation in architectural design, and the results in buildings have been hard and bare and mean; but in the hands of creative artists it has been a weapon of tremendous force.

Once it is understood that the conception of functionalism, as set forth by Sullivan and as it has since grown, calls for emotional and spiritual realities as well as physical realities, much confused thinking will be avoided. But they must be realities, not fantasies. It may be questioned by the skeptical: Of what use is such a theory of functionalism? If it is so broad as to include all kinds of vague mystical values and so loose as to permit all kinds of exceptions to mechanical truth—of what use is it in design?

The answer is definite. Functionalism as a theory of architecture is of absolutely no use to an architect who seeks a convenient rule-of-thumb, or set of proportions, or vocabulary of detail, or other prescription for our architectural ailments. It cannot make up for the lack of creative imagination, the lack of the ability to conceive strictly and to execute rightly. Functionalism is in reality only a system of thinking. It cannot by itself make a great architecture, but it can make a great architecture possible. That style has changed, and will continue to change, there can be no doubt. Even since Sullivan's day we have new needs, new materials, and new techniques, and all are finding expression. But Sullivan did not lay down a style to follow, he proposed a system of thinking, a system which is finally bearing fruit in a genuine modern architecture.

Sullivan may have been a great prophet of modernism, but he was equally a great traditionalist, for what he urged was the renewal of architecture as a creative art, based on those fundamentals which have always existed in the great architecture of the past. His work and his thinking have made architecture once more plastic in the hands of the creative artist, and rendered possible the development of a true architectural style in the present day.

[1] Fiske Kimball: "Louis Sullivan, an Old Master," *Architectural Record*, vol. 57, no. 4, pp. 289–304, April, 1925.

[2] Viollet-le-Duc: *Lectures on Architecture*, James Osgood & Co., Boston, 1881. Vol. II, p. 3.

[3] "The Young Man in Architecture." 1900.

[4] *Kindergarten Chats*. 1901–02.

# APPENDIX

# DANKMAR ADLER—
# A BIOGRAPHICAL SKETCH

DANKMAR ADLER was born at Stadt Lengsfeld, a small village about twenty miles southwest of Eisenach, Germany, on July 3, 1844. His father, Liebman Adler, was a teacher in the public school and cantor in the local synagogue. His mother died at his birth. It was this circumstance which caused his father to christen him Dankmar, a compound of the German *dank* (thanks) and the Hebrew *mar* (bitter). Liebman Adler came to America in 1854 and settled in Detroit, where he became the rabbi and cantor of the Jewish Congregation Bethel. Dankmar went to the public grammar schools in Detroit, and later to the Detroit and Ann Arbor high schools. Failing to pass the entrance examinations for the University of Michigan, he essayed a short apprenticeship in an exchange and shipping business which turned out to be unsatisfactory.

When about fifteen years old the boy had taken a course of instruction in free-hand drawing given by Mr. Jules Melchers, father of Gari Melchers. Dankmar's aptitude in the work and his special interest in architectural drawing led his father to place him under the tutelage of John Schaefer, a Detroit architect. Mr. Schaefer gave the youth a conventional training in the five orders, and taught him to draw a great deal of the alleged Byzantine and Romanesque ornament which was so popular in that day. His theoretical instruction in the origin and history of architectural styles, however, seems to have been rather eccentric. Among Mr. Schaefer's teachings was one to the effect that in erecting buildings devoted to the worship of God, our ancestors designed them in a style intended to illustrate by an upward tendency of lines their aspiration toward God, and that for this reason the style was called "Goddik," which has since been corrupted by the ignorant to "Gothic."

Dankmar Adler stayed but a short time with Mr. Schaefer, then in 1859 entered the office of E. Willard Smith in Detroit. In a brief autobiography written toward the end of his life Adler speaks of Mr. Smith as "an honor to his profession." "By him and by his able assistant, Mr. John M. Bancroft, now of Brooklyn and then just graduated from Dartmouth, I was introduced to a systematic study of architectural history and of the philosophy of architectural design, as also to neatness and finish of rendering of drawings and water colors. Under their guidance I worked indefatigably, often twelve and sixteen hours per day, and laid the foundation of whatever actual knowledge of my profession I may have acquired."

In May, 1861, Liebman Adler moved to Chicago to become the rabbi of the Congregation Anshe Ma'ariv. There he served with great distinction for over thirty years, and had the satisfaction of seeing the construction of a new synagogue designed by his son and Louis Sullivan just before his death in 1892. In the summer of 1861 Dankmar sought employment in a Chicago architect's office, but found such a dearth of business that at first no one was willing to take him on either as draftsman or student. After a few months, however, he obtained a position as draftsman in the office of Augustus Bauer. His stay in this office was cut short by the Civil War.

In July of 1862 Adler enlisted in Company M of the First Regiment of Illinois Light Artillery. He saw service in the campaigns of 1862, 1863, and 1864 in Kentucky, Tennessee and Georgia, and participated in some of the hardest fought battles of the war. Although wounded, he escaped serious injury and illness. Being an artillery man, he found opportunity to secrete several scientific and historical books in ammunition caissons, and to study them at intervals over several months. During the last nine months of his service he was detailed as draftsman in the Topographical Engineer's Office of the Military Division of Tennessee, where he had valuable engineering experience. Thus when he was discharged in August, 1865, he had made good use of his military experience in training himself for his future career.

After the war Adler returned to the office of Augustus Bauer in Chicago for a short time. He then entered the office of O. S. Kinney, first as a draftsman, then later as foreman. Kinney had quite a large practice in churches, schoolhouses and courthouses in various parts of Ohio, Indiana, and Illinois. Adler rose rapidly in the office, and on Mr. Kinney's death in 1869, he and A. J. Kinney, a son, assumed joint responsibility in finishing up the uncompleted commissions in the office.

In January, 1871, Adler left the younger Kinney to accept a partnership with Edward Burling. Adler worked with Burling for nine years, under the several firm names of E. Burling & Company, Burling & Adler, and Burling, Adler & Co. Eight months after the partnership was formed Chicago was devastated by the great fire of October, 1871. This meant a great rush of work in all architects' offices, and Burling & Adler played an important part in the reconstruction of the city. The Chicago *Tribune* of October 9, 1872, recorded that during the year following the fire Burling & Adler had designed a hundred buildings aggregating 8,875 feet of street frontage and costing $4,022,000.

In 1872 Adler married Dila Kohn, daughter of Abraham Kohn, a pioneer settler in Chicago and founder of the Anshe Ma'ariv Congregation.

The practice of Burling & Adler during the nine years from

1871 to 1879 was extensive. The office records of the firm have been lost, but the names of at least thirty-five buildings designed by the firm have been preserved. Among these were the old Chicago Tribune Building, at Dearborn and Madison Streets; Delmonico's, at Madison and Clark; Kingsbury Hall on Clark Street; the Garrett Biblical Institute on Lake Street; and the Methodist Church Block on Clark Street. Adler, as chief designer, was in charge of the drafting-room, but he was also responsible for a large part of the supervision of construction so that the designs of only nine or ten buildings were done by his own hand. One of these was the Sinai Temple at Indiana Avenue and 21st Street, Chicago, built in 1875–76; this building was completely remodelled in 1892 by the firm of Adler & Sullivan. During the course of years Burling progressively loaded more responsibilities on Adler, a policy which at first incurred his resentment, but which soon gave him an experience and resourcefulness in handling the business which might otherwise have taken many years to acquire. Adler gained the confidence of the firm's clients, and by the end of the decade felt himself in a position to cut loose from the partnership with Burling.

In 1879 Adler established an independent practice, and very shortly after this Louis Sullivan first entered the office as a draftsman. During the year 1879 Adler devoted most of his time to the design and construction of the Central Music Hall, on the corner of Randolph and State Streets, Chicago. It was torn down in 1900 to make room for the retail store of Marshall Field & Company. The building was entirely the work of Adler, except for the decorative organ grilles in the theatre, which were designed by Sullivan. It was finished in December, 1879. Adler was always very proud of this building, his first independent architectural undertaking, and wrote of it in his autobiography: "It has proved in many respects one of the most successful buildings ever erected in Chicago, and I shall always consider it the foundation of whatever professional standing I may have acquired."

The Central Music Hall was the ancestor or prototype of a long series of theatres designed by the firm of Adler & Sullivan; in it were already exemplified the acoustic principles which determined the lay-out of orchestra, balconies, and ceiling in all of the later theatres by the firm. The building as a whole was a combination of stores, offices, and theatre in a six-story structure costing $215,000. Although the exterior was not distinguished, it was nevertheless superior to most of its contemporaries, and in certain parts, notably the window groupings on the north side, quite dignified and forceful. John Wellborn Root, one of Chicago's most sensitive and discerning architects, wrote just before his death: "Among the highest in all the profession stands Mr. Adler. . . . Of late Mr. Adler has passed the artistic crayon to Mr. Sullivan, but work designed by him in the earlier days—such as the building at 97 Dearborn Street, and the Central Music Hall—shows a strength, simplicity, and straightforwardness, together with a certain refinement, which reveal the true architect. No professional man has pursued a more consistent and dignified course than he, and no man is more respected by his confrères." [1] The chief merits of the design lay in the arrangement of the interior and the acoustic properties of the theatre. The seventy offices were well-lighted and easily accessible; in addition to the theatre there was a concert hall of about one-quarter its size; and all these in combination with stores and the necessary corridors and stairs were so disposed as to gain much praise at the time as an example of practical planning. The acoustic properties of the theatre became nationally famous. These were partially due to the upward curve of the orchestra floor, greater than the mere line of vision required, to the transverse beams projecting below the ceiling, and to the lateral curve of the ceiling itself.

Adler's knowledge of acoustics seems to have been unique in that generation, and he must have obtained it entirely by himself, since it was not a subject which had been dealt with to any extent in scientific writings. Sullivan, discussing the Grand Opera House of a few years later, said: "I then discovered what Mr. Adler knew about acoustics. I did not know anything about them, and I did not believe that anyone else did. . . . It was not a matter of mathematics, nor a matter of science. There is a feeling, perception, instinct —and that Mr. Adler had. He had a grasp of the subject of acoustics which he could not have obtained from study, for it was not in books. He must have gotten it by feeling." [2] Adler learned a lesson in acoustics from the Mormon Tabernacle in Salt Lake City, which he visited in 1885. Woltersdorf gives the following account: "The Mormon Tabernacle, of turtle-back form, was conceived and executed by ship-builders, who thought of the structure as the upset hull of a ship, with rounded ends. Years after it was built necessity demanded more seating accommodations and a balcony was constructed at one end. Because of the rounded roof-end, head room would have been lacking in the last rows of seats, had the balcony been constructed and tied up against the dome. So this balcony was kept a few feet free of the rear wall, with the result that the sound waves under the balcony impaired in no way the acoustics at that end. Adler visited the Mormon Tabernacle to study the acoustics. He saw this balcony; he saw, too, the open back. He visited the place during services, when the tabernacle was crowded, and found that the open end was a great advantage to the acoustics and that the movement of sound waves was unimpaired. This theory was later reflected in much of Adler's theatre work, where open stair wells were constructed in back of the house to allow movement of the sound up the well. All this was before the day of city ordinances separating the auditorium from foyer by means of fireproof walls." [3]

Adler served at various times as a consultant on acoustics. He was called to Milwaukee to improve the acoustics of the Pabst Theatre, which he did simply by inserting transverse beams projecting below the ceiling of the auditorium to break up the reflecting area. He was also consultant on acoustics to the architect of Carnegie Hall, New York, when this building was designed by William B. Tuthill in 1889.

With the completion of the Central Music Hall, Adler found himself crowded with other commissions. The Borden Block, the Grand Opera House, the John Borden residence and other structures were in the office. It was at this time that he turned over more and more of the actual designing to Sullivan, and Sullivan's rise from draftsman to chief draftsman to junior partner to full partner was rapid, as related in the first chapter. Although the first few buildings after the Central Music Hall were nominally the work of Dankmar Adler & Company, Sullivan had an important part in their design, and for practical purposes they may be considered the first works of the firm of Adler & Sullivan.

During the years of the partnership with Sullivan, Adler was not only the guiding hand in all the business and engineering aspects of the work of the firm, but he was also very active in forwarding the activity of various architectural associations and in establishing a code of professional standards. When the Western Association of Architects was formed in a meeting at Chicago in November, 1884, Adler was elected first treasurer of the organization, and at the meeting in St. Louis in November, 1885, he was elected its second president. He remained an active member to the end of his life, serving on innumerable committees and on the board of directors. He was a member of the Chicago Chapter of the American Institute of Architects, and of the Illinois State Association of Architects, acting as president of the latter body in 1886–87. One of his most important achievements as a member of the latter organization was the proposal of a state law for the recognition and legal control of the architectural profession. The law which he drafted was enacted in 1888, resulting in the formation of the Illinois State Board of Examiners of Architects, and Adler was appointed its first chairman by the Governor. In 1890, when the Chicago Chapter of the A.I.A. and the Illinois State Association of Architects decided to merge into a single body to be called the Illinois Chapter of the A.I.A., Adler was one of the incorporators and helped to write the charter which was granted on February 8, 1890. He was at the same time elected treasurer of the new organization. He was active in the revision of the building ordinances of the City of Chicago, introducing many reforms of lasting benefit. He was also interested in the cause of labor and served on boards of arbitration in labor disputes on numerous occasions.

Adler wrote extensively during these years—chiefly on technical or legal aspects of architecture, or official reports in connection with his positions in architectural associations. There is hardly a single issue of the *Inland Architect* in the eighties and early nineties without some committee report, or treasurer's statement, or presidential address, short or long, from his pen. He wrote several papers on theatres, such as "The Paramount Requirements of Large Theatres" (an address before the Twenty-first Annual Convention of the A.I.A. in 1887), "The Chicago Auditorium" (a complete description, published in 1892), and "Convention Halls" (1895). On technical and legal questions, he wrote "Comment on Skyscrapers" (an extensive analysis of building foundations, 1891), "Light in Tall Office Buildings" (1893), and "Municipal Building Laws" (1895).

The account of the dissolution of the partnership of Adler & Sullivan in July, 1895, has been related in Chapter V. Adler's connection with the Crane Company as consultant architect and general sales manager was of short duration, and he returned to the independent practice of architecture in January, 1896. With the help of his two sons, Abraham and Sidney, he built several factories and warehouses for the Meyer Estate, the Chicago Dock Company, the Wright & Hill Linseed Oil Company, and some grain elevators. In 1897 and 1898 he designed a group of three buildings for the Morgan Park Military Academy, in a suburb of Chicago. The following year he designed the Isaiah Temple, at 45th Street and Vincennes Avenue, Chicago. The cornerstone was laid on September 11, 1898, and the building was dedicated on March 17, 1899. It was cruciform in shape, with the main façade fronted by a slightly projecting portico with four Ionic columns carrying an entablature and balustrade. This was his last work.

During his last years he continued to write, chiefly on technical and legal questions. Among the articles of this period were "Slow-Burning and Fireproof Construction" (1896), "The Influence of Steel Construction and of Plate Glass Upon the Development of Modern Style" (1896), "Architects and Trade Unions" (1896), "The Tarsney Act and the American Institute of Architects" (1897), and "The Architect's Duty Regarding the Enforcement of the Tarsney Law" (1897). Unfortunately, some of his articles were never completed. The writer has had the privilege of examining several manuscripts of considerable interest. One is a brief typewritten autobiography, written about 1894, from which Montgomery Schuyler drew some of the information for his review of the work of Adler & Sullivan published in 1895. Another is an article on "The Proposed Technological School of the University of Chicago from the Standpoint of the Architect," already in galley proof, but never published. Most interesting is a series of uncompleted articles on such terms as "Acoustics," "Auditorium," "Concert Hall," and "Theatre" in preparation for the Architectural Encyclopedia at the time of Adler's death. The parts finished show a great amount of scientific knowledge and a wealth of practical experience, and it is to be regretted that such authoritative discussions could not have been brought to completion.

Adler died on April 16, 1900, at the age of fifty-six.

## BIBLIOGRAPHY OF ADLER'S WRITINGS IN CHRONOLOGICAL ORDER

"Paramount Requirements of Large Theatres." A paper read before the 21st Annual Convention of the A.I.A. in Chicago, October 19, 1887. *Building Budget,* vol. 3, no. 9, pp. 127–129, October, 1887.

"Comment on Skyscrapers." *The Economist,* vol. 5, no. 26, pp. 1136–1138, June 27, 1891.

"The Chicago Auditorium." *Architectural Record,* vol. 1, no. 4, pp. 415–434, April–June, 1892.

"Some Notes upon the Earlier Chicago Architects." *Inland Architect & News Record,* vol. 19, no. 4, pp. 47–48, May, 1892.

"Tall Office Buildings—Past and Future." *Engineering Magazine,* vol. 3, no. 6, pp. 765–773, September, 1892.

"Light in Tall Office Buildings." *Engineering Magazine,* vol. 4, no. 2, pp. 171–186, November, 1892.

"Municipal Building Laws." *Inland Architect & News Record,* vol. 25, no. 4, pp. 36–38, May, 1895.

Open letter announcing his retirement from the profession. *Inland*

*Architect & News Record*, vol. 25, no. 6, p. 61, July, 1895.

"Convention Halls." *Inland Architect & News Record*, vol. 26, no. 2, pp. 13–14, September, 1895; and vol. 26, no. 3, pp. 22–23, October, 1895.

"Slow-Burning and Fireproof Construction." *Inland Architect & News Record*, vol. 26, no. 6, pp. 60–62, January, 1896; and vol. 27, no. 1, pp. 3–4, February, 1896.

"Architects and Trade Unions." *Inland Architect & News Record*, vol. 27, no. 4, p. 32, May, 1896.

"Influence of Steel Construction and of Plate Glass upon the Development of Modern Style." A series of four papers read before the 30th Annual Convention of the A.I.A. at Nashville, Tenn., October 21, 1896, by J. W. Yost, Dankmar Adler, George F. Newton, and Robert D. Andrews. Adler's paper is a critique of the doctrine "form follows function." *Inland Architect & News Record*, vol. 28, no. 4, pp. 34–37, November, 1896.

"Open Letter to Chicago Mason Builders." *Inland Architect & News Record*, vol. 29, no. 1, pp. 2–3, February, 1897.

"The Tarsney Act and the American Institute of Architects." *Inland Architect & News Record*, vol. 30, no. 4, p. 36, November, 1897.

"The Architect's Duty Regarding the Enforcement of the Tarsney Law." *Inland Architect & News Record*, vol. 30, no. 5, pp. 46–47, December, 1897.

[1] John Root: "Architects of Chicago," *Inland Architect & News Record*, vol. 16, no. 8, p. 91, January, 1891.

[2] Sullivan: "Development of Construction," *The Economist*, vol. 55, no. 26, p. 1252, June 24, 1916.

[3] Arthur Woltersdorf: "Dankmar Adler," *Western Architect*, vol. 33, no. 7, p. 75, July, 1924.

# CHRONOLOGICAL LIST OF
## BUILDINGS

*Buildings designed by the firm of Adler & Sullivan and by Louis Sullivan independently are listed as nearly as possible according to the chronological order of their construction. The following data are given for each building: name, address, date of construction, whether the building is still standing, its present name if different from the original one, dimensions of the ground plan, and cost or approximate cost. Addresses given are the present ones; for many of the buildings in downtown Chicago these are different from addresses given in old accounts, since the street numbers and in many instances the names of the streets have been changed since the buildings were constructed. Except for a few lists of buildings, no office records of the firm of Adler & Sullivan or of Louis Sullivan have been preserved; this has made the compilation of a complete list of their works difficult and many items of information are lacking. All data available through records of building permits, descriptions in old periodicals, correspondence with former owners, or examination of the buildings themselves have been included in this list.*

1. Central Music Hall, SE corner of Randolph & State Streets, Chicago. 1879. Dankmar Adler & Co. Demolished in 1900. Lot: 125′ x 151′. Cost: $156,463.

2. Borden Block, NW corner of Randolph & Dearborn Streets, Chicago. 1879–80. Dankmar Adler & Co. Demolished in 1910. Lot: 80′ x 90′. Cost: ca. $80,000.

3. Grand Opera House (remodelling), 119 North Clark Street, Chicago. 1880. Dankmar Adler & Co. Demolished in 1927. Cost: ca. $55,000.

4. John Borden residence, 3949 Lake Park Ave. Chicago. 1880. Dankmar Adler & Co. Still standing, now Vincennes Sanitarium.

5. Rothschild Store, 210 West Monroe Street, Chicago. 1881. Dankmar Adler & Co. Built for Max M. Rothschild, occupied by E. Rothschild & Bros. Wholesale Clothiers. Still standing, now the Milton F. Goodman Building. Lot: 50′ x 180′. Cost: $75,811.

6. Rosenfeld Building, SE corner Washington & Halsted Streets, Chicago. Built for Levi Rosenfeld in two sections: three-story section on east side of Halsted Street south to Meridian built in 1881 cost $42,850; five-story section occupying corner of the lot and extending 150′ east on Washington Street built in 1882 cost $92,091. Still standing.

7. Brunswick & Balke Factory (1881), Warehouse (1882), and Lumber-Drying-Plant (1883), entire block bounded by Orleans, Huron, Sedgwick & Superior Streets, Chicago. Still standing. Cost: $168,165.

8. Revell Building, NE corner of Wabash & Adams Streets, Chicago. 1881–83. Built for Martin A. Ryerson; long occupied by A. H. Revell Co. Still standing; lower stories remodelled in 1929. Lot: 116′ x 172′. Cost: $321,112.

9. Jewelers' Building, 15–19 South Wabash Ave. Chicago. 1881–82. Built for Martin A. Ryerson. Still standing. Lot: 58′ x 160′. Cost: $90,260.

10. Frankenthal Building, 141 South Wells Street, Chicago. 1882. Still standing. Lot: 22' x 72'. Cost: $21,407.

11. Hammond Library, 44 North Ashland Avenue, Chicago. 1882. Still standing, now Union Theological College. Lot: 43' x 65'. Cost: ca. $15,000.

12. Flat-building built for Max M. Rothschild, 3200 Prairie Ave. Chicago. 1882. Still standing. Lot: 19' x 74'. Cost: ca. $10,-000.

13. Henry Leopold residence, 2516 Indiana Ave. Chicago. ca. 1882. Demolished.

14. Sigmund Hyman residence, 2624 Wabash Ave. Chicago. ca. 1882. Demolished.

15. Knisely Store, Lake Street, Chicago. 1883. Built for Richard Knisely. Lot: 35' x 75'. Cost: ca. $16,000.

16. Three residences built for Max M. Rothschild, 3201–05 Indiana Ave. Chicago. 1883. Still standing. Lot: 50' x 65'. Cost: ca. $17,000.

17. E. L. Brand Store, Jackson Street, Chicago. 1883. Demolished. Cost: $3,000.

18. F. A. Kennedy & Co. Bakery, South Desplaines Street, Chicago. 1883–84. Cost: ca. $70,000.

19. Wright & Lowther Oil & Lead Mfg. Co., Chicago. 1883. Cost: ca. $40,000.

20. C. P. Kimball residence, 22 East Ontario Street, Chicago. 1883. Still standing, now "L'Aiglon" restaurant. Cost: ca. $45,000.

21. Sol Bloomenfeld residence, 8 West Chicago Ave. Chicago. 1883. Still standing, now "Cozy Hand Laundry."

22. Morris Selz residence, 1717 South Michigan Ave. Chicago. 1883. Still standing. Cost: ca. $30,000.

23. Charles H. Schwab residence, 1715 South Michigan Ave. Chicago. 1883. Still standing, much remodelled. Cost: ca. $18,000.

24. A. Halsted residence, Lincoln Avenue, Chicago. 1883. Cost: ca. $14,000.

25. Rubee Store, South Clark Street, Chicago. 1883. Cost: ca. $16,000.

26. Kauffmann Store, Lincoln Avenue, Chicago. 1883. Cost: ca. $10,000.

27. Schoolhouse, Marengo, Illinois. 1883. Cost: ca. $20,000.

28. E. L. Brand Building, East Jackson Street, Chicago. 1883. Demolished. Cost: ca. $15,000.

29. Three residences built for Max M. Rothschild, 32nd Street & Indiana Ave. Chicago. 1884. Still standing. Cost: ca. $12,000.

30. Three residences built for Mrs. N. Halsted, North Park Ave. Chicago. 1884. Cost: ca. $12,000.

31. Martin Barbe residence, 3157 Prairie Ave. Chicago. 1884. Still standing.

32. Abraham Strauss residence, 3337 Wabash Avenue, Chicago. 1884–85. Still standing. Cost: ca. $16,000.

33. Ryerson Building, 16–20 East Randolph Street, Chicago. 1884. Still standing. Lot: 68' x 171'. Cost: $152,127.

34. Troescher Building, 15–19 South Market Street, Chicago. 1884. Still standing, now the Daily Times Building. Lot: 80' x 80'. Cost: $90,614.

35. Knisely Building, 551–557 West Monroe Street, Chicago. 1884. Still standing. Cost: $86,928.

36. Zion Temple, SE corner Washington & Ogden Streets, Chicago. 1884–85. Demolished. Lot: 65′ x 115′. Cost: ca. $35,-000.

37. J. W. Scoville Building, 619–631 West Washington Street, Chicago. 1884–85. Still standing. Cost: $44,444.

38. Hooley's Theatre (remodelling), NE corner Randolph & LaSalle Streets, Chicago. 1884–85. Demolished 1927. Cost: ca. $50,000.

39. Chicago Opera Festival Auditorium, Interstate Exposition Building, Grant Park, Chicago. 1885. Demolished 1892.

40. McVicker's Theatre (remodelling), Madison Street, Chicago. 1885. Destroyed by fire, 1890. Cost: $95,074.

41. M. C. Stearns residence, Douglas Ave. Chicago. 1885. Demolished. Cost: ca. $8,000.

42. Benjamin Lindauer residence, 3312 Wabash Avenue, Chicago. 1885. Still standing. Cost: ca. $25,000.

43. Residence, Prairie Avenue & Gano Street, Chicago. 1885. Cost: ca. $13,000.

44. Henry Stern residence, 2915 Prairie Avenue, Chicago. 1885. Still standing. Lot: 25′ x 80′. Cost: ca. $13,000.

45. Samuel Stern residence, 2963 Prairie Ave. Chicago. 1885. Still standing. Cost: ca. $12,000.

46. Abraham Kuh residence, 3141 South Michigan Ave. Chicago. 1885. Demolished. Cost: ca. $10,000.

47. Mrs. Abraham Kohn residence, 3541 Ellis Ave. Chicago. 1885–86. Still standing.

48. Dankmar Adler residence, 3543 Ellis Ave. Chicago. 1885–86. Still standing.

49. Eli B. Felsenthal residence, 3545 Ellis Ave. Chicago. 1885–86. Still standing.

50. Hugo Goodman residence, 3333 Wabash Avenue, Chicago. 1885–86. Still standing.

51. Mrs. Eda Holzheimer residence, 3538 Ellis Ave. Chicago. ca. 1886. Still standing.

52. Gustav Eliel residence, 4122 Ellis Avenue, Chicago. ca. 1886. Still standing.

53. Peck Building, SW corner of LaSalle & Water Streets, Chicago. 1886. Demolished. Cost: $36,312.

54. West Chicago Club, 119 Throop Street, Chicago. 1886. Still standing, now Chicago Labor Temple.

55. Suburban Station, Illinois Central R. R., 39th Street, Chicago. 1886. Still standing.

56. Suburban Station, Illinois Central R. R., 43d Street, Chicago. 1886. Still standing.

57. Martin Ryerson Charities Trust Building, 318 West Adams Street, Chicago. 1886. Demolished. Cost: $100,282.

58. Selz, Schwab & Company Factory, NE corner of Superior & Roberts Streets, Chicago. 1886–87. Still standing. Lot: 111' x 204'. Cost: $75,773.

59. Wirt Dexter Building, 630 South Wabash Ave. Chicago. 1887. Still standing. Lot: 70' x 160'. Cost: $99,636.

60. Joseph Diemal residence, 3143 Calumet Ave. Chicago. 1887. Lot: 25' x 27'.

61. Springer Building (remodelling), corner of State & Randolph Streets, Chicago. 1887. Demolished.

62. John Kranz Building (remodelling), State Street, Chicago. 1887.

63. Mrs. Mary M. Lively residence, Oak Ave. Chicago. 1887. Lot: 20′ x 45′. Cost: ca. $4,500.

64. Auditorium Building, Chicago. 1887–89. Still standing. Lot: 187′ frontage on Michigan Ave., 362′ frontage on Congress Street, 162′ frontage on Wabash Ave. Cost: $3,-145,291.

65. Standard Club, SW corner of Michigan Ave. & 24th Street, Chicago. 1887–88. Demolished 1931. Lot: 60′ x 162′. Cost: $108,139.

66. Walker Warehouse, 200–214 South Market Street, Chicago. 1888–89. Still standing. Cost: $325,942.

67. Felsenthal Building, 63–71 North Canal Street, Chicago. 1889. Demolished 1908. Lot: 38′ x 150′. Cost: $32,022.

68. Ira A. Heath residence, 3132 Prairie Ave. Chicago. 1889. Still standing. Cost: ca. $15,000.

69. Wirt Dexter residence (addition), 232 Irving Ave. Chicago. 1889. Lot: 20′ x 50′. Cost: ca. $25,000.

70. Martin Ryerson Tomb, Graceland Cemetery, Chicago. 1889. Still standing.

71. Jewish Training School, 554 West 12th Place, Chicago. 1889–90. Still standing. Lot: 60′ x 100′. Cost: $48,730.

72. Crane Company Factory, Judd Street, Chicago. 1890. Demolished. Lot: 100′ x 203′. Cost: ca. $50,000.

73. Carrie Eliza Getty Tomb, Graceland Cemetery, Chicago. 1890. Still standing.

74. Louis Sullivan Cottages, Ocean Springs, Miss. 1890. Still standing, remodelled. Lot: 300′ x 1800′.

75. Three residences built for Victor Falkenau, 3420–24 Wabash Ave. Chicago. 1890. Still standing.

76. Opera House Block, Pueblo, Colorado. 1890. Destroyed by fire 1922.

77. Design for Opera House Block, Seattle, Wash. 1890. Never built.

78. Design for Hotel Ontario, Salt Lake City, Utah. 1890. Never built.

79. Das Deutsche Haus, Milwaukee, Wis. (remodelling). 1890.

80. Dooly Block, 111 West 2nd South Street, Salt Lake City, Utah. 1890–91. Still standing.

81. McVicker's Theatre, Madison Street, Chicago (remodelling). 1890–91. Demolished 1925. Cost: $106,120.

82. Wainwright Building, NW corner Seventh & Chestnut Streets, St. Louis. 1890–91. Still standing. Adler & Sullivan; Charles K. Ramsey, Assoc. Lot: 127′ x 114′. Cost: $561,-255.

83. Kehilath Anshe Ma'ariv Synagogue, SE corner of 33d Street & Indiana Ave. Chicago. 1890–91. Still standing, now Pilgrim Baptist Church. Cost: $91,005.

84. Chicago Cold Storage Exchange Warehouse, West Water Street between Randolph & Lake Streets, Chicago. 1891. Demolished 1902. Cost: $442,896.

85. Design for a Hotel, Chicago. 1891. Never built.

86. Design for an Apartment-hotel, South Michigan Ave. Chicago. 1891. Never built.

87. Design for Mercantile Club, St. Louis. 1891. Never built.

88. Design for Fraternity Temple, Chicago. 1891. Never built.

89. Schiller Building, 64 West Randolph Street, Chicago. 1891–92. Still standing, now Garrick Theatre Building, remodelled 1935. Lot: 80′ x 181′. Cost: $737,099.

90. J. W. Oakley Building, 141–143 West Austin Street, Chicago. 1892. Still standing, completely remodelled. Cost: $95,017.

91. James Charnley residence, 1365 Astor Street, Chicago. 1892. Still standing.

92. Albert W. Sullivan residence, 4575 Lake Park Ave. Chicago. 1892. Still standing.

93. Charlotte Dickson Wainwright Tomb, Bellefontaine Cemetery, St. Louis. 1892. Still standing.

94. Sinai Temple, SW corner of Indiana Ave. & 21st Street, Chicago. Remodelling. 1892. Demolished.

95. Passenger Station, Illinois Central R. R., New Orleans. 1892. Still standing.

96. Union Trust Building, NW corner of Seventh & Olive Streets, St. Louis. 1892–93. Adler & Sullivan; Charles K. Ramsey, Assoc. Still standing, now Central National Bank Building. Lot: 84′ x 127′. Cost: $631,076.

97. Design for Trust & Savings Bank Building, Seventh & Olive Streets, St. Louis. 1892–93. Adler & Sullivan; Charles K. Ramsey, Assoc. Never built.

98. St. Nicholas Hotel, Eighth & Locust Streets, St. Louis. 1892–93. Adler & Sullivan; Charles K. Ramsey, Assoc. Still standing, much remodelled. Cost: $334,187.

99. Victoria Hotel, Chicago Heights, Illinois. 1892–93. Still standing, remodelled.

100. Meyer Building, 307 West VanBuren Street, Chicago. 1893. Still standing, remodelled. Cost: $205,825.

101. Transportation Building, World's Columbian Exposition, Chicago. 1893. Demolished.

102. Stock Exchange Building, 30 North LaSalle Street, Chicago. 1893–94. Still standing. Lot: 101' x 181'. Cost: $1,131,555.

103. Guaranty Building, SW corner Church & Pearl Streets, Buffalo. 1894–95. Still standing, now Prudential Building. Lot: 93' x 116'.

*Dissolution of the partnership, July, 1895*

104. Bayard Building, 65–69 Bleecker Street, New York. 1897–98. Louis Sullivan; Lyndon P. Smith, Assoc. Still standing, now Condict Building.

105. Gage Building, 18 South Michigan Ave. Chicago. 1898–99. Still standing, remodelled. Louis Sullivan; Holabird & Roche, Assoc.

106. Schlesinger & Mayer Department Store, SE corner of State & Madison Streets, Chicago. Nine-story section on Madison Street, 1899. Twelve-story section on corner of lot and extending 150' south on State Street, 1903–04. Five southernmost bays on State Street, 1906, by D. H. Burnham & Co. Still standing, now Carson Pirie Scott Store.

107. Euston & Company Linseed Oil Plant, Blackhawk Street, Chicago. ca. 1899–1900.

108. Euston & Company Linoleum Plant, Chicago. ca. 1899–1900.

109. Crane Company Foundry & Machine Shop, SE corner Canal

& 12th Streets, Chicago. 1899–1900. Still standing, completely remodelled.

110. Crane Company Office Building, Canal Street & West 12th Place, Chicago. 1903–04. Demolished.

111. Store built for Eli B. Felsenthal, 701–703 East 47th Street, Chicago. 1905. Still standing.

112. National Farmers' Bank, NE corner of Broadway & Cedar Streets, Owatonna, Minn. 1907–08. Still standing, now Security Bank. Lot: 68′ x 154′.

113. Henry Babson residence, 230 Riverside Drive, Riverside, Ill. 1907. Still standing.

114. Mrs. Josephine Crane Bradley residence, 106 North Prospect St., Madison, Wis. 1909. Still standing, now Sigma Phi Fraternity House.

115. People's Savings Bank, 3d Ave. S. W. & 1st St. S. W., Cedar Rapids, Iowa. 1911. Still standing. Lot: 50′ x 90′.

116. St. Paul's Methodist Episcopal Church, 3d Ave. S. E. & 14th St. S. E., Cedar Rapids, Iowa. 1913–14. Still standing.

117. John D. Van Allen & Son Company Dry-Goods Store, NW corner 5th Ave. & So. 2nd St., Clinton, Iowa. 1913–15. Still standing.

118. Henry C. Adams Building, NW corner Moore & State Streets, Algona, Iowa. 1913. Still standing, now Druggists' Mutual Insurance Co.

119. Merchants' National Bank, NW corner 4th Ave. & Broad Street, Grinnell, Iowa. 1914. Still standing, now Poweshiek County National Bank.

120. Home Building Association Bank, NW corner West Main &

North 3d Streets, Newark, Ohio. 1914. Still standing, now Union Trust Company.

121. Purdue State Bank, State & Vine Streets, West Lafayette, Ind. 1914. Still standing.

122. People's Savings & Loan Association Bank, SE corner Court Street & Ohio Avenue, Sidney, Ohio. 1917–18. Still standing.

123. Farmers' & Merchants' Union Bank, NW corner James Street & Broadway, Columbus, Wis. 1919. Still standing.

124. William P. Krause Music Store and residence, 4611 Lincoln Ave. Chicago. 1922. Louis Sullivan; William C. Presto, Assoc. Still standing.

# A BIBLIOGRAPHY OF THE
# WRITINGS OF LOUIS SULLIVAN

*Listed in Chronological Order*

"Characteristics and Tendencies of American Architecture." A paper read before a meeting of the Western Association of Architects in St. Louis in 1885. Published in the *Builders' Weekly Reporter* (London) in 1885. No ref.

"Inspiration." A paper read before the Third Annual Convention of the Western Association of Architects in Chicago, November 17, 1886. Published in brochure by the Inland Architect Press, Chicago, 1886.

"What is the Just Subordination, in Architectural Design, of Details to Mass?" A symposium at a meeting of the Illinois Association of Architects in Chicago, April 2, 1887, with talks by Louis Sullivan, L. D. Cleveland, and O. J. Pierce, with a summary by Louis Sullivan. Published in the *Inland Architect & News Record*, vol. 9, no. 5, pp. 51–54, April, 1887, and in *Building Budget*, vol. 3, no. 3, pp. 62–63, April, 1887.

"Ornamentation of the Auditorium." A paper quoted in part in *Industrial Chicago*, vol. 2, pp. 490–491.

"Ornament in Architecture." *Engineering Magazine*, vol. 3, no. 5, pp. 633–644, August, 1892.

"Objective and Subjective." A paper read before the 28th Annual

Convention of the A.I.A. in New York, October, 1894. Published in brochure by the Inland Architect Press, Chicago, 1895.

"Emotional Architecture as Compared With Classical, a Study in Objective and Subjective." *Inland Architect & News Record*, vol. 24, no. 4, pp. 32–34, November, 1894.

"The Tall Office Building Artistically Considered." *Lippincott's*, vol. 57, pp. 403–409, March, 1896; *Inland Architect & News Record*, vol. 27, no. 4, pp. 32–34, May, 1896; *Western Architect*, vol. 31, no. 1, pp. 3–11, January, 1922.

"An Unaffected School of Modern Architecture: Will It Come?" *Artist* (N.Y.), vol. 24, pp. xxxiii–xxxiv, January, 1899.

Address to the Chicago Architectural Club, read at the Art Institute, Chicago, May 30, 1899. Unpublished.

"The Master." Part 2 of Inspiration series. Completed July 1, 1899. Unpublished.

"The Young Man in Architecture." A paper read before the Architectural League of America, June 12, 1900. Published in *The Brickbuilder*, vol. 9, no. 6, pp. 115–119, June, 1900; *Western Architect*, vol. 34, no. 1, pp. 4–10, January, 1925.

"Reality in the Architectural Art." *Interstate Architect & Builder*, vol. 2, no. 25, pp. 6–7, August 11, 1900.

*Kindergarten Chats. Interstate Architect & Builder*, vol. 2, no. 52–vol. 3, no. 51; 52 issues from February 16, 1901 to February 8, 1902. Sullivan's revision of June–December, 1918, edited by Claude Bragdon, published in book form by the Scarab Fraternity Press, 306 Marvin Hall, Lawrence, Kansas, 1934.

"Education." A paper read before the Annual Convention of the

Architectural League of America in Toronto in 1902. Unpublished.

"Sympathy—A Romanza." A short poem written about 1904. Unpublished.

"Natural Thinking: A Study in Democracy." A paper read before the Chicago Architectural Club, February 13, 1905. Unpublished.

"The Possibility of a New Architectural Style." A reply to an article by Frederick Stymetz Lamb on "Modern Use of the Gothic." *The Craftsman*, vol. 8, pp. 336–338, June, 1905.

"Form and Function Artistically Considered." A reprinting of "The Tall Office Building Artistically Considered" in the "Architectural Discussion" department of *The Craftsman*, vol. 8, pp. 453–458, July, 1905.

"What is Architecture? A Study in the American People of Today." *American Contractor*, vol. 27, no. 1, pp. 48–54, January 6, 1906. Reprinted in *The Craftsman*, vol. 10, no. 2, pp. 145–149; no. 3, pp. 352–358; and no. 4, pp. 507–513; May, June, July, 1906.

*Democracy: A Man Search*. A book in 44 chapters, ca. 180,000 words. First draft completed July 1, 1907; revision completed April 18, 1908. Unpublished.

"Is Our Art a Betrayal Rather Than an Expression of American Life?" *The Craftsman*, vol. 15, no. 4, pp. 402–404, January, 1909.

Letter replying to an article by Gutzon Borglum. *The Craftsman*, vol. 17, no. 3, December, 1909.

"Suggestions in Artistic Brickwork." Foreword to a pamphlet entitled "Artistic Brick," pp. 5–13, published by the Hydraulic-Press Brick Company, St. Louis. N.d. (ca. 1910).

"Wherefore the Poet?" *Poetry*, vol. 7, pp. 305–307, March, 1916.

"Development of Construction." A paper read before the Illinois Chapter of the A.I.A. Published in *The Economist*, vol. 55, no. 26, p. 1252, June 24, 1916; and vol. 56, no. 1, pp. 39–40, July 1, 1916.

*The Autobiography of an Idea.* Published serially in the *Journal of the American Institute of Architects*, June, 1922–August, 1923. Published in book form by the Press of the A.I.A., 1924; reprinted in the "White Oak Library" series, W. W. Norton, 1934.

*A System of Architectural Ornament According with a Philosophy of Man's Powers.* A series of nineteen plates drawn from January, 1922, to May, 1923. Published in folio by the Press of the American Institute of Architects, 1924.

"The Chicago Tribune Competition." *Architectural Record*, vol. 53, no. 2, pp. 151–157, February, 1923.

"Concerning the Imperial Hotel, Tokyo." *Architectural Record*, vol. 53, no. 4, pp. 333–352, April, 1923.

"Reflections on the Tokyo Disaster." *Architectural Record*, vol. 55, no. 2, pp. 113–117, February, 1924.

# GENERAL BIBLIOGRAPHY

*BOOKS*

Bragdon, Claude: *Architecture and Democracy*, Knopf (N.Y.) 1926. Ch. 4: "Louis Sullivan, Prophet of Democracy."

Dredge, James: A Record of the Transportation Exhibits of the World's Columbian Exposition of 1893, John Wiley & Sons (N.Y.) 1894.

Gilbert, Paul, and Bryson, Charles Lee: *Chicago and Its Makers*, Felix Mendelsohn (Chicago) 1929.

Glover, Lyman B.: *The Story of a Theatre*, R. R. Donnelley & Sons (Chicago) N.d. (ca. 1898).

Goodspeed Publ'g. Co.: *Industrial Chicago*, vols. I & II: The Building Interests. Chicago, 1891.

Meites, Hyman L. (ed.): *History of the Jews in Chicago*, Jewish Historical Society of Illinois (Chicago) 1924.

Monroe, Harriet: *John Wellborn Root*, Houghton, Mifflin & Co. (Boston) 1896.

Moore, Charles H.: *Daniel H. Burnham, Architect, Planner of Cities*, Houghton, Mifflin & Co. (Boston) 1921.

Mujica, Francisco: *History of the Skyscraper*, Archaeology and Architecture Press (Paris) 1929.

Mumford, Lewis: *The Brown Decades*, Harcourt Brace (N.Y.) 1931.

Schuyler, Montgomery: *Studies in American Architecture*, Harper & Bros. (N.Y.) 1892.

Tallmadge, Thomas E.: *The Story of Architecture in America*, W. W. Norton (N.Y.) 1927.

Woltersdorf, Arthur (ed.): *Living Architecture*, Kroch's (Chicago) 1930.

World's Columbian Exposition: Memorial Volume, Dedicatory and Opening Ceremonies, Stone Kastler & Painter (Chicago) 1893.

Wright, Frank Lloyd: *An Autobiography*, Longmans Green (N.Y.) 1932.

*PERIODICAL LITERATURE*

Anonymous: "Characteristics and Tendencies of American Architecture," a Note on a Paper Read Before the Western Association of Architects by Louis H. Sullivan. *Inland Architect & Builder*, vol. 7, no. 1, p. 6, February, 1886.

————: "The Standard Club's New Building." *American Architect & Building News*, vol. 25, no. 691, p. 137, March 23, 1889.

————: "The Chicago Auditorium." *American Architect & Building News*, vol. 26, no. 724, pp. 223–224, November 9, 1889.

————: "The Auditorium Building." *American Architect & Building News*, vol. 26. no. 731, pp. 299–300, December 28, 1889.

————: "Structures Designed by Louis H. Sullivan." *Interstate Architect & Builder*, vol. 2, no. 44, pp. 11–20, December 22, 1900.

————: "A Departure from Classic Tradition: Two Unusual Houses by Louis Sullivan and Frank Lloyd Wright." *Architectural Record*, vol. 30, no. 4, pp. 327–338, October, 1911.

————: "A Unique Church Building." *American Contractor*, vol. 32, no. 44, pp. 92–93, November 4, 1911.

————: "Louis Sullivan, the First American Architect." *Current Literature*, vol. 52, no. 6, pp. 703–707, June, 1912.

————: "A Sullivan Design That Is Not Sullivan's." *Western Architect*, vol. 20, no. 8, p. 85, August, 1914.

————: "St. Paul's Methodist Episcopal Church." *Western Architect*, vol. 20, no. 8, pp. 87–88, August, 1914.

————: "The Merchants' National Bank, Grinnell, Iowa." *Western Architect*, vol. 23, no. 2, p. 20, February, 1916.

————: "The 33d Annual Chicago Architectural Exhibition." *Western Architect*, vol. 29, no. 4, pp. 33–34, April, 1920.

————: Louis Sullivan, Obituary. *Architectural Record*, vol. 55, no. 5, p. 503, May, 1924.

————: A Review of "A System of Architectural Ornament." *American Architect*, vol. 126, no. 2455, pp. 14–16, September 24, 1924.

————: "Memorial to Louis H. Sullivan." *American Magazine of Art*, vol. 19, no. 5, pp. 276–277, May, 1928.

————: "Memorial to Louis Sullivan." *Western Architect*, vol. 38, no. 6, p. 100, June, 1929.

Barker, A. W.: "Louis H. Sullivan, Thinker and Architect." *Architectural Annual*, 2nd edition, pp. 49–66, 1901.

Bennett, Carl K.: "A Bank Built for Farmers." *The Craftsman*, vol. 15, no. 2, pp. 176–185, November, 1908.

Bouilhet, André: "L'Exposition de Chicago." *Révue des Arts Décoratifs*, vol. 14, p. 68, 1893–94.

Bragdon, Claude: "Letters from Louis Sullivan." *Architecture*, vol. 64, no. 1, pp. 7–10, July, 1931.

Caffin, Charles H.: "Louis H. Sullivan, Artist Among Architects, American Among Americans." *The Criterion* (N.Y.) vol. 20, no. 471, p. 20, January 28, 1899. Reprinted in *Architectural Annual*, 2nd edition, pp. 67–68, 1901.

Dean, George R.: "A New Movement in American Architecture." *Brush and Pencil*, vol. 5, no. 6, pp. 254–259, March, 1900.

Desmond, H. W.: "Another View—What Mr. Louis Sullivan Stands For." *Architectural Record*, vol. 16, no. 1, pp. 61–67, July, 1904.

Ferree, Barr: "The High Building and Its Art." *Scribner's*, vol. 15, no. 3, pp. 297–318, March, 1894.

————: "The Modern Office Building." *Inland Architect & News Record*, vol. 27, nos. 1–5, pp. 4, 12, 23, 34, 45, February-June, 1896.

Grey, Elmer: "Indigenous and Inventive Architecture for America." *Inland Architect & News Record*, vol. 35, no. 5, p. 36, June, 1900.

Hamlin, A. D. F.: "The Ten Most Beautiful Buildings in the United States." *Brochure Series of Architectural Illustrations*, vol. 6, no. 1, January, 1900.

————: L'Art Nouveau. *The Craftsman*, vol. 3, p. 129.

Kimball, S. Fiske: "Louis Sullivan, an Old Master." *Architectural Record*, vol. 57, no. 4, pp. 289–304, April, 1925.

McLean, Robert Craik: "Architects and Architecture in the United States." *Inland Architect & News Record*, vol. 28, no. 6, pp. 58–62, January, 1897.

————: "Dankmar Adler." *Inland Architect & News Record*, vol. 35, no. 4, p. 26, May, 1900.

————: "Louis Henry Sullivan, Sept. 3, 1856–April 14, 1924; An Appreciation." *Western Architect*, vol. 33, no. 5, pp. 53–55, May, 1924.

Millett, Louis J.: "The National Farmers' Bank of Owatonna, Minn." *Architectural Record*, vol. 24, no. 4, pp. 249–254, October, 1908.

Pond, Irving K.: "Louis Sullivan's *The Autobiography of an Idea*, a Review and an Estimate." *Western Architect*, vol. 33, no. 6, pp. 67–69, June, 1924.

Rebori, A. N.: "An Architecture of Democracy." *Architectural Record*, vol. 39, no. 5, pp. 437–465, May, 1916.

————: "Louis H. Sullivan, an Obituary." *Architectural Record*, vol. 55, no. 6, p. 587, June, 1924.

Rice, Wallace: "Louis Sullivan as Author." *Western Architect*, vol. 33, no. 6, pp. 70–71, June, 1924.

Robertson, Howard: "The Work of Louis H. Sullivan." *Architect's Journal*, vol. 59, no. 1537, pp. 1000–1009, June 18, 1924.

Root, John W.: "Architects of Chicago." *Inland Architect & News Record*, vol. 16, no. 8, pp. 91–92, January, 1891.

Sabine, Paul E.: "Acoustics of the Chicago Civic Opera House." *Architectural Forum*, vol. 52, no. 4, pp. 599–604, April, 1930.

Schopfer, Jean: "American Architecture from a Foreign Point of View: New York City." *Architectural Review*, vol. 7 old series, vol. 2 new series, no. 3, pp. 25–30, March, 1900.

Schuyler, Montgomery: "A Critique of the Works of Adler & Sullivan." *Architectural Record*, Great American Architects Series, no. 2 (published separately), December, 1895.

————: "The 'Skyscraper' Up To Date." *Architectural Record*, vol. 8, no. 3, pp. 231–257, January-March, 1899.

———: "The People's Savings Bank of Cedar Rapids, Iowa." *Architectural Record*, vol. 31, no. 1, pp. 45–56, January, 1912.

Smith, Lyndon P.: "The Schlesinger & Mayer Building—An Attempt to Give Functional Expression to the Architecture of a Department Store." *Architectural Record*, vol. 16, no. 1, pp. 53–60, July, 1904.

———: "The Home of an Artist-Architect—Louis H. Sullivan's Place at Ocean Springs, Miss." *Architectural Record*, vol. 17, no. 6, pp. 471–490, June, 1905.

Sturgis, Russell: "Good Things in Modern Architecture." *Architectural Record*, vol. 8, no. 1, pp. 92–110, July-September, 1898.

Tallmadge, Thomas E.: "The Chicago School." *Architectural Review*, vol. 15, no. 4, pp. 69–74, April, 1908.

———: "The People's Savings & Loan Association Building of Sidney, Ohio." *American Architect*, vol. 114, no. 2235, pp. 477–482, October 23, 1918.

———: "The Farmers' & Merchants' Bank of Columbus, Wisconsin." *Western Architect*, vol. 29, no. 7, pp. 63–65, July, 1920.

———: "Louis Henri Sullivan, His Claim to Fame." *Building for the Future* series publ. by Peoples Gas Light & Coke Co. Chicago, July, 1933.

Winkler, Franz K.: "Building in Salt Lake City." *Architectural Record*, vol. 22, no. 1, pp. 15–37, July, 1907.

Woltersdorf, Arthur: "Dankmar Adler" (A Portrait-Gallery of Chicago Architects, II). *Western Architect*, vol. 33, no. 7, pp. 75–79, July, 1924.

Wright, Frank Lloyd: "Louis Sullivan, Beloved Master." *Western Architect*, vol. 33, no. 6, pp. 64–66, June, 1924.

————: "Louis H. Sullivan—His Work." *Architectural Record*, vol. 56, no. 1, pp. 28–32, July, 1924.


*PAMPHLETS*

Auction Catalogue: Catalogue of Auction of Household Effects, Library, Oriental Rugs, Paintings, Etc., of Mr. Louis Sullivan. November 29, 1909. Williams, Barker & Severn Company, Chicago.

Fraternity Temple: An Announcement to the Independent Order of Odd Fellows of Chicago and the State of Illinois, by Wm. C. McClintock, President, J. P. Ellacott, Vice-President, and Norman Totten, Secretary-Treasurer; published in brochure, September, 1891.

Mercantile Club: An Announcement to the Members of the Mercantile Club, St. Louis, by W. A. & A. E. Wells, Chicago, June 1, 1891.

St. Paul's Church: St. Paul's Methodist Episcopal Church at Cedar Rapids, Iowa. Descriptive pamphlet, with history of the project and account of the dedication ceremonies, May 31, 1914.

Schiller Building: Rental pamphlet publ. by C. P. Dose & Co. Chicago, 1892.

Wainwright Building: Rental pamphlet publ. by the Wainwright Real Estate Co. St. Louis, 1891.


*NEWSPAPER ARTICLES*

Auditorium: The Dedication of the Auditorium. Chicago *Tribune*, December 10, 1889.

————: Auditorium Supplement. *Sunday Inter-Ocean* (Chicago), December 8, 1889.

Exposition Building: The Remodelling of the Exposition Building in Grant Park into an Opera Hall. Chicago *Sunday Tribune*, March 1, 1885.

McVicker's Theatre: The Restoration of the McVicker's Theatre. *Evening News* (Chicago), November 22, 1890.

————: Opening of the New McVicker's. *Daily Inter-Ocean* (Chicago), March 31, 1891.

Sullivan, Louis: America's Foremost Architect and Some of His Work. *New York Press*, Sunday, January 7, 1912.

# INDEX

# INDEX

# INDEX

# INDEX

# INDEX

# THE NORTON LIBRARY

Morey, C. R. *Christian Art.* With 49 illustrations. N103

Morrison, Hugh. *Louis Sullivan:* Prophet of Modern Architecture. Illustrated. N116

Ortega y Gasset, José. *Man and Crisis.* Translated from the Spanish by Mildred Adams. N121

Richardson, Henry Handel. *Australia Felix (The Fortunes of Richard Mahony:* 1). N117

Richardson, Henry Handel. *The Way Home (The Fortunes of Richard Mahony:* 2). N118

Richardson, Henry Handel. *Ultima Thule (The Fortunes of Richard Mahony:* 3). N119

Richardson, Samuel. *Pamela.* Introduction by William M. Sale, Jr. N166

Rilke, Rainer Maria. *Translations from the Poetry* by M. D. Herter Norton. N156

Russell, Bertrand. *Freedom Versus Organization:* 1814-1914. N136

Simms, William Gilmore. *Woodcraft.* Introduction by Richmond Croom Beatty. N107

Spender, Stephen. *The Making of a Poem.* N120

Stravinsky, Igor. *An Autobiography.* N161

Ward, Barbara. *The Interplay of East and West:* Points of Conflict and Cooperation. With a new epilogue by the author. N162

## NORTON/BATSFORD PAPERBACKS

Clutton, C., C. Posthumus & D. Jenkinson. *The Racing Car.* B18

Clutton, C., & J. Stanford. *The Vintage Motor Car.* B7

Cox, J. C., & C. B. Ford. *Parish Churches.* B5

Crossley, F. H. *The English Abbey.* B19

Dutton, Ralph. *The English Country House.* B16

Ford, C. B., Editor. *England's Heritage.* B8

Gibbon, Monk. *Austria.* B14

Harvey, John. *English Cathedrals.* B2

More, Jasper. *Land of Italy.* B4

Nock, O. S. *Railways of Britain.* B17

Priestley, J. B. *The Beauty of Britain.* B15

Russell, John. *Shakespeare's Country.* B6

Russell, John. *Switzerland.* B20

Scott-Moncrieff, D. *Veteran and Edwardian Motor Cars.* B3

Sitwell, Sacheverell. *Spain.* B1

Stanford, John. *The Sports Car.* B13